BETWEEN CLASS AND MARKET

BETWEEN CLASS
AND MARKET

POSTWAR UNIONIZATION IN THE CAPITALIST DEMOCRACIES

Bruce Western

PRINCETON UNIVERSITY PRESS   PRINCETON, NEW JERSEY

Second printing, and first paperback printing, 1999
Paperback ISBN 0-691-01033-1

The Library of Congress has cataloged the cloth edition of this book as follows

Western, Bruce, 1964–
Between class and market : postwar unionization
in the capitalist democracies / Bruce Western.
p.   cm.
Includes bibliographical references and index.
ISBN 0-691-01617-8 (cl : alk. paper)
1. Trade-unions—History—20th century.   I. Title
HD6476.W467   1997
331.88'09'045—dc21   97-5236   CIP

This book has been composed in Times Roman

The paper used in this publication meets the minimum requirements
of ANSI/NISO Z39.48-1992 (R1997) (*Permanence of Paper*)

http://pup.princeton.edu

Printed in the United States of America

10 9 8 7 6 5 4 3 2

For My Parents, John and Tasnee Western

_____

Contents

Figures ————————————————————————

Tables

Acknowledgments —————————————————————

RESEARCH for this book was completed in three phases, in Los Angeles, Princeton, and Florence. I began dissertation research on trade unions in Los Angeles at UCLA in 1992. My committee of Dick Berk, Sandy Jacoby, Ivan Szelenyi, Michael Wallerstein, and Maurice Zeitlin were engaging and demanding readers. I hope I've done justice to Dick Berk's rather daunting respect for the challenge of empirical research and Ivan Szelenyi's macroscopic vision of economic sociology. At UCLA I also benefited greatly from discussions with Kathy Beckett, Alec Campbell, Dahlia Elazar, Michael Mann, Andrew McLean, Ruth Milkman, Bill Roy, and Eleanor Townsley. Bill Mason taught me a lot about the hierarchical models that form the core of several data analyses reported in the book. While at UCLA, I first gained access to Jelle Visser's superb "Trade Union Membership Database." Professor Visser's compilation of aggregate unionization statistics has provided a wonderful resource for all students of comparative industrial relations.

I continued work on the manuscript at Princeton University where I field-tested a number of ideas about the state of union movements in the 1980s. My colleagues, Gene Burns and Frank Dobbin in particular, gave me extremely helpful suggestions for Chapter 10 on the decentralization of collective bargaining. Germán Rodríguez introduced me to the dangers of Gibbs sampling, which allowed estimation of several of the models. During this time I also received valuable comments on drafts of various chapters from Ed Amenta, Chris Anderson, Miguel Centeno, Frank Dobbin, Bernhard Ebbinghaus, John Hartman, Alex Hicks, Peter Lange, Jane Poulsen, and Andy Sobel. I am especially indebted to Gøsta Esping-Andersen, Larry Griffin, Alex Hicks, and Wolfgang Streeck, who provided splendid comments during journal review. I gratefully acknowledge the helpful advice from journal editors Paula England, Gerry Marwell, Dick Simpson, Marta Tienda, and my more anonymous journal referees.

A complete draft of the manuscript was finished while I was on leave from Princeton at the European University Institute in Florence. At the Institute, I was fortunate to come into contact with Colin Crouch, John McCormick, Yasemin Soysal, and Jim Walsh, all of whom commented on drafts of several of the early chapters. Charles Tilly and Alex Hicks both read the entire manuscript, helping enormously to draw the book together into a more coherent project. The manuscript was also improved by the advice of anonymous reviewers and Bernhard Ebbinghaus and the research assistance of Erin Kelly, Cath Woollard, and Jackie Gordon.

In addition to these intellectual debts I greatly appreciate the encourage-
ment and support of Viviana Zelizer and Paul DiMaggio, who each chaired
the Sociology Department while I was working on the book. Peter Dougherty
and Beth Gianfagna at Princeton University Press provided excellent editorial
assistance. I also thank Lyn Grossman for her copyediting and Shirley Kessel
for the index.

Research for this book would have been impossible without financial support from UCLA, the 1994 Summer Institute of the Center for Advanced
Study, the National Science Foundation, Princeton University, and the European University Institute.

While all of the data analysis presented here is new, parts of a few chapters
were adapted from journal articles. Chapter 6 draws from "Unionization and
Labor Market Institutions in Advanced Capitalism, 1950–1985," *American
Journal of Sociology* 99:1314–41. (© 1994 by the University of Chicago
Press. All rights reserved.) Chapter 7 builds on "Postwar Unionization in 18
Advanced Capitalist Countries," *American Sociological Review* 58:266–
82 (1993). Chapter 8 adapts the analysis of "Institutional Mechanisms for
Unionization: An Analysis of Social Survey Data from 16 OECD Countries,"
Social Forces 73:497–520 (1994). An earlier version of Chapter 10 appeared
as "A Comparative Study of Working Class Disorganization: Union Decline
in 18 Advanced Capitalist Countries," *American Sociological Review* 60:
179–201 (1995).

Abbreviations

Australia

ACTU   Australian Council of Trade Unions
ALP   Australian Labor Party

Austria

ÖGB   Österreichischer Gewerkschaftsbund (Austrian Confederation of Trade Unions)

Belgium

ABVV-FGTB   Algemeen Belgisch Vakverbond, Fédération Générale du Travail de Belgique (General Belgian Trade Union Federation)
ACV-CSC   Algemeen Christelijk Vakverbond, Confédération des Syndicats Chrétiens (General Christian Trade Union Federation
BSP-PSB   Belgische Socialistiche Partij, Parti Socialiste Belge, (Belgian Socialist Party)
PSC   Parti Social Chrétien (Social Christian Party)

Canada

CCF   Cooperative Commonwealth Federation
NDP   New Democratic Party

Denmark

LO   Landsorganisationen i Danmark (Danish Confederation of Trade Unions)

Finland

SAJ   Suomen Ammattijärjestö (Finnish Trade Union Federation)

SAK   Suomen Ammattiliittojen Keskusjärjestö (Central Organization
             of Finnish Trade Unions)

France

CFTC   Confédération Française di Travailleurs Chrétiens (French
             Federation of Christian Workers)
CGT   Confédération Générale du Travail (General Federation of Labor)
CGT-FO   Confédération Générale du Travail-Force Ouvrière (Reformist
             Federation of Labor)
PCF   Parti Communiste Français (French Communist Party)
PS   Parti Socialiste (Socialist Party)
UDF   Union pour la Démocratie Française (Union for French
             Democracy)

Germany

CDU   Christlich-Demokratische Union (Christian Democratic Union)
DGB   Deutscher Gewerkschaftsbund (German Confederation of Trade
             Unions)
SPD   Sozialdemokratische Partei Deutschlands (German Social
             Democratic Party)

Ireland

ICTU   Irish Congress of Trade Unions

Italy

CGIL   Confederazione Generale Italiana del Lavoro (General Confed-
             eration of Italian Labor)
CISL   Confederazione Italiana Sindacati Lavoratori (Italian Confed-
             eration of Labor Unions)
UIL   Unione Italiana del Lavoro (Italian Confederation of Labor)

Japan

JSP   Japan Socialist Party

Netherlands

CDA   Christen Democratisch Appèl (Christian Democratic Appeal)
KVP   Katholieke Volkspartij (Catholic People's Party)
NKV   Nederlands Katholiek Vakverbond (Dutch Catholic Trade
           Union Confederation)
NVV   Nederlands Verbond van Vakverenigingen (Dutch Confederation
           of Trade Unions)
PvdA   Partij van de Arbeid (Labor Party)

Norway

DNA   Det Norske Arbeiderparti (Norwegian Labor Party)
LO   Landsorganisasjonen i Norge (Norwegian Confederation of
           Trade Unions)
NAF   Norges Arbeidsgiver Forening (Norwegian Employers
           Federation)

Sweden

LO   Landsorganisationen i Sverige (Swedish Confederation of
           Trade Unions)
SACO   Sverige Akademikers Centralorganisation (Swedish Confederation
           of Professional Associations)
SAF   Svenska Arbetsgivaresöföreningen (Swedish Employers Confed-
           eration)
SAP   Sveriges Socialdemokratiska Arbetareparti (Swedish Social
           Democratic Party)
TCO   Tjänstemännens Centralorganisation (Confederation of
           Salaried Employees)

Switzerland

CNG   Christlich-Nationaler Gewerkschaftsbund (Christian-National
           Confederation of Swiss Trade Unions)
SGB   Schweizerischer Gewerkschaftsbund (Confederation of Swiss Trade
           Unions)
SPS   Sozialdemokratische Partei der Schweiz (Swiss Social Democratic
           Party)

United Kingdom

TUC   Trades Union Congress

United States

AFL-CIO   American Federation of Labor–Congress of Industrial
           Organizations
PATCO   Professional Air Traffic Controllers Organization

Part I

THE PROBLEM

One

Class Power, Market Power, and the Comparative Method

BY 1950, trade unions had become key players in the capitalist democracies of Europe, North America, and the Pacific region. In each of the advanced capitalist countries, unions organized between a third and two-thirds of all workers. For many observers, strong unions in the smokestack industries were at the heart of a compromise between labor and capital that could drive economic growth and social improvement (Dahl and Lindblom 1953; Dahrendorf 1959; Crosland 1956). Forty years later, things had changed markedly. Some union movements had grown to organize entire labor markets, others represented only a rump in traditional manufacturing sectors, and the relevance of big industrial unions to economic development was being questioned even by sympathetic commentators (Bluestone and Bluestone 1992; Sabel 1995). How did we get from there to here? Why did some labor movements enjoy remarkable growth in the postwar period, while others withered, and why has the last decade been so hostile to organized labor? To answer these questions, this book examines the growth and decline of trade union organization in the postwar capitalist democracies. This involves a study of eighteen countries over a period of four decades, from 1950 to 1990.

My main argument is briefly stated: *Labor movements grow where they are institutionally insulated from the market forces that drive up competition among workers.* Three institutional conditions have been essential for union growth. First, working-class parties enlisted the power of the state to promote union organizing. Second, centralized industrial relations reduced employer resistance to unions and enabled a coordinated approach to unionization. Third, unions that managed unemployment insurance successfully recruited those at the margins of the labor market. Working-class parties, labor market centralization, and union-managed unemployment insurance contribute to a powerful account of union organization that explains variation within national labor markets, across countries, and over time for the three decades since 1950. From the late 1970s, the institutional contours of the capitalist democracies were increasingly buffeted by the global economy. The institutional and organizational power of unions eroded as a result. This story, in a nutshell, describes the main findings of this book.

This analysis stands between traditional perspectives in sociology and economics. From a Marxist perspective in sociology, union growth is a political process. Workers and employers wrestle over class-based collective interests on an institutional surface marked by the accumulation of previous struggles. In the neoclassical view of economics, power in these struggles originates with the conditions of supply and demand in the marketplace. Without market power, unions have little chance of growth.

The sociological and economic perspectives offer important insights, but neither side quite gets it right. Economic conditions are important, but they must be understood in their institutional context. I present an institutional sociology of the labor market that views unions as the joint product of class institutions and market forces. In this contextual approach, collective action in the labor market is shaped by economic conditions that are filtered through the prism of the surrounding institutions.

Class Power and Market Power

Trade unions—much maligned but often studied—raise basic questions about social change and the nature of capitalist societies. Theorists beginning with widely different assumptions have commonly asked whether unions can alter the basic logic of capitalist economies. The question has been treated in two main ways. One side views unions as class representatives advancing a collective interest in freedom from the uncertainty of the labor market. The other sees unions as market agents extracting a rent for their members in collective bargaining.

Unions as Class Representatives

The Marxist analysis of trade unions begins most famously with Lenin. In the context of prerevolutionary Russia, Lenin worried that unions delivered only limited and short-run gains to workers. Modest advances in wages and conditions obstructed revolutionary action led by a vanguard party. Without the party, the labor movement would succumb to a "trade-unionist striving to come under the wing of the bourgeoisie" (Lenin 1968 [1902], pp. 45–46). This question of whether unions could play a significant role in the transformation of capitalism set the terms for political debate on the left after World War II. From the Leninist perspective, unions that helped to administer capitalist economies and enterprises were essentially creatures of capitalism, incapable of radical social change (see Kelly [1988, 186–193] for a short review). Works councils, joint consultation committees, and political exchange between unions and the state were demonized. From this point of view, unions were either dupes in a management power play or collaborators in the class war (e.g., Kelly 1988, 191; Panitch 1981).

Comparative sociologists countered that large unions were class representatives, equipped with power resources to pursue significant social reforms. In this research, high unionization was shown to be strongly associated with the success of social democratic parties, union influence in economic policy, and the development of generous welfare states. Where unionization was low, labor leaders were marginal to economic and social policy. In countries with weak labor parties and flimsy welfare states, the market emerged as an axial principle of social life. The level of union membership was thus seen as a vital influence on the trajectory of capitalist development (Stephens 1979; Hicks 1988; Korpi 1983, 1989; Esping-Andersen 1985, 1990).

Unions as Market Agents

From the neoclassical viewpoint, unions are market agents rather than class representatives. Milton Friedman stakes out one corner of the paradigm, treating unions as monopolistic aberrations that damage the quality of democracy and economic efficiency: "Unions have not only . . . harmed the public at large and workers as a whole by distorting the use of labor; they have also made the incomes of the working class more unequal by reducing the opportunities available to the most disadvantaged workers" (1962, 124). In response to this market distortion, "the first and most urgent necessity in the area of government policy is the elimination of those measures which directly support monopoly" (ibid., 132). From this neoclassical position, there is no real difference between monopoly in labor and monopoly in business. Both are threats to capitalism and freedom and both should be eradicated (Freeman [1986a] cites more sources).

As for the Marxist analysis, social science research challenged the normative claims. Applied economists found that encompassing union movements pursued broad interests in full employment and economic growth. Economies with high unionization and centralized labor markets performed strongly during the postwar period. This was especially true through the recessions of the 1970s. Leaders of encompassing unions restrained their wage claims to help control inflation and unemployment at a time of contracting demand and rising oil prices. Union membership was thus closely related to robust economic performance in hard times (Flanagan, Soskice, and Ulman 1983; Bruno and Sachs 1985; Layard, Nickell, and Jackman 1991).

Unions between Class and Market

If Lenin and Milton Friedman were united in anything, it was in their mutual
suspicion of unions. These political instincts reflect the ambiguous place of
organized labor in capitalist economies. The contrast between the Marxist and
neoclassical positions makes this ambiguity clear. For Lenin, unions betrayed
the true interests of the working class by obstructing meaningful social change.
For Friedman, unions advanced the collective interest too effectively, sub-
verting the efficiency of an unfettered capitalism. Both positions appear to
lack a strong empirical foundation. Union organization has muted the caprice
of the market and maintained prosperity. Unlike more transient forms of collective action, such as strike activity, union organization exerts an ongoing and
pervasive influence on the development of capitalist democracy. Whatever the
empirical limitations, however, viewing unions as class representatives or as
market agents illuminates the problem of unionization.

From the Marxist perspective, relations between workers and employers
have a collective significance. Capitalist societies are rooted in institutions
that express the importance of class as a principle of social organization.
Sometimes the unity of interest among workers on one side and among employers on the other is clearly inscribed in the rules regulating work and
employment. For instance, representation is class-wide where union officers
meet with government and business leaders to make national economic
policy. In other settings, classes as organized social forces are virtually in-
visible. The scope of representation in industrial relations is narrow, and collective interests span only certain firms or occupations. Class provides a way
of describing this sort of institutional variation. Instead of referring to an abstract social category, the notion of class refers to how institutions actively
consolidate or fragment collective interests in the labor market. For the unionization story, the important point is that class institutions—institutions expressing a market-wide unity of interest among workers—assist broadly based
collective action. In short, institutions are a source of class power that drives
union growth.

In the neoclassical analysis, labor organizing relies on overcoming competition among workers for jobs. Competition is keen when economic conditions
are poor—when labor markets are slack and firms are cutting back on production. Commons (1918, 10) makes this observation at an early point for the
United States: "the movement of American prices shows also the movements
of American labour." Modern economic studies follow this line by arguing
that the costs of union membership for workers and the incentives for union
opposition among employers are highest in the troughs of the business cycle
(Ashenfelter and Pencavel 1969; Bain and Elsheikh 1976). The same argument
helps explain why unions find it difficult to penetrate the fringes of the labor

market, dominated by women, young workers, immigrants, and ethnic minorities. Here, labor market competition is particularly intense and employment too precarious to justify union membership. In contrast to the class analysis, this theory of union growth is essentially structural. The union-organizing problem is a general feature of capitalist labor markets which operates in the same way across times and places. In this structural logic, union growth depends on workers' market power.

An Institutional Sociology of the Labor Market

Does union growth rely on class power rooted in encompassing institutions or market power arising from supply and demand in the labor market? The class and market perspectives pose a false choice. Instead of asking if markets *or* institutions determine union growth, I take the view that markets *are* institutional settings. In Polanyi's (1957) phrase, labor markets are "instituted processes." The main implication of this institutional sociology of the labor market is captured by Schumpeter (1954, 34), who argues that economic laws "work out differently under different institutional conditions." From this point of view, labor markets are not simply generic forums for wage-labor exchanges. Instead, they are historically formed institutional settings that show rich cross-national variation beyond the bare bones of capitalist property relations. These institutions are causally implicated in union organizing by providing workers, employers, and their representatives with opportunities for generating and resisting collective action. They provide the historical context in which the structural logic of capitalist labor markets is played out. Where class relations are strongly imprinted on the institutional framework, the framework provides a powerful mechanism for collective action. Class institutions are thus more than power resources for labor leaders; they also reshape the logic of the market to help union organizing. Where class has no institutional reality, unions and employers appear to each other as market agents. In this setting, collective action is insecure, fluctuating with market power.

These ideas suggest two sorts of institutional effects. First, union membership has grown in the presence of institutions that broadly reward collective, rather than individual, action on the labor market. In this case, class institutions raise the general level of union organization. We can think of this as the direct effect of institutions on union growth. In addition to this direct effect, the institutional conditions for labor movement growth also create incentives for union membership even when economic times are hard and labor's market power is weak. Here, institutions are working indirectly on the impact of market conditions on union growth. The logic of labor movement growth is institutionally variable, but structurally constrained. From the structural point of view, the costs of union organizing are high when competition among workers is keen. The level of competition, however, depends on the salience of class in the surrounding institutional context.

Institutional regulation extends to the two main spheres of capitalist economies—the state and the market. Within the state, working-class parties fostered union growth by providing resources for collective action that were beyond the reach of market forces. Social democratic governments reformed industrial relations institutions to support union organizing and expand union power. Perhaps most important in the postwar experience, labor governments supported public sector unionization and included unions at the highest levels of economic decisionmaking. These measures diluted labor market competition among workers by raising the returns to union membership and lowering the costs of labor organizing. Although parties of the left have widely supported trade unions, links between parties and unions show a great deal of variation, and much of the causal action is found in the institutional detail. Where central unions have collective membership in political parties and where unions are integrated into state policymaking bodies, parties have the largest effects on union growth.

Beyond the state, labor market institutions have provided a major impetus to unionization. Labor market centralization encourages union membership among employed workers; union-run unemployment insurance integrates the margins of the work force into trade unions.

Let us look first at labor market centralization. Industrial relations experts often classify collective bargaining rules according to whether workers are represented at the level of the firm, the industry, or the national economy. In some cases—in Scandinavia and the Low Countries—collective bargaining has been centralized at the national level. Labor leaders act as class representatives, recognized as such by government and business. The legitimacy of organized labor has historically grown from mutual recognition pacts that concede an indispensable role to unions in regulating the labor market. Under these conditions, employers have been less resistant to union organizing and union membership has risen steadily. Centralized labor markets also allow a coordinated approach to unionization. Relations between unions are cooperative rather than competitive, and union leaders redistribute organizing costs across different sectors of the economy. When centralized unions take a role in national economic management, they also direct policy to support employment in unionized sectors. Although the level of labor market centralization correlates with unionization across the capitalist democracies, stronger evidence of causality is given by developments in Italian industrial relations. Before 1969, the Italian labor market was largely unregulated and industrial relations institutions were weak. Italian unions were shrinking for the first two decades after the war. After the Hot Autumn strike wave of 1969, competition among the three major union groups was replaced by cooperation, major wage agreements were signed at the national level, and labor law reform established union rights across the country. Italian union membership rose steadily from this time. Importantly, of the eighteen countries studied, Italy is the only one with radical institutional change before the late 1970s, and it is the only one in this period to show a sharp change in unionization trend.

While labor market centralization gives union leaders control over market competition among the employed, union-run unemployment funds provide some control over the market position of the jobless. Union officials who staff the labor exchanges direct the unemployed to union jobs, and unions retain contact with those out of work. Contrast unemployment in countries with public unemployment insurance. Here, exit from the labor movement usually follows exit from the labor market. Union-run unemployment funds were common before World War II. The earliest schemes developed in Switzerland and Belgium. A program of municipal subsidies in the Belgian town of Ghent gave its name to the system in 1901, and was widely emulated throughout Europe over the next twenty years. However, as control of unemployment insurance passed to the state, only four Ghent systems—in Belgium, Denmark, Finland, and Sweden—survived the postwar period. While union organization remained steady or declined in most countries, unionization grew in these four countries in the forty years since World War II. Control of unemployment funds by organized labor not only raises the overall level of unionization; it also shapes the market mechanisms for unionization that operate within national economies. While rising unemployment depleted union membership through the late 1970s in most of Europe, union membership rose rapidly with the unemployment rate in Belgium and Denmark. The Ghent system provides a key lesson. Institutions not only directly boost union organization; they also filter the effects of market forces.

These institutional conditions for union growth underline the historical dimension of this story. The institutions in nearly all the countries under study established stable contexts for union organizing. Enduring institutional variation produced divergent trends in unionization for most of the postwar period. Unions grew continuously in some countries, while steadily shrinking in others. Through the 1980s, however, the institutional conditions deteriorated. Social democratic parties filled the opposition benches, and labor markets became more decentralized. Researchers argue that these changes were driven by the expansion of the global economy (Pontusson 1992a, 1992b; Katz 1993; Piven 1992). The nation-class institutions that shaped postwar labor movements were penetrated by international market conditions that were difficult to control domestically. The resulting decline of social democracy and the decentralization of collective bargaining threatened the unionization trends that characterized most of the postwar period. While most of the book's analysis is taken up with the long period of continuity from 1950 to 1980, the final empirical chapters focus specifically on these institutional changes and labor organizing trends during the 1980s.

The Comparative Method

The institutional account of unionization presents significant methodological challenges. Not only should the analysis evaluate the effects of three institutional conditions on union organization in eighteen countries; it should also examine the leading alternative explanations that emphasize the impact of the business cycle and the structure of employment on union growth. With so many different explanations, we quickly encounter the fundamental problem of comparative research: The number of explanatory variables is large relative to the number of cases available to compare.

I tackle this difficulty through a "problem-driven" approach to the analysis. In contrast to the "model-driven" approach of econometrics, where the assumptions stem from deductive theory, the problem-driven approach aims to saturate the analysis with substantive information about the research question. In this way, the weight of a wide variety of evidence is enlisted to draw sharp conclusions about the causes of unionization. The Bayesian branch of statistics occupies a special place in the problem-driven approach because it provides a method for combining different kinds of information. In comparative research, where we have data from many different countries, and many different kinds of data, combining information is a key research task. The problem-driven approach to comparative research consists of four specific strategies: (1) a willingness to make strong assumptions on the basis of substantive knowledge, (2) the use of multiple tests and research designs, (3) the admission of heterogeneous sources of uncertainty, and (4) the need to tailor models to fit substantive conjectures.

Assumptions and Substantive Knowledge

Assumptions are ubiquitous in empirical research. We pretend to know some things with certainty in order to find out about other things that are not well understood. Because comparative unionization data are often thin, sustaining only vague conclusions, we need to make strong assumptions to obtain strong conclusions. Throughout this book, I try to choose these assumptions on the basis of substantive knowledge, not statistical or other sorts of convenience. This knowledge draws on the rich comparative histories, area studies, and institutional descriptions that often guide quantitative work in an informal way. Substantively motivated assumptions are applied explicitly in a Bayesian analysis with prior information. For the Bayesian analysis, evidence from labor history and case studies in industrial relations are combined with sample data to obtain estimates of institutional effects.

Sometimes substantive knowledge doesn't help much in choosing assumptions. The *ceteris paribus* disclaimer that underpins most empirical research is a prime example. We may be interested in the effect of a variable, "all other things equal," but we are often uncertain what all these other things might be. When substantive knowledge is vague in this way, we need to investigate the sensitivity of our conclusions to the assumptions. If the data admit a relatively narrow range of conclusions from a wide class of assumptions, the plausibility of those conclusions is enhanced. In short, I willingly use the extensive historical record of postwar unionization to make assumptions. Where this information is unavailable, it is important to assess the sensitivity of conclusions to assumptions.

Multiple Tests and Designs

Another way of enriching the fund of information used for analysis involves examining many different kinds of unionization data, generated by a variety of research designs. We can begin by elaborating the simple cross-sectional design that takes a single observation from each country. Time series analysis presents one way forward. Analyzing forty-year postwar unionization series from eighteen countries substantially enlarges the sample size from the eighteen data points of the cross-sectional design and introduces information about the dynamics of union growth. Social survey data also include more information than does the simple aggregate cross-section and provide insight into how institutions shape patterns of union organization within national labor markets. In addition to the quantitative analysis, qualitative historical evidence puts some meat on the skeleton of the statistics. The historical evidence also offers quasi-experimental comparisons—such as the Italian exceptionalism discussed above—in which rival explanations are controlled through common histories or anomalous developments. With multiple tests such as these, weaknesses in any one research design are compensated by the strengths of others.

The empirical analysis can also be reinforced by studying alternative implications of the institutional theories. The institutional mechanisms are more likely to be operating as we think if these alternative implications are associated with the institutional conditions (e.g., Stinchcombe 1968, 18–20). The institutional explanations of unionization lend themselves naturally to this idea because they carry two types of empirical implications. First, they suggest that unionization varies with the power of working-class parties, labor market centralization, and Ghent systems of unemployment insurance. Second, they also suggest that the effects of economic forces vary with the institutions.

The strength of the evidence for the institutional mechanisms relies on showing both types of empirical relationships. Here, then, the methodology is very much driven by the idea that the logic of labor markets is embedded in an institutional context.

The Heterogeneity of Uncertainty

Examining many kinds of data from a range of sources introduces a variety of uncertainties into the analysis. These uncertainties are rooted in the idea that the data could have been at least slightly different. Why might the data have been different? To start with, they are socially produced by processes that introduce noise and bias. The actual events of interest represented by the data also could have been different because of openness in the historical process. If we were to analyze surveys of union membership, we might obtain different results because of variability introduced by the survey sampling process. Uncertainty may vary cross-nationally along all these dimensions in comparative research. Interpreting comparative data partly involves taking account of heterogeneous uncertainty. In a statistical framework, resampling methods, cross-validation, and hierarchical models can all be specified to allow for heterogeneous sources of uncertainty. (These procedures are described in the following chapters.) At a minimum, I reject determinism in social explanation and take uncertainty assessment to be an important objective for this work. Despite the recent popularity of deterministic methods in comparative sociology (Ragin 1987; Skocpol 1984), evaluating uncertainty about conclusions remains a major research problem wherever there is uncertainty about data. Statistics provides a powerful vocabulary for dealing with this problem. In a comparative setting, where uncertainty is rife and varied, statistical methods that allow for multiple sources of error are a key research tool.

Statistical Modeling

Finally, we need to choose our models to fit our substantive problems. From this perspective, the popular linear regression equations are like cheap suits. One size fits all—badly. The problem is that we often think about our theories in a more complicated way than our models admit. In the analysis below, I am sometimes interested in explaining particular events—such as institutional change or turning points in union density time series—rather than generic variation. The institutional approach also suggests that the process of union growth obeys no master logic, but instead varies across institutional contexts. As we will see, unionization time series are sometimes not Normal, and outliers are common. In these situations, we need to go beyond the conventional toolbox of social science research. The added complication comes at a price, however. We may need more, or different, assumptions to extract strong conclusions. Here, we come full circle in the problem-driven approach to data analysis. For these assumptions, we can turn to the rich fund of historical information that abounds in comparative research.

Plan of the Book

Chapter 2 introduces different kinds of variation in unionization, which an adequate explanation must address. This establishes the dependent variable for the remainder of the book. Chapters 3 through 5 present historical material and institutional description linking unionization to labor market centralization, the Ghent system, and political parties. These historical chapters set the stage for the statistics. Chapter 6 examines the cross-sectional data, integrating the historical material through a Bayesian analysis. Issues in the sociology of data are also considered here. This cross-sectional analysis is expanded with time series data in Chapter 7. The time series analysis assesses how the effects of the business cycle and other longitudinal variables depend on the institutional setting. Chapter 8 examines the effect of labor market structure on unionization. Using social survey data, this chapter studies the connection between institutions and the influence of industry, occupation, and demography on union membership. Chapters 7 and 8 thus take on the major research styles of the neoclassical analysis of unionization—analysis of time series and survey data—and place them in the context of an institutional theory. Chapters 9, 10, and 11 take the story into the 1980s. This starts with an examination of changes in unionization trends in the 1980s and consideration of some leading explanations. Neither structural changes in employment nor an institutional time series analysis adequately accounts for the latest downturns in union organization. This motivates a more dynamic treatment of labor market institutions in Chapter 10, which studies recent trends in decentralized collective bargaining. Next, the impact of this institutional change on widespread declining unionization in the late 1970s and 1980s is explored. The conclusion draws together the empirical story and uses the analysis to offer some conjectures about the future of unions in the advanced capitalist countries.

Two

Variation in Union Membership

UNION MEMBERSHIP varies in many different ways. The number of union members in a country can change over time and vary across industries, and, most important, the percentage of union members in a national labor market can vary a great deal across countries. This variation in union membership is the dependent variable for this study. Although previous studies have focused on just one type of variability in unionization, part of the power of the institutional explanation is that it provides some insight into the range of variability that unionization shows. In this chapter, I introduce the key ideas of "union" and "union density." I next describe several kinds of variation in union membership that an adequate explanation must address.

Unions and Union Density

How should we compare unions in a large number of countries, given the many different forms they take and many different roles they play? Take, for example, the relationship between unions and the political arena. In Belgium and the Netherlands, union leaders are formally integrated into the process of social and economic policymaking through governmental advisory boards. In France, on the other hand, unions have largely been excluded from the corridors of state power. Instead, French unions try to influence the political process through surges in industrial militancy. Similar variety can be found in the relationship between unions and political parties. The British scene represents one pole where trade unions have formal organizational standing in the Labour party. The opposite pole, Japan, features company unions that are largely divorced from partisan politics.

There are also large differences in the roles that unions play in the labor market—an area where we might expect stronger cross-national similarities. Australian union leaders present their case for a new wage agreement in a quasi-legal tribunal. The new collective agreement arrives in a judicial ruling, which extends to all workers in the industry, regardless of whether they are union members. Contrast the North American labor markets. American and Canadian unions bargain with employers over a procedurally informal bargaining table. Collective agreements from this process cover only working conditions at an authorized bargaining unit, which the union represents exclusively. The British case suggests a third variant, in which, unlike the Australian or North American case, unions bargain without legal recognition.

We can begin to think more systematically about the "immense variety of trade unions" (Clegg 1976) by first defining what is meant by a "union," and a "union member." Bain and Price (1980, 2) in their comprehensive statistical study define a union as "an organization of employees which seeks to represent the job interests of its members to employers and in some circumstances to the state, but which is not dominated by either of them." This definition conveys the main idea of a voluntary organization of employees whose chief purpose is collective bargaining over wages and working conditions. Unions—commonly "trade unions" in Britain, but "labor unions" in the United States—can then be distinguished from professional associations, such as the American Medical Association. Professional associations, while representing members' "job interests," generally include significant numbers of self-employed professionals in private practice. With the Bain and Price definition, professional associations are excluded, but organizations of credentialed wage-earners, such as teachers, nurses, or social workers, are included in union membership counts.

An overall measure of union organization in a labor market is given by the union density statistic. Union density is the number of union members expressed as a percentage of the number of people who could potentially be union members. This potential constituency is called the dependent labor force. It is often defined to include all wage-earners plus the unemployed. Employers and the self-employed are thus excluded as part of labor's potential constituency. The unemployed are counted as potential union members principally because unions retain jobless members on their rolls and because the unemployed retain their membership in the labor force by seeking work (Bain and Price 1980, 6–9). If jobless workers were excluded from union density statistics, labor's organizational strength would fluctuate purely as an artifact of the unemployment rate. A distinction is sometimes drawn between gross density statistics, which count unemployed and retired members, and net density statistics, which include only employed union members. This study uses mostly gross densities because these data are more complete. In practice, gross and net densities are generally highly correlated.

From a sociological point of view, these definitions, taken from the industrial relations literature, imply an old-fashioned but serviceable map of the basic class division in capitalist societies—that between wage-earners and employers. Instead of drawing a multiplicity of class cleavages based on relations of ownership or authority, the students of unions take their maps of social division from the concrete facts of collective action in the labor market. The study of unionization can thus be seen as an empirical test of this simple class map. In this test, unionization expresses the salience of the class division as a principle of collective action.

Variation in Union Membership

Studies of unionization have distinguished four major types of variation. In the research traditions of industrial relations and labor economics, researchers have focused on how unionization varies across industries and over time within a single country. Comparative research in sociology and political science has examined cross-national variability. Finally, several recent studies have identified a widespread tendency for the decline of union density across all advanced capitalist countries since the late 1970s.

Sectoral and Demographic Variation

The earliest studies of unionization in Britain and the United States observed substantial sectoral variation. The traditional industrial working class of the early twentieth century grew out of manufacturing industries. Unionization was widely found to be higher in those industries than in services or agriculture. For instance, early union density statistics show that 32 percent of British workers in metals and engineering industries were union members in 1892, compared to only 5 percent in local government and education (Bain and Price 1980, 50 & 76). More recently, sectoral variation has been an important part of the unionization story in the context of public sector growth. Through the 1960s, unions increasingly acquired collective bargaining rights for public sector workers. Union membership in this area grew rapidly as the employment share of government workers sharply rose through the late 1960s and 1970s.

Table 2.1 shows sectoral differences in union membership for eighteen OECD countries in 1985. We see large sectoral effects for manufacturing and public sector workers. Across eighteen OECD countries, union density in manufacturing is higher than the average level across the whole labor force. In Denmark, Sweden, and Belgium, all or nearly all manufacturing sector workers were union members by 1985. France is the notable exception, having virtually no union members in manufacturing industries. Public sector unionization is also relatively high. Public sector union organization is particularly strong where the national union density is low. In Japan, for example, the proportion of public sector workers who were union members was more than twice the national average. In the United States, less than a fifth of all American workers were union members in 1985, but more than a third of those in the public sector had joined unions.

Researchers have argued that this general pattern of sectoral variation is related to the costs and benefits of unionization. For the unions, organizing manufacturing industries and the public sector is relatively inexpensive be-

TABLE 2.1

Union Density by Sector and Sex, Eighteen OECD Countries, 1985

	National	Manufacturing Sector	Public Sector	Women	Men
Australia	57	51	71	45	63
Austria	61	56	61	37	57
Belgium	81	90	—	—	—
Canada	36	45	63	30	39
Denmark	91	100	75	72	78
Finland	87	80	86	75	69
France	16	below 5	35	11	21
Germany	44	50	50	22	47
Ireland	62	—	—	47	60
Italy	60	49	56	—	—
Japan	29	33	62	22	32
Netherlands	34	34	49	13	37
New Zealand	54	58	—	—	—
Norway	65	85	77	—	—
Sweden	94	100	88	86	83
Switzerland	33	33	71	13	39
United Kingdom	51	58	69	37	55
United States	18	25	36	13	22

Source: Visser 1991.

Notes: National densities are gross figures that include unemployed and retired members. French figures include employed members only. French men's and women's figures are averages of 1981 and 1989 densities. The French manufacturing sector density is for 1988. All Finnish figures, except national union density, are for 1989. Swiss manufacturing and public sector figures and Canadian manufacturing figures are for 1984, as are all British statistics except national union density. Irish data for men and women are from 1988. Danish men's and women's figures are for 1986.

cause workers are typically collected together in large shops sharing similar employment conditions. For employers in these sectors, either wages tend to be a small part of total production costs or at least wage increases can be passed on to consumers. Employers are less likely to resist union organizing under these conditions.

This type of argument can be extended to other kinds of variability in unionization within national labor markets. For instance, union membership varies across occupations. Just as manufacturing sector workers are more likely to be union members, manual workers within particular industries are much more likely to be union members than nonmanual workers. Although there are few good aggregate data on unionization by occupation for a large number of countries, analyses of social survey data commonly find this pattern (Hirsch and Addison 1986).

Finally, researchers have argued that the benefits of union membership vary with characteristics of the workers themselves. This is because the types of benefits unions provide can vary across workers, so the incentives for union membership also vary. This suggests that unionization differs across demographic groups. The gender gap in unionization is a clear illustration. In all the advanced capitalist countries, men are more likely to be union members than women. This is sometimes attributed to the weakness of women's labor force attachment. Because family obligations have historically taken women out of the labor force, they have benefited less from seniority provisions in collective agreements. The gender gap in unionization is largest in the Netherlands, Germany, and Switzerland. In these countries, women's labor force participation is low and declines quickly with age and marriage. Where women hold a less marginalized place in the labor market, as in the Scandinavian countries, the gender gap in union membership is small.

Cross-National Variation

Studies of sectoral and demographic variation in union membership usually ignore large differences in union size across countries. Indeed, the statistics shown in Table 2.1 suggest that sectoral and demographic variation is small compared to the enormous cross-national differences in union density. Comparative researchers often remark on the considerable strength of the Swedish labor movement, and this is reflected in the level of union membership (e.g., Galenson 1952; Clegg 1976; Korpi 1983). In 1985, the most organized labor market in the world could be found in Sweden, where nearly all workers were union members. On the other hand, the United States is often painted as a labor movement laggard, and U.S. unions are organizationally among the weakest in the advanced capitalist world. The Swedish labor market contrasts with the American and French ones, where less than a fifth of all workers are in unions. The other countries of the OECD are distributed between these extremes.

    Interestingly, with the exception of Scandinavia, regional patterns of variation in union density are quite weak, perhaps casting doubt on cultural explanations of unionization. In the Romance countries, Italian and French union densities differ by more than 40 percentage points. In the Low Countries, the difference between Belgian and Dutch union organization exceeds 45 percentage points. In the German-speaking countries, union density ranges from around 60 percent in Austria to around 30 percent in Switzerland. Even within closely defined regions, large differences can be found. For example, Canadian workers are now about twice as likely to be union members than their counterparts south of the border in the United States. If cross-national variability in union density is rooted in cultural variability, it is difficult to find broad evidence of cultural effects anywhere but Scandinavia.

Change over Time

While one research tradition has focused on variation in union membership across structural cleavages of industry and demography, another has associated change over time with fluctuations in the business cycle. Neither tradition has been comparative. Researchers in the business cycle tradition have typically studied how union membership changes with the rise and fall in inflation and unemployment. When several countries are studied, reports emphasize the generality of cyclical fluctuations, rather than cross-national variability (Bain and Elsheikh 1976).

However, when time series of union density are placed in comparative perspective, a number of interesting patterns emerge. Figure 2.1 shows one way of graphically examining the eighteen union density time series from our population of eighteen OECD countries. This figure provides a time series of boxplots showing the distribution of union densities for the eighteen countries for each year from 1950 to 1989. Each box marks the interquartile range (the distance from the 25th to the 75th percentile) of the annual union density distribution. The line within the box shows the median. The "whiskers" of the box extend to the 5th and 95th percentiles.

In the aggregate pattern revealed by this figure, the general level of union density in the advanced capitalist countries increased slowly through the 1950s and 1960s, and then increased quite quickly during the 1970s. This is indicated by movements in the median union density, which increased by about 20 percentage points from the late 1960s. Unionization has also diverged throughout most of the postwar period. In 1950, union density varied in a fairly narrow band between about 35 percent and 55 percent. Thirty years later, the range of union densities had increased by more than three times. The most heavily unionized country (Sweden) now organized around 90 percent of its dependent labor force, while the least unionized country (the United States) could claim less than one-fifth of its work force as union members. The most unionized countries at the beginning of the time period were not always the most unionized at the end. Rapid union growth moved Finland into the top tier of advanced capitalist labor movements. Australia and Austria were among the most unionized in 1950, but subsequently fell behind their Nordic counterparts. In short, the labor markets of the advanced capitalist countries looked much more similar in 1951 than they did three decades later.

A more disaggregated picture is given by the individual time series shown in Figure 2.2. In this figure, we can distinguish three broad trajectories of labor movement development. First, some countries show more or less continuous increase in unionization. Four countries—Belgium, Denmark, Finland, and Sweden—show large increases in union density. Except for Finland, all four began the 1950s with about 60 percent of their labor forces unionized, and now

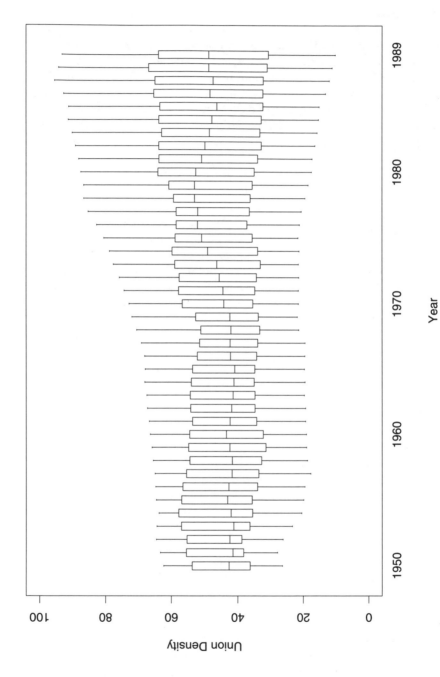

Figure 2.1. Boxplots of the annual distribution of union density, eighteen OECD countries, 1950–1989. *Source:* See Appendix.

all four, including Finland, have union density in excess of 80 percent. The size of the union movement increases smoothly in Belgium and Sweden. In Finland, the increase does not begin until the late 1950s. In Denmark, the sharpest increase started in the mid-1970s.

Second, a large group of countries show a steady level of unionization throughout the postwar period. This group includes Australia, Austria, Canada, Germany, Ireland, New Zealand, Norway, and the United Kingdom. The general level of unionization in the second group is, lower than in the first, varying in a band between 30 and 60 percent, with Austria and Norway at the top and Canada at the bottom. Shifts are found in Britain and Ireland (increase through the 1970s, decline in the 1980s). Italy can be added to this group. Although Italy has a unique and strongly redescending pattern of union organization, it shares the same general level of unionization—around 40 percent—with the other middle-density countries.

Third, the union densities of five countries—France, Japan, the Netherlands, Switzerland, and the United States—contracted between 1950 and the end of the 1980s. By 1990, the level of labor organization in these countries varied between about 14 and 25 percent. The timing of decline also varied, beginning first in the United States and Switzerland, where densities have dropped steadily since the mid-1950s. Decline in Japan came in two stages, first in the 1950s and then in the 1970s. In France and the Netherlands, union decline began in the 1970s.

In sum, any account of postwar unionization in the advanced capitalist countries must account for two patterns of longitudinal variation. First, there is increasing variability in union densities in the three decades after 1950. Second, there are three general trajectories of labor movement development: increasing organization among the high-density countries, constant union density in the moderately organized countries, and declining density among the least organized.

Union Decline in the 1980s

The boxplots in Figure 2.1 also reveal another distinctive type of variation in postwar unionization. While union density was diverging in the advanced capitalist countries for the thirty years from 1950 to 1980, union density was generally falling during the 1980s. The prolonged pattern of divergence had been replaced by the convergent trajectories of union decline. The 1980s thus mark a novel development in the history of the postwar labor movements.

A clearer picture of the union decline is given in Table 2.2, which compares the change in union density during 1973–1980 to the change during 1981–1989. The table shows that, although many union movements did relatively well in the 1970s, nearly all lost ground in the 1980s. Generally, the low-

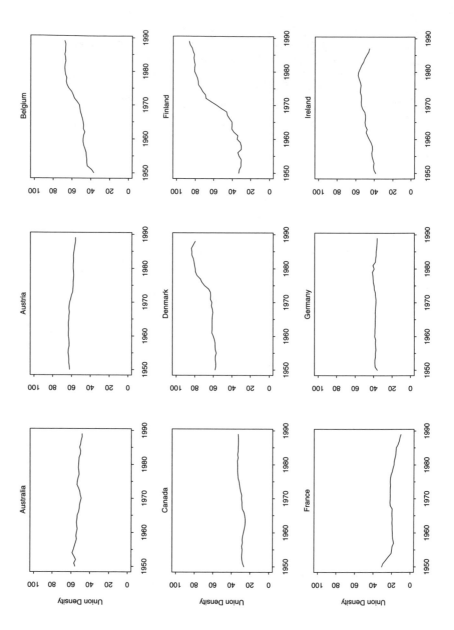

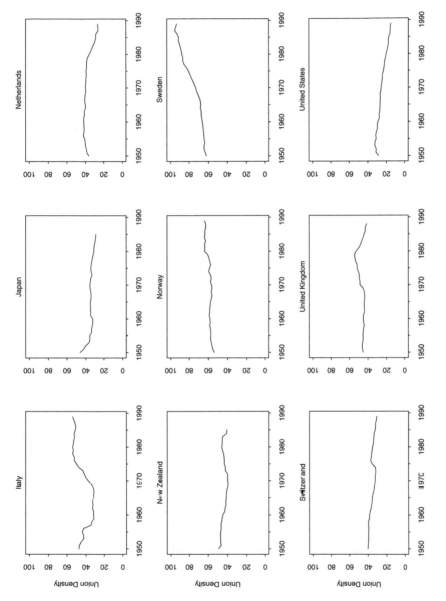

Figure 2.2. Time series of union density. 18 OECD countries, 1951–1989.

TABLE 2.2

Changes in Union Density, Eighteen OECD Countries, 1973–1980
and 1981–1989

	1973 Density	Change 1973–1980	Change 1981–1989
High-density countries			
Belgium	59	8.7	−0.2
Denmark	63	16.3	−0.8
Finland	69	12.0	5.8
Sweden	78	9.9	5.0
Middle-density countries			
Australia	52	0.0	−3.3
Austria	59	−0.5	−2.4
Canada	31	2.4	−0.9
France	22	−3.9	−7.2
Germany	39	1.3	−4.5
Ireland	54	3.0	−10.5
Italy	43	10.9	0.8
New Zealand	42	3.6	−4.9
Norway	58	6.1	0.2
United Kingdom	49	3.5	−8.2
Low-density countries			
Japan	33	−2.6	−4.6
Netherlands	39	−3.4	−7.0
Switzerland	32	3.2	−3.6
United States	25	−4.3	−4.5

Notes: Latest year for Denmark is 1988. Latest year for Ireland is 1987.
Latest year for Japan and New Zealand is 1985.

density countries fared worst, accelerating their decline of the 1970s. However, the largest declines in union density are found in two moderately organized countries—Ireland and the United Kingdom. Unionization in both countries shrank by about 10 percentage points, a decline in union membership of about one-quarter. Only the four highly organized countries resisted the membership declines. Even here, however, union density by the end of the 1980s was growing at a much slower rate than before.

In sum, unions play a variety of roles in the labor markets of Western Europe, North America, and Australasia. Despite this variation, union membership is a broadly similar type of organizational affiliation that we can compare across countries. A common and useful overall measure of union membership is union density—union membership as a percentage of the dependent labor force. Union density has shown four main kinds of variation in the postwar period. First, there are general differences in unionization across structural and demographic lines within national labor markets. Second, there are broad cross-national differences in union density. France and the United States are lowest in union density, while all the Nordic countries except Norway are highest. Third, there is longitudinal variation, which reveals increasing divergence in union organization over the course of the postwar period. Finally, there is the uniquely convergent pattern of union decline, coming in the 1980s. Any adequate explanation of the development of labor movements in the postwar capitalist democracies must account for these four types of variation in union membership.

Part II

THE INSTITUTIONAL SOURCES
OF UNION GROWTH

Three _____

Labor Market Centralization

LABOR MARKETS are embedded in institutions that aggregate and fragment the interests of workers and employers. Rules that regulate collective bargaining and internal union affairs are particularly important in this way. They determine whether unions represent workers by plant, by industry, or at the level of the national economy. These systems of representation draw lines of competition and cooperation in the labor market. For this reason, the patterns of labor market representation are closely connected to the process of unionization.

The breadth of collective interest that develops among workers depends importantly on the centralization of the institutions of interest representation. Centralized labor markets condense representation into a single union covering all workers. Decentralized representation, by contrast, creates many local contests between workers and employers. Industrial relations specialists often distinguish three types of interest representation in collective bargaining (e.g., Clegg 1976; Traxler 1994). At the highest level of centralization, national representatives of employers and unions negotiate wages and conditions for the entire labor market. Union confederations—representing affiliated unions—bargain for labor. Central employer associations—representing industry-level business groups—bargain for owners. Effective bargaining hinges on peak associations powerful enough to bind their members to collective agreements. Thus central unions often hold strike funds, and central employer associations often have the power to levy fines on their members (Headey 1970; Windmuller 1984, 19–20). More decentralized bargaining is found in countries where employers and unions negotiate wages for particular industries, rather than the entire national economy. In these countries, organizational power resides with industry unions and employer groups. The central organizations of labor and capital play an advisory role, or act as representatives in national politics. Finally, in decentralized labor markets, collective relations between employers and workers are found in individual firms or plants. In this case, employers are usually directly involved in wage talks with local unions, dispensing with the agency of the employer association.

Variations on this three-level model of interest representation have been proposed by students of corporatism (Cameron 1984; Lehmbruch 1984; Lange, Wallerstein, and Golden 1995). In that research, centralized, or corporatist, bargaining provides a way of subordinating sectional concerns to broad class-wide interests in full employment and universal welfare pro-vision (Calmfors and Driffill 1988; Korpi 1989; Esping-Andersen 1990). The work on corporatism goes beyond the sphere of industrial relations by emphasizing the influence of unions on national economic and social policy. Where bargaining is highly centralized, the range of issues on the table often extends beyond wages and working conditions. Social welfare, unemploy-ment, inflation, and economic growth are also at stake. Sometimes influence on these policy areas is formally expressed in three-cornered forums represent-ing the government, the unions, and employers. Just as commonly, govern-ments also informally consult with union confederations on economic and social policy.

So far, I have used the term "labor market centralization" a little loosely to refer to (1) the level of collective bargaining, (2) the centralization of unions' and employers' own internal administration, and (3) the role of unions in eco-nomic and social policy. In practice, these distinctions may not be so important for this analysis. All three aspects of labor market centralization contribute to union growth, and all three are closely related empirically. Thus, confedera-tions engaged in national bargaining usually have significant control over the strike activity of union affiliates, and they are also represented in public policy. Similarly, union confederations in decentralized labor markets have little formal control over union affiliates and are unrepresented in state economic management. Labor market centralization can thus be viewed as a closely knit constellation of institutional characteristics, underpinned by a single principle of representation. In the highly centralized setting, labor market representation is broad and unified. Under decentralization, labor market representation is narrow and fragmented.

Research on corporatism often adds union density to the institutional ingre-dients of labor market centralization. In this view, union density and central-ized labor markets form part of a single cluster of labor movement power resources (e.g., Hicks 1988; Alvarez, Garrett, and Lange 1991; see also the review of Esping-Andersen and van Kersbergen [1992, 202]). I take a different view here. In this chapter, I tease out the possible causal links between labor market centralization and union organizing. From this approach, union density and labor market centralization are not just different aspects of the same insti-tutional complex; instead, the patterns of centralization drive variation in union organization. After describing how labor market institutions influence union growth, I present three pieces of evidence for this causal link. First, an overview of collective bargaining in the advanced capitalist countries re-veals institutional stability and a correlation between unionization and levels of centralization. This suggests that collective bargaining institutions provided stable contexts for divergent union density trends, at least until the early 1980s. Second, when labor market institutions in Italy were strengthened and central-ized following the Hot Autumn of 1969, union density increased rapidly. This exceptional case provides some longitudinal evidence for the relationship between union growth and centralization, and for the causal priority of centralization. Finally, a brief comparative case analysis of Sweden, Britain, and the United States illustrates in more detail how centralization influences the process of union organizing.

The Case for Labor Market Centralization

Three causal mechanisms connect centralized labor markets to union growth. First, with labor market centralization, employers have few opportunities or incentives to oppose union organizing. In one version of this argument, the extension of union wages to unorganized workers defuses employer opposition to unionism in highly centralized settings (Freeman 1989). Employers are forced to pay the costs of unionism regardless of whether their workers are union members. More generally, labor market centralization defuses employer opposition by establishing the institutional legitimacy of organized labor. Because centralized collective bargaining institutions are usually underwritten by mutual recognition pacts, employers are less likely to view unions as intrusions on capitalist property rights or managerial prerogatives. In more decentralized labor markets, the legitimacy of organized labor is much more tenuous and employers have greater opportunity to contest union organizing.

Second, powerful confederations in centralized labor markets coordinate the organizing effort and redistribute organizing costs from highly unionized industries to weakly unionized industries. Coordination also reduces competition among unions over membership. Where union organizing is coordinated, resources are seldom wasted on jurisdictional disputes. In decentralized labor markets, the central union confederation is not powerful enough to direct the organizing effort and unions in poorly organized sectors are unable to attract resources for organizing. Union movements are also less cohesive under decentralized bargaining, so competition among unions for members is more common.

Third, centralized labor markets involve union confederations in developing and applying economic policy. A centralized influence over the size of the national wage bill provides unions with some control over unemployment and its distribution across industries. Where unions actively participate in other economic policy areas, they can protect organized industries and occupations by directing investment and subsequent employment to these or other unionizable sectors. Central union support for expanding highly unionized public sector employment is a notable example (Masters and Robertson 1988). Without this influence on the economy, unions are placed in a passive position, reacting to exogenous changes in the structure of employment and market conditions.

A Survey of Labor Market Institutions

The historical roots of centralized labor market representation can be traced to coordinated union activity, not in collective bargaining, but in strike activity. Unions in Austria, Belgium, Finland, the Netherlands, Norway, and Sweden were all involved in mass strikes directed by socialist and social democratic parties pressing for suffrage reform (Therborn 1977; Esping-Andersen 1985, 59; Knoellinger 1960, 48; Windmuller 1969, 32). The original impulse for centralized bargaining in the first decades of the twentieth century also came from outside the union movement. In Sweden and Norway, employers responded to isolated pockets of strike activity with multiemployer lockouts. Cooperation among the bosses reduced competition for workers under conditions of acute labor scarcity during a period of mass Scandinavian migration to the United States (Swenson 1991). Low-wage workers also favored centralized bargaining as their market power and wages rose in the more encompassing forum (Swenson 1989). The route to contemporary labor market institutions, however, was often interrupted and sometimes spurred by war, depression, and political foment.

The High-Density Countries

The centralized Swedish labor market moved toward its modern form in 1938, when the Basic Agreement was signed between the employers, represented by the Swedish Employers Confederation (SAF), and blue-collar workers, represented by Sweden's Landsorganisationen (LO), the Scandinavian-style national confederation of trade unions (Korpi 1978, 83). Regular wage bargaining rounds between the LO and SAF began in 1956. Parallel talks for white-collar workers also began at this time. The Swedish pattern of occupationally divided, but centralized, unionism originated in the 1940s, when the main white-collar confederations, the Central Organization of Salaried Employees (TCO) and the Swedish Confederation of Professional Associations (SACO), were formed. As in most centralized labor markets, the national wage agreement accounted for only part of all wage movements. Upward departures from the agreement ("wage drift") pushed up pay in high-income jobs in response to the LO's solidaristic policy of wage compression (Flanagan et al. 1983, 313–15). Centralized bargaining deteriorated from 1983, when the high-wage metalworkers split from the central bargaining rounds, negotiating independently with the metal trades employer federation (Lash 1985).

Less centralized than in Sweden, Belgian industrial relations show elements of national and industry bargaining. As in several countries of continental Europe, a national framework for labor market regulation developed in wartime. Secret talks between union leaders and employers during the German occupation yielded a social pact establishing the rights of the labor market representatives and procedures for collective bargaining. Although wage talks were held at the industry level in the decades after the war, negotiations from the 1960s on were framed by national social programming agreements. These national agreements provided broad guidelines for welfare, wages, and economic development (Hancke 1991; Blanpain 1971). The mixture of national and industry-level labor market representation is cross-cut by political and linguistic differences among the blue-collar unions. The Catholic Flanders-based General Christian Trade Union Federation (CSC) is strong in the private sector, while the socialist Walloon General Belgian Trade Union Federation (FGTB) is the dominant public sector confederation. Still, the two pillars within the union movement have coordinated bargaining since 1962, and the confederations assert a national influence on economic and social policy through the "social parliament," the National Labor Council (Molitor 1978; Blanpain 1984, 327; Lorwin 1975).

Finnish and Danish labor markets are less centralized than in Belgium and Sweden. In Finland, labor unity is limited by communist union leaders, who play a strong independent role in the blue-collar confederation (Elvander 1990, 8). A stable framework for industrial relations also developed late in Finland. A Basic Agreement initiating centralized bargaining over nonwage issues was signed in 1940, but the first centralized wage talks were held only after a general strike in 1956 (Knoellinger 1960). Industry bargaining periodically surfaced throughout the 1960s, but regular national bargaining involving peak representatives from the union, employers, and farmers did not begin until 1968 (Elvander 1974, 432).

The Danish union movement is decentralized compared to those of the other high-density countries. Danish unions were organized by craft from the late nineteenth century on. Despite this fragmented structure, the Danish LO was the first to sign a mutual recognition pact with employers—the 1898 September Agreement. This agreement formed the constitution for national wage talks, which began in the 1930s, and has remained largely intact since World War II (Jacobsen 1989, 25–26; Flanagan et al. 1983, 452). Although the confederation represents only about half of all Danish labor organizations (Esping-Andersen 1985, 62), the central agreements shape bargaining for unaffiliated unions. Craft fragmentation of the union movement was also balanced by the LO's policy of reducing wage inequality across skill levels during the 1970s (Flanagan et al. 1983, 459).

Labor market institutions in the four high-density countries show broadly similar patterns of centralization. Throughout the postwar period, union confederations were involved in national and industry bargaining. Mutual recognition of the rights of peak associations to bargain for union and employer affiliates was established by the end of the war in all the high-density countries except Finland. Finnish centralized bargaining institutions began to assume their contemporary shape in the late 1950s.

The Middle-Density Countries

The seven moderately organized countries of the postwar period can be divided into two groups. Labor market institutions are centralized in Austria and Norway, while wages are set at the industry and enterprise levels in Australia, Britain, Canada, Germany, and New Zealand.

Austrian and Norwegian centralized bargaining resembles industrial relations in the high-density countries. Indeed, the Austrian Confederation of Trade Unions (ÖGB), representing sixteen industrial unions, is the most centralized of all confederations in the OECD. The ÖGB was formed in 1945 by Austrian trade union leaders, who fundamentally reformed the decentralized and conflictual union structure of the interwar years. Sweeping institutional change placed bargaining, financial, and disciplinary responsibilities in the hands of the new confederation. The Austrian unions of the postwar period have no independent legal personality and submit to the ÖGB's direction in collective bargaining (Duda and Tödtling 1986, 238–42; Strasser 1982). Agreements are generally made for each industry, however, and the affiliates have some wage-bargaining autonomy (OECD 1979a, 11–12; Flanagan et al. 1983, 52). Consistent with the dominance of industry bargaining in Austria, the ÖGB has not pursued the solidaristic wage policy characteristic of the Scandinavian confederations (Korpi and Esping-Andersen 1984, 194).

Norwegian labor market institutions are similar to those in Sweden. Like the Swedish LO, the central union of Norwegian manual workers holds strike funds and directs the industrial action of union affiliates. The Norwegian Landsorganisasjon (LO) has been authorized to negotiate for affiliates since its Basic Agreement in 1935 (Visser 1990a, 157). Collective agreements between the LO and the employers' association, the Norwegian Employers Federation (NAF), were reached at the industry and at the national level through the 1950s and biennial national bargaining began in 1964 (Elvander 1974, 423). Peak-level wage rounds were threatened by the parliamentary left, which urged higher wage increases in lieu of centralized bargaining in 1961 and 1974 (Flanagan et al. 1983, 168). As in Sweden at the same time, pressure for wage solidarity from the Norwegian LO and the low-wage unions endangered the participation of high-wage workers in the central agreement.

In Germany, Australia, New Zealand, and Britain, multiemployer agreements at the industry level characterize labor relations. The German system is most centralized, with sixteen large industrial unions monopolizing wage bargaining (Markovits 1986, 12–13). Wage-setting by industry can be traced to early experiments with tripartism in the Weimar period (Maier 1988, 61). After the repression of organized labor during the Nazi years, the legislative framework for industry bargaining was reestablished in the Adenauer government's Collective Agreement Act (1949) (Markovits 1986, 39). The basic form of pattern bargaining, led by the metalworkers' union, IG Metall, began in the early 1950s. The prominence of the industry level in industrial relations accompanied relatively weak shop floor organization until the late 1960s. Since then, union power within enterprises was expanded by law through the development of local works councils (Markovits 1986, 54–60).

Although more fragmented than the German system, industry bargaining is also found in three British Commonwealth countries. In Australia procedures for industry union registration date from the turn of the century. Weak national bargaining began in the 1930s, with a regular hearing of the National Wage Case, in which employer groups were pitted against the Australian Council of Trade Unions (ACTU). The role of the ACTU in collective bargaining was recast in 1983, when the incoming Labor government sponsored the national Prices and Incomes Accord (Brooks 1988). In New Zealand, a similar procedure for union registration began in 1894 (Howells 1982, 52–53). As in Germany, wage rounds in New Zealand follow pattern-setting agreements by the metalworkers, but the New Zealand Federation of Labor, unlike the German central union, actively participated in bargaining by contesting employer groups over the General Wage Order (Roth 1973).

In Britain and Ireland, labor market institutions are outwardly similar, consisting of a mix of general, industrial, and craft unions. More legally informal than in the Southern Hemisphere (McCarthy 1984, 132; Clegg 1979, 290–96), the British system of two-tier bargaining emerged when shop stewards took up wage bargaining, first in engineering industries, in the late 1930s and early 1940s (Clegg 1979, 23). The move to local bargaining was periodically arrested by state incomes policies that set national guidelines for pay raises. Legal informality in British industrial relations eroded gradually until the early 1980s, when Thatcher's Conservative government passed a sequence of laws decisively restricting trade union rights (Marsh 1992). In Ireland, by contrast, regular industry bargaining dominated Irish labor relations between 1946 and 1969, while the central confederation, the Irish Congress of Trade Unions (ICTU), periodically negotiated "rudimentary and unsophisticated" central agreements (Hardimann 1988, 45). Growing wage competition in this period resulted in a series of National Wage Agreements through the 1970s and 1980s.

Unlike the other middle-density countries, Canadian labor market institutions have strong similarities to the American ones. The importance of local bargaining in Canada stems from the impact of the U.S. National Labor Relations Act (1935). Canadian labor law emerged during the emergency conditions of wartime in 1944 and was built on the U.S. model (Arthurs, Carter, Glasbeck, and Fudge 1988, 46). While the wartime provisions and peacetime variants instituted American-style procedures for local union certification, Canadian certification and collective agreements are generally less restrictive of unions than the U.S. procedures (Riddell 1993). Elections are usually not required (except in British Columbia and Nova Scotia), and union shop clauses are broadly enforceable. While the bargaining environment developed in the late 1940s, craft and industrial confederations had emerged by the 1930s. The union movement was unified by merger of the two confederations to form the Canadian Labor Congress in 1956.

In sum, the institutions and actors of the postwar labor markets in the middle-density countries generally remained stable in the three decades after 1950. Industrial relations had already taken shape during the 1930s in all but two countries. In different ways, institutional developments in Canada and Austria were profoundly shaped by war, and the main contours of the labor markets in those countries were not clear until the 1940s. A correlation is also beginning to emerge between labor market centralization and unionization. The highly organized middle-density countries are also the most centralized; Canada has the weakest central union and lowest union density.

The Low-Density Countries

Although collective bargaining is generally uncoordinated, the pattern of labor market decentralization varies within the low-density group. In Japan and the United States, bargaining and other union activity is focused at the enterprise level. Swiss and French unions bargained by industry for most of the postwar period, but the unions were weak compared to employer groups. By comparison, Dutch confederations have been strong, with extensive control over their affiliates.

Japan provides the limiting case of labor market decentralization. The Japanese system of enterprise unionism emerged in the mid-1950s, following intense struggles between employers and industry unions (Gordon 1985, chs. 9 & 10). Bargaining in Japan is reasonably synchronized, beginning with the Spring wage round, the Shunto. Still, unions are organized at the plant level and enterprise agreements increasingly reflect the economic performance of individual firms (Kuwahara 1987). Enterprise unionism shapes labor organizing as union leaders generally negotiate with employers for

consent to unionization. Thus a routine opportunity for employers to oppose unionization is built into the organizing process (Freeman and Rebick
1989, 591).

In the United States, a decentralized principle of labor organization was
established in the late 1930s by early Labor Board rulings on workplace
certification elections (Bernstein 1969, 653). Unknown in Europe, the system
of union elections allowed U.S. employers to run antiunion campaigns as
a normal part of the organizing process. After the war, industrial unions
were still comparatively decentralized, presenting a common front to U.S.
employers through pattern bargaining rather than through industry agreements (Kochan, Katz, and McKersie 1986, 34). In 1947, the Taft-Hartley Act
allowed states to pass "right-to-work" legislation, prohibiting union shops.
This power was subsequently exercised by twenty, mostly southern, states
(Goldfield 1987, 187). Certification elections, in combination with right-to-
work legislation, provide employers with regular opportunities for actively
opposing unions.

As in Japan and the United States, the legitimacy of trade unionism in
France was not woven into the institutional fabric of the labor market. Although the legal framework for labor relations was established in 1950 and
some industry and local wage agreements emerged from this point, collective bargaining was not common until after 1968. Unions secured some
recognition at the plant level at this point when the Law on Trade Union Rights
was passed. Still, the development of collective bargaining since the 1970s
was restricted largely to the public sector, and private sector employers often
ignored collective agreements until labor law reforms of the early 1980s
(Howell 1992). As in the United States and Japan, and in contrast to most
other countries, decentralization of the French labor market gave employers
the chance to resist unions in their workplaces. Nationally, the weakness of
French industrial relations is compounded by the close interdependence between government and private industry. Consequently, labor is excluded from
economic management.

Labor markets in Switzerland and the Netherlands are more centralized
than in France, the United States, or Japan. In Switzerland, industry agreements often set working conditions, but wages are negotiated within the firm.
The main labor confederation, the Confederation of Swiss Trade Unions
(SGB), represents sixteen industrial affiliates. It has maintained cooperative
relations with the Christian confederation, the Christian-National Confederation of Swiss Trade Unions (CNG), since the 1930s. The most powerful
union, representing metalworkers and watchmakers, began regular collective
bargaining in 1937. The institutionalized position of unions in the Swiss
labor market began in the same year, with the adoption of the Code of Obligation. The code established the legal force of collective agreements. Passage of

the code and regular bargaining in metals and watchmaking industries in the late 1930s marked the end of employer resistance to unions in large industries (Aubert 1989).

In the Netherlands, the union movement is divided by the Calvinist, Catholic, and Socialist pillars of Dutch society, but the three main confederations were themselves highly centralized, controlling strike funds, and contributing to national wage-setting (Headey 1970, 413–14). As in Belgium, wartime conditions provided a context for centralization, as unions negotiated with employers to establish the bipartite consultative forum, the Foundation of Labor. Through the 1950s and 1960s, wages were set by a central government authority in consultation with the central representatives of labor and business. Unions gained more room for industry bargaining through the 1960s, a process culminating with the abolition of government wage guidelines in 1968. The system gradually recentralized through the 1970s, as the government regained some control over prices and wages. The union movement itself became more unified in 1976, following a merger of two of the main confederations (Windmuller 1968; Rood 1993, 62–69).

The five low-density countries share postwar continuity in their labor market institutions. With the exception of Japan, the basic institutions were set by 1950. The Japanese style of enterprise unionism had developed by the late 1950s. Once established, however, the framework for industrial relations was not radically reformulated in any of the low-density countries before the 1980s. The French and Dutch cases are partial exceptions. In the Netherlands, government influence over central wage talks was relaxed and industrial unions gained greater autonomy in the late 1960s and early 1970s, but an array of forums for national consultation remained intact (e.g., Visser 1990b, 201). In France, labor law reform created new legal protections for unions on the shop floor. In that case, however, formal institutional changes did little to curb French employers after 1968 (Lange, Ross, and Vannicelli 1982, 125; Flanagan et al. 1983, 612).

In all the low-density countries except the Netherlands, union confederations were excluded from a role in economic management and were weak in relation to affiliated unions and rival employer associations. Labor was generally strongest at the local level. In Lehmbruch's (1984, 66) phrase, Japan, the United States, France, and Switzerland are examples of "concertation without labor" (Lash and Urry [1987] make this argument for the United States; for Switzerland, see Katzenstein [1984]). Additionally, in France, Japan, and the United States, local organization features an institutionalized basis for employer opposition to unionization. The Dutch case, with the highest organization of the low-density countries, is a striking outlier: the Dutch union confederations are strong in relation to their affiliates, and unions have been integrated into the policy process through their institutionalized representation on state advisory bodies.

Quantitative Approaches

Instead of the institutional description presented so far, many researchers have taken a quantitative approach to describing labor market centralization. Studies in this tradition agree substantially about the most and least centralized labor markets. The Nordic countries and Austria are placed at the top, while the United States is at the bottom. Because slightly different institutional characteristics can be emphasized in measuring labor market centralization, there tends to be greater disagreement about the intermediate cases. One way of addressing the problem is to consider a variety of institutional indicators. This approach is taken by Bruno and Sachs (1985, 228). In their analysis of the economic effects of industrial relations institutions, they use a scale of labor market centralization that combines information about the centralization of union movements, the autonomy of union locals, the co-ordination among employers, and the presence of formal institutions for workplace representation.

Table 3.1 compares this scale to a brief summary of the institutional characteristics of labor markets in each of the eighteen countries. The qualitative institutional attributes and the quantitative scores are largely in line. Germany is perhaps the most discrepant case: the German confederation is relatively uninvolved in collective bargaining compared to the Scandinavian or Austrian case, yet Germany ranks at the top of the centralization scale, along with Austria, Norway, and Sweden. This may well be because, although the German confederation plays a relatively small bargaining role, it is closely involved in public policy. This was particularly true of the concerted-action period from the late 1960s to the mid-1970s. The centralization scores also confirm the correlation between labor market centralization and union density. There are no decentralized countries in the high-density group, and most low-density countries have low centralization scores.

My analysis in subsequent chapters relies heavily on the labor market centralization score. It is therefore important to show that the measure does not differ markedly from other quantitative indicators of centralized labor market representation and thus that my main results do not crucially depend on this choice of indicator. Table 3.2 illustrates this point, showing the rankings of countries in four leading studies using other measures of centralized industrial relations. The centralization ranking of Calmfors and Driffill (1988) is based on characteristics of union and employer organization. The Schmitter (1981) ranking was derived by combining information about the centralized organization of unions and the number of confederations. The final two measures, of Cameron (1984) and Stephens (1979), rank countries according to the degree of union centralization. The rankings shown in the table are all in agreement as to the high centralization of Austria and the Nordic countries, and the decen-

TABLE 3.1
Labor Market Institutions and Labor Market Centralization Scores,
Eighteen OECD Countries

	Labor Market Institutions	Labor Market Centralization
High-density countries		
Belgium	Industry bargaining, two coordinated blue-collar confederations	3.0
Denmark	National bargaining, blue-collar confederation coordinates craft unions	3.0
Finland	National bargaining by the late 1960s by politically divided confederation	3.0
Sweden	National bargaining, blue-collar confederation coordinates industry affiliates	4.0
Middle-density countries		
Australia	Industry bargaining, but confederation has limited role in collective bargaining	0.0
Austria	Industry bargaining, one confederation controlling sixteen industry affiliates	4.0
Canada	Local bargaining patterned by province, one major and two smaller confederations with little control over affiliates	0.0
Germany	Industry bargaining, confederation plays consultative role to sixteen industry unions	4.0
Ireland	Some national bargaining, but industry and local unions most powerful	0.0
Italy	Industry bargaining, three competitive confederations unified in 1971	0.5
New Zealand	Industry bargaining, confederation with weak collective bargaining role	0.5
Norway	National bargaining, coordinated by blue-collar confederation	4.0
United Kingdom	Industry bargaining, weak confederation, but strong industry and local unions	0.0

tralization of North American labor markets. Underlining the reliability of the centralization scores, all the indicators are themselves closely related, correlating at about .8 or .9. (Crouch [1993, 12–17] lists a similar array of indicators that provide similar results.)

To summarize, postwar labor market institutions were stable over time but varied greatly across countries from the 1950s to the early 1980s. The centralization of labor market institutions is also closely associated with levels of union organization. This suggests that patterns of centralization established

TABLE 3.1, continued

	Labor Market Institutions	Labor Market Centralization
Low-density countries		
France	Weak industry bargaining, multiple competing confederations divided across partisan lines	0.0
Japan	Coordinated enterprise bargaining, confederation has little control over local unions	1.5
Netherlands	National bargaining until 1968, industry unions gained more bargaining autonomy in 1970s and 1980s	2.0
Switzerland	Industry bargaining, two cooperative but politically divided confederations	1.0
United States	Local bargaining, weak confederation, but strong industry and local unions	0.0

Notes: Labor market centralization scores have been adapted from Bruno and Sachs 1985, 226. Scores were adjusted for union centralization in Belgium and Finland and for low union shop floor autonomy in Belgium and Japan.

durable contexts for union organizing, resulting in three distinct trajectories of union organizing in the 35 years since 1950. The Italian case provides a key exception to the pattern of institutional continuity. Italian industrial relations were transformed by the Hot Autumn of 1969 and the Italian labor movement made a radical break with its past.

Italian Exceptionalism

As in France, Italian collective bargaining before 1968 was conducted mostly at the industry level, but in practice employers were not bound by collective agreements. Unions had little legitimacy with employers and only a few hundred collective agreements were in force by the late 1950s, compared to more than 150,000 at the same time in the United States (Barkan 1984, 41). The two largest union confederations, the General Confederation of Italian Labor (CGIL) and the Italian Confederation of Labor Unions (CISL), were closely tied to political parties (the Communists, the Socialists, and the Christian Democrats). As a result, bargaining was uncoordinated, with frequent disputes and competition between the confederations. Employers and their association, Confindustria, capitalized on these political differences, often dealing only with the noncommunist unionists (Barkan 1984, 40–48; Neufeld 1961, ch. 10). Weak shop floor organization accompanied weak industrial unionism (Contini 1985). The CGIL provided little support for plant-level representation, and union activists commonly faced repressive measures inside the workplace. In-

TABLE 3.2

Rankings Based on Alternative Indicators of Labor Market Centralization and Correlations with Labor Market Centralization Score

Labor Market Centralization	Degree of Centralization	Societal Corporatism	Organizational Unity of Labor	Union Centralization
Austria	Austria	Austria	Austria	Austria
Germany	Norway	Norway	Denmark	Netherlands
Norway	Sweden	Denmark	Finland	Belgium
Sweden	Denmark	Finland	Germany	Norway
Belgium	Finland	Sweden	Norway	Sweden
Denmark	Germany	Netherlands	Sweden	Finland
Finland	Netherlands	Belgium	Belgium	Denmark
Netherlands	Belgium	Germany	Netherlands	Australia
Japan	New Zealand	Switzerland	Switzerland	Germany
Switzerland	Australia	Canada	Australia	Switzerland
Italy	France	Ireland	Canada	France
New Zealand	United Kingdom	United States	Ireland	Canada
Australia	Italy	France	U.K.	Ireland
Canada	Japan	U.K.	U.S.	Italy
France	Switzerland	Italy	France	New Zealand
Ireland	U.S.		Italy	U.K.
U.K.	Canada		Japan	U.S.
U.S.				
CORRELATION .9	.9	.9	.8	

Sources: Degree of centralization—Calmfors and Driffill 1988; societal corporatism—Schmitter 1981; organizational unity of labor—Cameron 1984; union centralization—Stephens 1979.

Note: Correlations between the labor market centralization score and the alternative indicators are based on ranks reported by Calmfors and Driffill and by Schmitter.

effective organization at the workplace and a complicated method of dues payment resulted in the confederations collecting only 30 to 40 percent of the membership fees owed to them in the late 1950s (Neufeld 1961, 513).

Toward the end of the 1960s, rising economic growth increased the demand for labor and thus its market power. This shift in the balance of power in Italian industrial relations combined with an intensification of the production process and substantial migration from the south to the north in the mid-1960s. On the political front, the Communists had expanded their parliamentary representation, while the Socialists had been decimated in the 1968 elections. This development made Communist participation in government a real possibility for the first time since the 1940s (Flanagan et al. 1983, 520–23; Lange et al. 1982, 127). By 1969, a rising stock of discontent had collected among the younger semiskilled migrant workers from the south, who were excluded from the weak industrial relations institutions. This discontent resulted in the widespread unofficial strike waves of the Hot Autumn in 1969 (Lange et al. 1982, 127–28; Contini 1985). Beginning with strikes in Turin at Pirelli in 1968 and at Fiat the following spring, the wave of militancy culminated in massive marches on Turin and Rome by workers from all sectors in the fall of 1969. In all, 5.5 million workers—a quarter of the Italian labor force—took part in the strikes, and 520 million worker hours were lost to industrial action (Barkan 1984, 75; Bedani 1995, 151–53).

The strike waves triggered far-reaching institutional change, both on the shop floor and at the national level. Within the factories, union rights were significantly strengthened by labor law reform contained in the Statuto dei lavoratori (1970). The new labor legislation provided rights to plant-level organization, bargaining, and assembly and allowed appeals against employer decisions to fire and transfer. Unlike parallel legislation in France, the Italian law was used extensively by the unions, and local bargaining flourished. In short, the law reform helped "institutionalize a new system of labor relations in which unions became legitimate actors in the firms with specific rights under the law" (Franzosi 1995, 304). At the national level, deep divisions within the union leadership were resolved to an important degree. An early step to consolidating the Italian labor movement was taken in July 1969, when the metalworkers union from each confederation jointly developed a single slate of demands for Confindustria (Bedani 1995, 153). Led by the metalworkers, the confederations cooperated closely through the early 1970s. In 1972, conflicts within the Italian union movement were significantly tempered when the confederations collected under the auspices of the Unitary Federation. Although the confederations remained separate entities under the umbrella federation, they jointly signed the *scala mobile* wage indexation agreement in 1975. This national agreement had an enormous effect on the Italian labor market by substantially raising wages and compressing the wage structure over the following decade. Labor movement unity was not seriously reversed until the mid-1980s, when the confederations split over the scala mobile and an autonomous confederation was formed for skilled public sector workers (Visser 1990a, 133).

The institutional reforms of the Hot Autumn offer a unique opportunity. With this case, we can observe in a dynamic way many of the institutional mechanisms of labor market centralization that we have so far seen only in a static cross-national comparison. To be sure, the Italian institutional transformation of the late 1960s and early 1970s is not a clear-cut case of centralization. Law reform attacked the arbitrary authority of management in the workplace, and local unions were fortified. Currents of labor market centralization are also clear, however. Political differences among the confederations were swapped for greater cooperation and the landmark agreement on wage indexation was signed at the national level. Even the gains unions made at the local level provide some functional equivalents to labor market centralization.

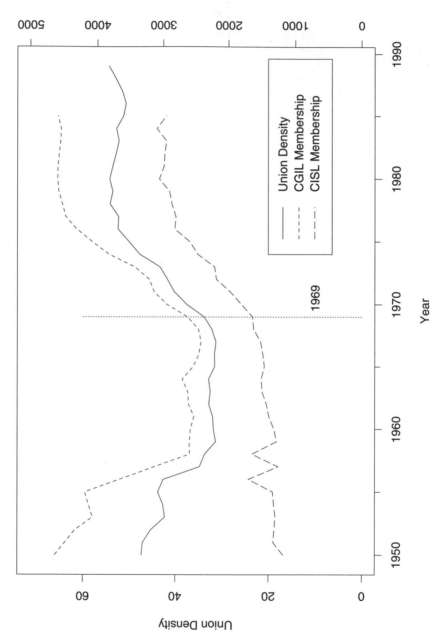

Figure 3.1. Time series of union density and union membership in Italy, 1950–1990. *Source:* Visser (1989; 1991).

Labor law reform moderated employer opposition and provided unions with unprecedented legitimacy. Like the mutual recognition pacts that established centralized bargaining in northern Europe, the Hot Autumn reforms substantially reconciled employers to the reality of strong and institutionalized union representation (Franzosi 1995, 314–15).

Some of the Hot Autumn reforms can also be found in several other countries. Splits between union confederations were healed in Finland in the late 1960s, and confederations merged in the Netherlands in the mid-1970s. Industrial relations law was broadly revised in France after 1968 and in Britain after 1979. However, Italy is the only country in the postwar period to experience significant reconciliation of a politically divided union movement, sweeping legal reform, and fundamental change in the practice of industrial relations. Italy is alone therefore in undergoing a radical reform of labor market institutions in the three decades after the war.

Even more provocative for the argument here: Italy is the only country to show strongly resurgent union membership growth after a prolonged period of decline (see Figure 3.1). Italian union density dropped dramatically in the fifteen years following 1950. The unionized proportion of the labor force shrank by half between 1950 and 1967. Density and CGIL membership both increased through the late 1960s, however. After the Hot Autumn, growth in membership and density accelerated. The organized labor movement continued to expand until the early 1980s (see also Lange et al. 1982, 128). Membership growth in the predominantly Catholic CISL was particularly strong— nearly doubling from 1969 to 1980. In the Italian case, the cross-national pattern of covariation between union centralization and union organization was maintained over time. Thus the only country with a sharp reversal in its unionization trend is the exception that provides some evidence for the rule. While durable labor market institutions, widely established in the OECD by the 1950s, shaped trends in unionization over the following thirty-five years, labor market institutions were transformed in Italy. Only here do we see a radical reversal in deunionization.

Sweden, Britain, and the United States

So far in this chapter I have made some arguments about how centralized labor market institutions contribute to the growth of unions. I have also presented some evidence of covariation. There is a cross-national association between labor market centralization and union density. The Italian case provides some longitudinal evidence for the same relationship. In this section I try to illustrate the causal links more directly by a closer examination of the Swedish, British, and U.S. cases. These three countries represent three trajectories of labor movement development. In Sweden, union densities were high and increasing throughout the postwar period; British union organization remained roughly constant, at least until the 1980s; and labor organization was low and declining from the mid-1950s in the United States. The three countries also display different levels of labor market centralization. Sweden provides the paradigmatic case of social democratic corporatism. In Britain, collective management of the labor market is weaker than in Sweden, but industry bargaining and strong ties between the unions and the Labour party offer some institutional conditions for encompassing representation of workers. Finally, the U.S. labor market is highly decentralized, and market logic dominates the logic of class-wide interest representation.

The Swedish union movement is occupationally divided, with the LO representing blue-collar workers and the TCO representing white-collar workers. Industry unions affiliate with these two confederations. Within confederations, relations among unions are coordinated and jurisdictional disputes are rare (Korpi 1978, 65). The LO and the TCO were historically cooperative, establishing a special interconfederation board in the late 1940s to manage jurisdictional disputes at the national level (Nilstein 1966, 286–87). Wage and jurisdictional competition intensified in Sweden through the 1980s, but demarcation disputes remained infrequent compared to more decentralized industrial relations systems. With this collegiality among the unions and their confederations, the organizing effort is seldom duplicated in interunion competition.

In Sweden, the centralized structure of the LO facilitates national-level bargaining. Industrial relations at the national level produce "frame agreements," which set the terms for later rounds of industry and local negotiations. Centralized bargaining secures employer acceptance of the union movement in two ways. First, mutual recognition was initially established by union and employer representatives in 1906 and extended in the Basic Agreement of Saltsjöbaden in 1938. This agreement instituted procedures for dispute resolution by the LO and central employer association (SAF) officials. As Swenson (1989, 50) observes, the cooperative "spirit of Saltsjöbaden" persisted through most of the postwar period. Second, the institutional legitimacy of unionism was reinforced by frame agreements that bound individual employers to centrally agreed-upon wage rates through their SAF membership. SAF enforced frame agreements through central control of strike insurance and managerial expertise. Union recognition among Swedish employers, however, is also underscored by industrial relations outside the employer association. Unions often negotiate additional agreements with non-SAF employers. In 1991, for instance, these subsidiary agreements covered 12 percent of blue-collar workers (Traxler 1994, 178–79).

Swedish centralized bargaining also gave the LO substantial informal influence over economic policy. By shaping the level of the national wage bill through the central agreement, the LO controlled aggregate investment to some degree. However, this influence steadily declined from the beginning of regular national bargaining in 1957 as an increasing proportion of the wage bill was consumed by locally negotiated wage drift. The LO and SAF were also involved in making economic policy with postwar social democratic governments. By influencing the direction of investment and subsequent employment, the LO could direct job growth to economic sectors with strong union representation. The Swedish active labor market policy is the prime example. Formulated by LO economists Gøsta Rehn and Rudolf Meidner, the active labor market policy provided extensive state support for training and remobilizing unemployed workers. This policy retained employment in manufacturing export industries, a highly unionized sector dominated by the powerful metalworkers' union. The central confederation's influence on employment policy thus maintained employment in a core union constituency.

Class-wide representation is less developed in the British labor market. At the peak level, British labor is formally more centralized than Swedish labor. Only one central union, the Trades Union Congress (TUC), has affiliates from all industries and crafts. Unlike the Swedish confederations, however, the TUC has little real control over affiliates. Interunion rivalry is also sharper than in Sweden. As in Sweden though, the British union movement internalizes the costs of jurisdictional disputes, resolving them through the unions' own structures without resort to state authority (Ball 1980). Although union cooperation is lower than in Sweden, demarcation disputes account for only a small fraction of strike activity. From 1946 to 1973, the percentage of strikes caused by demarcation disputes dropped from 6 percent to 1 percent as the union movement became more concentrated in the course of a steady merger movement (Durcan, McCarthy, and Redman 1983; Windmuller 1981).

Institutional resources for employer challenges to British unions have fluctuated with labor legislation through the 1970s and 1980s. Until the early 1970s, the legal position of unions gradually improved with repeal of wartime limits on strike activity and legislation preventing compulsory public sector unionism. Wilson's Labour government provided positive rights of association and other legal protections in the 1975 Employment Protection Act. Employers' recognition of unions was gradually withdrawn through the 1980s under Prime Minister Thatcher's Conservative party legislative program. The first Employment Act (1980) restricted the closed shop and secondary boycotts (sympathy strikes). The second Employment Act (1982) removed union immunities from prosecution, imposed further restrictions on the closed shop, and facilitated the selective dismissal of strikers (Marsh 1992, 76–77). Institutional support for employer resistance in the 1980s was strengthened by the weak and decentralized organization of the employer associations. Although they play a role in industry bargaining, British employer associations, unlike SAF, cannot enforce collective agreements on employers. A Donovan Commission survey that interviewed representatives from twenty-four industry-level employer associations in 1967 found that only two claimed to bind employers to collective agreements, using "diplomatic letters" and "pure . . . persuasion" for enforcement (Clegg 1978, 137). In contrast to the Swedish case, no central agency in Britain could commit employers to dealing with the unions.

The role of British unions in economic policy is also small compared to their role in Sweden. Although unions were increasingly represented in government authorities during World War II and Atlee's postwar Labour government, they carried little real power over economic planning (Crouch 1979, 21). Union influence on economic policy was fitfully expanded by Labour governments in the late 1940s, the mid-1960s, and mid-1970s. All attempted incomes policies for wage restraint with TUC participation. The TUC was an unwilling participant in the first two, defying the government policy after a year or so of co-operation (Crouch 1979). In the 1970s, Wilson's Labour cabinet sought voluntary wage restraint in return for social welfare and labor law reforms. The policy was initially successful but was subsequently undermined by wildcat strikes toward the end of Callaghan's administration in 1978–1979 (Regini 1984). In each of these experiments in economic planning, the centralized influence of labor over the economy was slight, as the TUC was typically placed in a reactive position to Labour's inducements.

Compared to those of Britain and Sweden, U.S. labor market institutions are highly decentralized. As in Britain, there is only one union confederation, the AFL-CIO, which has little formal influence over its industrial and craft affiliates. The role of the confederation as a central representative has been further undermined by the independence of several of the largest unions—the Teamsters, the United Auto Workers, and the teacher's union, the National Education Association. Jurisdictional disputes, more common in the United States than in Sweden and Britain, originated with the AFL's policy of exclusive jurisdiction from the turn of the century on (Galenson 1986, 48). Exclusive jurisdiction gives a union a monopoly on representation in a particular workplace. This principle was institutionalized in the Wagner Act, and formal mechanisms for jurisdictional conflict were installed in procedures for multiunion elections established by early Labor Board rulings (Bernstein 1969, 654–57). In contrast to the internal resolution of disputes between rival unions in Sweden and Britain, U.S. unions can actively campaign against one another in the external forum of the certification election.

The contestability of United States unionism is suggested by the growth of "employer resistance" explanations of American labor movement decline. This argument relates the growing union wage premium in the 1970s to employers' militant antiunion offensive in the 1980s. The rising incidence of unfair labor practices, lengthening delays before certification elections, and growing popularity of professional union-busting management consultants all indicate an intensified effort by employers to resist unionization (Freeman 1986b; Goldfield 1987; Farber 1990). From a comparative point of view, however, decentralized secret ballot elections with oppositional employer campaigns provide unique opportunities for employer resistance (see also Jacoby 1991; Bok 1971). Of the three case study countries, only the United States provided formal procedures for deunionization and opposition to union representation throughout the postwar period. It may be true that American employers are more opposed to unionism than their counterparts in Sweden and Britain; it is clearly the case that their institutional opportunities for opposing unionism are more extensive.

The influence of unions on economic policy is also weak in the United States (Goldfield 1987, 26; Wilson 1982). Labor representatives have been only slightly involved in economic policymaking bodies, while large corporations have continuously provided a pool of influential economic advisors for Democratic and Republican administrations (Domhoff 1967, 1990). Compared to Europe, institutions for economic policy implementation in the United States are regulatory rather than planning agencies. This "arm's length" management of U.S. capitalism further weakens union influence on the economy (Zysman 1983, 266–73; Wilson 1982, 227–29). However, unions were not always unimportant for economic policy. Organized labor historically influenced economic planning in wartime tripartite Production Boards and through the Democratic party. The institutional legitimacy conferred by the centralization was reflected in strong union membership growth during the war. Still, the wartime influence of labor was limited and short lived (Brody 1975), and the links between unions and the Democrats are typically weaker than those between unions and labor parties in Europe (Greenstone 1977).

In sum, labor market centralization promotes the growth of organized labor by reducing employer opposition, providing an efficient framework for a coordinated organizing effort, and giving unions influence over national economic trends. An institutional description showed that patterns of centralization were established in most countries by the early 1950s, and most survived largely unchanged until the early 1980s. Qualitative descriptions and quantitative scores of labor market centralization correlate with postwar union densities. Italy provides a telling exception. Italian union density increased following the transformation of labor market institutions in the wake of the Hot Autumn of 1969. A more focused examination of Sweden, Britain, and the United States shows how the institutional conditions translate into differences in collective action in the labor market. This discussion of labor market centralization has so far emphasized institutions that affect employed workers. The next chapter examines systems of unemployment insurance that connect the jobless to trade unions.

Four

The Ghent System

A CENTRAL function of the earliest unions was control over entry into jobs. Most famously perhaps, the British craft guilds developed apprenticeship systems that restricted the entry of unskilled workers into the labor market. Control of the labor supply motivated some of the earliest union-controlled unemployment insurance funds that emerged in Europe through the nineteenth century. As well as providing relief to unemployed union members, these unemployment insurance funds helped to reinforce the role of unions in wage bargaining. Benefits were often paid only if alternative work at union rates was not available. Members were also eligible for payments during strikes or lockouts. Transplanted to the landscape of industrial unionism, these unemployment insurance plans provided a powerful mechanism for union growth.

In this chapter I examine how systems of unemployment insurance either integrate the jobless into organized labor movements or reinforce the division between unionized insiders and marginalized outsiders. I begin with a review of the role of unions in the development of unemployment insurance. This is followed by a description of postwar institutions for the payment of unemployment benefits. This shows that high union densities are found in countries with union-run unemployment funds. Next, as for labor market centralization, I examine the link between institutions and unionization in Sweden, Britain, and the United States. These cases show that strong labor movements secured control over unemployment insurance, turning the welfare scheme into an instrument for unionization.

Labor and Unemployment Insurance

Modern forms of relief from unemployment are organized in three ways. First, the earliest schemes, called Ghent systems, involved government subsidies to unemployment funds run by trade unions. Membership in the insurance plans was voluntary, and historically contingent on union membership. Second, following the development of the Ghent system, governments widely assumed control of unemployment relief in compulsory insurance plans. In these systems, mandatory payments into the unemployment fund by employ-

ers and workers are levied as payroll and income taxes. Finally, a third generation of unemployment relief came to supplement the contributory schemes.
These unemployment assistance programs pay benefits without specially ear-
marked taxpayer contributions.

Early Schemes

As its name suggests, the Ghent system was popularized in Belgium when the
Ghent municipal authority supplemented local trade union unemployment insurance schemes with public funds in 1901 (Kiehel 1932). This system of
subsidized insurance was widely emulated in the early 1900s. Shortly after the
establishment of the Belgian scheme, locally supported Ghent systems could
also be found in Britain, Denmark, France, Germany, Italy, the Netherlands,
Norway, Sweden, and Switzerland (ILO 1955, 15). Control of the funds remained with local unions, which paid benefits through their own labor exchanges. Eligibility requirements in these schemes were usually supportive of
trade unionism. Workers often received benefits during industrial disputes.
Members were commonly obliged to accept jobs offered by the exchanges
only if the jobs paid union rates (Spates and Rabinovitch 1931, 37; Kiehel
1932, 108, 116; Rothstein 1989, 330; Harris 1972, 297). Unemployment insurance became more centralized when provincial governments began to supplement municipal funds. The first national Ghent system began in France in
1905. Norway and Denmark followed in the next two years. Over the next
three decades, the Netherlands (1916), Finland (1917), Belgium (1920), Switzerland (1924), and Sweden (1934) all adopted national voluntary unemployment plans (Alber 1981, 153).
    Many of these national Ghent systems were instituted under recessionary
conditions by governments of a variety of partisan complexions (Alber 1981,
170). In Belgium and the Netherlands, state subsidies emerged as unemployment rapidly increased during and immediately after World War I (Kiehel
1932; Windmuller 1969, 42). Similarly, consolidation of the Danish and
Swedish Ghent systems followed in consecutive years at the height of the
depression (Rothstein 1989; Pedersen 1982, 584). In each of these countries,
reforms establishing or expanding unemployment subsidies were passed by
governments with social democratic or socialist party involvement. Left parties dominated the construction of national Ghent systems in three countries.
The Belgian system, instituted by the Socialist party in 1920, was rolled back
in 1922 under a Conservative government, but reinvigorated several years later
when the Socialists returned to power (Kiehel 1932). The two Scandinavian
legislative programs were developed in parliaments under Social Democratic
control (Rothstein 1989; ILO 1955, 45). In the Netherlands, state support for
the Ghent system emerged in the social disruption of World War I. Military

threat galvanized the Dutch Socialist party and the unions behind the Catholic government. The government, in turn, replenished the near-bankrupt union unemployment funds and acceded to union control at the local level in return for industrial peace (Windmuller 1969, 42–43).

In the early debates on unemployment relief, the Ghent system was just one option open to policymakers. Compulsory insurance was discussed by British architects of welfare reform in the first decade of the twentieth century. Low union organization—especially among unskilled workers—made the expansive compulsory scheme an attractive alternative. Lloyd George's Liberal government initiated the first national compulsory system of out-of-work benefits in Britain in 1909. The British plan provided the model for later developments. Its key characteristics were a waiting period for payment of benefits to discourage false claims, and eligibility requirements that ensured payments only to the involuntarily unemployed (Alber 1981, 154). Unlike many of the union-run schemes at the time, the British plan supported only "standard" rather than union wages in its eligibility provisions (King 1995, 43–49). Following the expansion of the British plan, compulsory unemployment insurance was adopted in Italy (1919), Austria (1920), Ireland (1923), and Germany (1927). From the outset, then, the market position of unions was not protected in the state-run compulsory programs.

By the early 1930s, the development of national unemployment insurance programs was largely complete in Western Europe. By this time, central governments had taken a large financial responsibility for the unemployed, through either compulsory insurance funds or Ghent systems. The trend toward strengthening unemployment insurance at higher levels of government was general in Europe but not elsewhere.

Outside Europe, unemployment insurance was not publicly supported until the 1930s. In North America, the first statutory plan began in Wisconsin in 1932. No national initiative was taken until the passage of the Social Security Act in 1935. A Canadian unemployment insurance system was successfully created in the first years of World War II, following a constitutional amendment (ILO 1955, 38–39). The history of Australian and New Zealand state unemployment benefits also diverges from the European experience. In New Zealand a compulsory contributory plan was passed in 1930, eight years before the New Zealand Labour party set up the public assistance scheme that continued after World War II (ILO 1955, 40). The Australian Labor party, under Prime Minister John Curtin, played a similar role, legislating a system of noncontributory benefits in 1944 (Castles 1985, 65). Finally, in Japan, a national plan for unemployment insurance was established only in 1947, when a compulsory system for employer contributions was organized (ILO 1955, 43).

The next wave of welfare reform passed control of unemployment relief from the unions to the states. In most cases this was less a rejection of union power, than an effort at comprehensive welfare provision. Thus social demo-

cratic governments were instrumental in the establishment of compulsory unemployment insurance in Norway in 1938 and in the Netherlands in 1952. In
Belgium, the first postwar Christian Democratic government also set up a
compulsory insurance fund in 1945. The Belgian plan was not a conservative
initiative, but rather the product of prior clandestine negotiations between employers and union leaders during wartime occupation. In contrast to the Norwegian and Dutch measures for unemployment relief, Belgian unions retained
a vital administrative role in the payment of benefits. The three Belgian trade
union confederations each established payment offices, in addition to the state
office for nonunion workers (Degans 1975). This partial Ghent system was
maintained throughout the postwar period.

Developments in France and Switzerland took a different turn. In France,
the unions were severely repressed during the war. With the union movement
driven underground by the Occupation, the number of state-subsidized unemployment funds shrank from over two hundred in 1938 to only one by 1951.
To expand the delivery of unemployment benefits, a large state-run noncontributory scheme was introduced in 1951 (ILO 1955, 18–19). In Switzerland
responsibility for unemployment relief was largely shouldered at the provincial level. Constitutional reform facilitated federal control of unemployment
insurance in 1946. As a consequence, the national government assumed a su-
pervisory role in relation to a large number of cantonal, union, and bipartite
plans. By 1961, only two cantons had not introduced compulsory unemployment insurance, and a majority of insured workers belonged to the public or
jointly managed funds. Because fund membership depended on income, however, coverage of the local funds was low (Federal Social Insurance Office
1961, 499–500). In 1976, the piecemeal system was rationalized when the
government set up a national compulsory system in response to the threat of
mounting unemployment.

Postwar Unemployment Insurance

Table 4.1 summarizes the role of unions in the administration of unemployment benefits in the postwar period. In only four countries—Belgium, Denmark, Finland, and Sweden—unions retained a strong national role in the
administration of relief from unemployment. In the three Nordic countries,
unemployment insurance was organized in Ghent systems of union-run unemployment insurance throughout the postwar period. The Finnish case is a little
unusual. Although unions in Finland had a long-standing role in the administration of unemployment insurance, unemployment relief did not receive significant state support until the early 1960s (Ministry of Social Affairs 1953,
101; Alestalo and Uusitalo 1987, 141). Union membership also conferred unemployment fund membership, but in Sweden and Denmark, nonunion members could voluntarily affiliate with the fund (Olsson 1987, 17; Johansen 1987,

TABLE 4.1
Union Involvement in Administration of Unemployment Policy,
Eighteen OECD Countries

	Unemployment Insurance Scheme
Ghent system countries	
Belgium	Compulsory insurance (1945), but unemployment benefits paid by state-approved unions
Denmark	Voluntary union-run insurance funds; special payments to union members for early retirement since 1978
Finland	Voluntary union-run insurance funds; unemployment insurance linked to union membership
Sweden	Voluntary union-run insurance funds; local labor exchanges work in cooperation with unions
Public insurance countries	
Australia	Public system of unemployment assistance (1944)
Austria	Compulsory insurance in private sector (1920)
Canada	Compulsory insurance (1941)
Germany	Compulsory insurance (1927)
France	Compulsory insurance and public assistance (1958–1967)
Ireland	Compulsory insurance (1923)
Italy	Compulsory insurance for nonfarm workers (1919); unions sometimes negotiate added unemployment benefits
Japan	Compulsory insurance for all workers, except those on small farms
Netherlands	Public compulsory insurance (1952) in private sector; unions retained unemployment payments in construction industry
New Zealand	Public system of unemployment assistance (1938)
Norway	Compulsory insurance (1938)
Switzerland	Public compulsory insurance (1976); previously compulsory insurance run by cantons, bipartite plans, and unions
United Kingdom	Compulsory insurance (1911)
United States	Compulsory insurance (1935), varying across states

Sources: Flora 1983–1987; Alber 1981; OECD 1979b, 1988a, 1991a.
Note: Year of establishment in parentheses.

204–05; Alestalo and Uusitalo 1987, 142). Trade unionism as a principle of labor market organization is preserved in the unemployment benefit eligibility requirements. In Denmark, the union placement services would direct workers to jobs in the union's trade. This practice was retained even after the state took over the placement services in 1969 (OECD 1991a, 212). By Swedish law, a job offer from a placement service is considered suitable only if "wages and benefits are comparable to those determined by a collective agreement" (Bjørklund and Holmlund 1991, 114). Thus the benefit system curtails wage competition from the unemployed.

Belgium no longer has private unemployment insurance funds, but unions still are heavily involved in paying benefits and running unemployment offices. Industrial relations specialists report that the unions perform this task "much more efficiently than the public authorities," so the union funds attract much higher enrollment than the state system (Vilrokx and Leemput 1992, 370). We can see the popularity of the union-disbursed funds in the unusually high proportion of unemployed among Belgian union members. Union members prefer the union-run schemes, and retain their union membership while unemployed. In the last decade, when more than 10 percent of the Belgian labor force was out of work, as much as one-fifth of the entire union membership was unemployed (Visser 1991). In all the Ghent systems, including the Belgian one, the key feature of unemployment insurance is not its organization at the top, but its execution at the bottom. In the four Ghent system countries, unions are closely involved with workers at local labor exchanges both in job-seeking and in the payment of benefits.

In the countries without Ghent systems, unions have been largely excluded from influencing labor market competition at the national level. Partial exceptions include a number of countries where unions negotiate special payments for unemployment. In Grais's (1983) review of unemployment compensation for layoffs and short-time work in eleven OECD countries, he found unemployment payments were sometimes negotiated by unions. In North America, supplementary unemployment insurance is a feature of some collective agreements. Canadian provisions cover mostly uninsured public sector workers in Quebec. In the United States, unemployment insurance is provided in collective agreements in the metal and garment industries. These agreements, however, cover only a small fraction of the total labor force. Similar provisions can be found in Italy, where unions are also involved in the payment of a range of welfare benefits. Elsewhere in Europe, unions are represented in tripartite bodies administering labor market policy. Germany and the Netherlands are notable examples (Janoski 1990; Cox 1993). In these cases however, unions are usually quite distant from the street-level delivery of services.

The Case for the Ghent System

The Ghent system boosts unionization by giving unions control over labor market competition from unemployed workers, and by maintaining contact between workers and unions during spells of unemployment. Two processes allow unions to control labor market competition. First, eligibility provisions in Ghent systems are more likely to be explicitly permissive of unionism. Many of the early Ghent systems protected union wages, strike action, and collective bargaining. We have also seen how contemporary Swedish laws respect collective agreements. Second, unions can control labor market competition simply because of how unemployment services are delivered. Roth-stein (1989) argues that the importance of the Ghent system for unionization thus derives from the unique inseparability of labor as a commodity from its seller, the worker. Because labor is inseparable from the worker, policy on eligibility for unemployment benefits is determined locally when workers pre-sent themselves at the labor exchange. Union officials working at the local labor offices have considerable discretion in determining alternative employ-ment and conditions under which unemployment becomes "involuntary."

The significance of union control over labor market competition is illus-trated by the emergence of the Belgian Ghent system after World War I. The scheme was introduced in 1920 by a Socialist government, and wide eligibility criteria were originally defined. Unusual by modern standards, the scheme provided unemployment benefits during strikes and lockouts, and unemploy-ment insurance was guaranteed if an employer refused to arbitrate an industrial dispute. When conservatives took power two years later eligibility criteria were narrowed. Rights to unemployment benefits during industrial disputes were restricted, and the new measures also limited union discretion in paying benefits. Many of the measures sought to achieve a "standardization of prac-tice, more careful definition of terms, improved accounting and inspection service and reduction of expenditures which they considered too liberal" (Kiehel 1932, 290). By limiting discretion in the payment of benefits, these measures reduced the ability of union officials in labor offices to protect the market position of unionized workers.

The Ghent system also raises unionization by connecting workers with trade unions during spells of unemployment. In non-Ghent countries, unemploy-ment typically causes a worker's withdrawal from the labor market and the labor movement. In Ghent countries, however, unions take an active role in a worker's welfare even though the worker's place in the labor market may be marginal. With this reasoning, the effect of the tie between unions and the unemployed varies across different segments of the labor market. Ghent sys-tems should be particularly influential for organizing workers for whom the risk of unemployment is especially high. Instead of concentrating union pres-ence in the monopoly sectors of the labor market, Ghent systems are integra-tive mechanisms that draw the margins of the labor market into the labor movement.

Some Historical Examples and Quasi-Experiments

The effect of the Ghent system on unionization can be seen in historical and comparative contexts. An early observation is provided in Perlman's (1928) account of the growth of German trade unions in the late nineteenth century. Unemployment relief was one of the few programs omitted from Bismarck's welfare plan. In this context, German industrial unions initially adopted unemployment insurance schemes to insulate their membership from fluctuating economic conditions. For more militant unions, the schemes also enhanced the capacity for strike activity. Recruiting strikebreakers from the unemployed became more costly for employers when unions paid unemployment benefits. By 1917, all national industrial unions provided unemployment benefits, and union membership grew rapidly in the first two decades of the twentieth century (Perlman 1928, 90–91).

Some recent examples of the effects of the Ghent system can be found in Scandinavia during the large rises in unemployment in the early 1970s. In an econometric context, Pedersen (1990, 1982) observed a dramatic procyclical relationship between unemployment and unionization in Denmark, which he attributed to the effects of the Ghent system. Unemployment climbed from below 2 percent in 1973 to a high of around 10 percent in 1982 after the first oil price shock. In this period union growth accelerated, with union density growing from well under 65 percent to over 80 percent (Neumann, Pedersen, and Westergaard-Nielsen 1989; Pedersen 1990; see also Pedersen 1982). A contrasting trend is observed in Finland, where, after the Ghent system was supplemented by a state-administered scheme in 1972, a period of rapid union growth leveled off despite rising unemployment (Neumann et al. 1989, 26).

From a comparative point of view we can contrast the Dutch and Belgian experiences, and those of Sweden and Norway. Both pairs of countries provide useful quasi-experiments because they are similar in many respects, but differ in their experiences with the Ghent system. In the Netherlands, where unions are strongly represented at the highest level on labor market and social policy advisory units, Belgium developments are sometimes viewed as the road not taken (Visser 1992b, 25). In the early 1950s, the Dutch welfare state was erected slowly by a sequence of labor governments in negotiations with the Catholic and labor pillars of Dutch society (Cox 1993). In 1952 the government established a universal system of unemployment insurance, replacing the voluntary scheme run by the trade unions in the prewar period (Roebroek and Berben 1987; Rothstein 1992, 44). From then on, Dutch and Belgian union densities steadily diverged, accelerating when unemployment rose rapidly in the Low Countries through the 1970s and 1980s.

Only construction unions in the Netherlands retained control over unemployment insurance, and unionization in this sector has remained relatively high (Windmuller 1969, 206). This can be seen in Table 4.2, which compares union density in construction with the national level in the Netherlands. Although the figures in the table are somewhat rough, they show that union organization in construction exceeds the average level. The more recent figures show that since the dissolution of the Dutch Ghent system in 1952, the gap between construction industry union density and national union

TABLE 4.2
Union Density in Construction and the
Nation, the Netherlands, 1920–1985

	Union Density	
	Construction	*National*
Under the Ghent system		
1920	63	37
1930	46	31
1939	60	37
1947	77	41
Under public unemployment insurance		
1960	50	40
1971	48	36
1979	43	35
1985	42	28

Sources and Notes: Union membership in construction and national union density are from Visser (1989). Construction industry employment is taken from the *Statistical Yearbook of the Netherlands.* Figures for employees were available only after the 1960s, so for earlier years, gross employment statistics were adjusted downwards, using the ratio of dependent labor force to the economically active population.

density has widened. (The gap is wider in the earliest period, but the figures are less accurate here.) From the early 1970s, as union density has declined with rising unemployment in the Netherlands, union density in construction has held steady.

A similar comparison can be drawn between Sweden and Norway. The two countries share structurally similar union movements, a similar cultural heritage, and ethnic homogeneity. Despite these similarities, the Norwegian Ghent system was replaced by a compulsory state system of unemployment insurance in 1938, and since then, Swedish union density has persistently exceeded the Norwegian by 20 to 30 percentage points (Neumann et al. 1989, 26). Time series of Norwegian and Swedish union density from 1921 to 1950 show that union growth in both countries had been strong until the late 1930s (Figure 4.1). In 1938 Norwegian union density trailed the Swedish density by only 9 percentage points. By 1950 the gap had widened to nearly 20 points. The two union density trends continued to diverge through the postwar period.

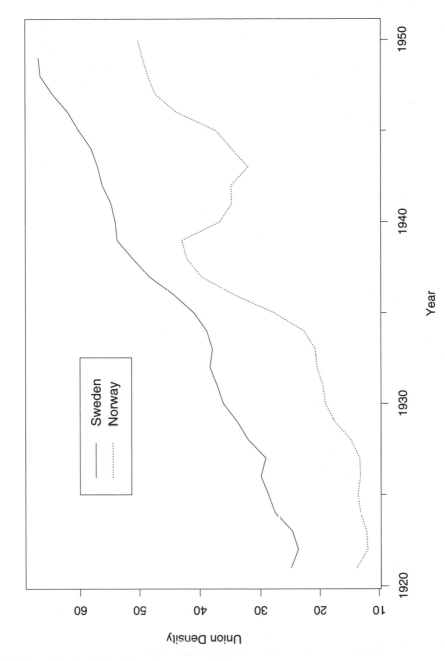

Figure 4.1. Union density time series for Sweden and Norway, 1920–1950. *Source:* Visser (1989).

Sweden, Britain, and the United States

A closer look at the origins of unemployment insurance in Sweden, Britain, and the United States helps show the logic of institutional regulation. In Sweden, the Ghent system was a social democratic program and has been closely associated with the rise in postwar unionization. In Britain, unions pressed for a Ghent-style scheme but ultimately were too weak to permanently effect the passage of compulsory insurance. The British union movement was thus vulnerable to the rise in unemployment in the 1930s. In the United States, unions initially rejected a role in unemployment insurance, and the resulting system reinforced the growth of a largely unregulated American labor market in the postwar period.

Sweden was a relative latecomer to state-supported unemployment insurance. In 1934 the Swedish parliament endorsed subsidies to union unemployment funds, nearly thirty years after the French had established the first national Ghent system and fifteen years after the Belgians had done so. Pressure for a national Ghent system began in the 1920s, when the unions' unemployment funds were depleted by severe recession (Heclo 1974, 92–94). Although the Social Democrats had supported a Ghent system, the unstable coalition governments of the 1920s made the left reliant on broad-based support from the bourgeois parties. United opposition from the Conservative, Liberal, and Agrarian parties prevented majority support for the scheme. The opposition forces objected that a national Ghent system would prevent labor markets from clearing, and—perhaps less disingenuously—that the policy amounted to a state intervention in favor of union power (Rothstein 1989, 328; Heclo 1974, 97).

By the 1930s, the electoral position of the Social Democrats had improved, and a coalition government with the Liberal party in 1934 opened the possibility of Ghent system legislation. To secure Liberal party support, the original plan was diluted by provisions for state oversight of the funds, the admission of nonunion workers to fund membership, the rejection of employer contributions, and a low level of benefits. In return, the unions retained control over job placement. Importantly, workers would not be directed to jobs at workplaces affected by strikes; neither would they be forced to accept jobs at below the union wage. While the economic significance of the scheme was modest, its qualitative impact on union control of the labor supply was large. As Rothstein (1989, 329–30) observed, substance in policy was traded for "institutional principles."

In the postwar period the unemployment insurance funds played only a residual role in the Social Democratic government's employment policy. Shortly after the war, the local labor exchanges were nationalized, coming under the control of the newly created National Labor Market Board. Still, labor exchanges continued to work closely with unions on job placement, and unemployment insurance remained a voluntary union-run scheme. The insurance funds monopolized unemployment relief until 1974 when a public noncontributory assistance program was established. The numbers of workers insured under the Swedish Ghent system increased slowly through the 1950s and early 1960s, but growth accelerated through the 1960s, preceding the growth in union density. The unionization and insurance enrollment time series shown in Figure 4.2 move together, correlating at .98. Following recent unionization trends, the latest members of the insurance funds were mostly women and white-collar workers (Olsson 1986, 34).

The chance for British unions to have an institutionalized presence among the unemployed was decided in the two decades after 1900. Before national unemployment insurance, British unions, like the Swedish, had been extensively involved in paying unemployment benefits. Between 1892 and 1906, about two-thirds of all union members belonged to unions that paid some type of unemployment benefit (Royal Commission on Poor Laws 1910, 614). As in Sweden, this significantly influenced policy debates. During the early 1900s, momentum for a national unemployment policy gathered within the British labor movement. By 1907 Labour members had spoken in Parliament in favor of a national Ghent system (Harris 1972, 240). However, the decisive impetus for unemployment policy came from the Royal Commission on the Poor Laws and Relief from Distress, empaneled by a Conservative government in 1905.

The commission faced two major questions: would unemployment insurance be voluntary or compulsory, and how would the funds be administered? The question of administration was addressed first in the debate over labor exchanges. In 1907, William Beveridge published two articles in the *Morning Post* endorsing the expansion of trade union labor exchanges. As Beveridge observed: "Trade unions are able to assist their unemployed members cheaply and effectively because they can constantly check the need for assistance and test the claimant's ability and willingness to accept employment by the offer of a vacancy" (1953, 60).

For Beveridge, the unions exemplified an administrative mechanism that could be expanded into a national public authority. The idea of a national system of public labor exchanges engaged the Webbs and, later, the majority of the Royal Commission. The link between union membership and unemployment was nearly severed at this point, although union protests ensured that workers registered at labor exchanges would not be penalized for refusing substandard wages or work at strike-affected workplaces (Harris 1972, 291).

The labor exchanges provided a way of paying benefits, but a plan for contribution to unemployment insurance remained unresolved. The commission reviewed continental experiments, and the Ghent system received strong support from the minority. The commission majority countered that employers would refuse to subsidize trade union funds. In any event, unskilled workers,

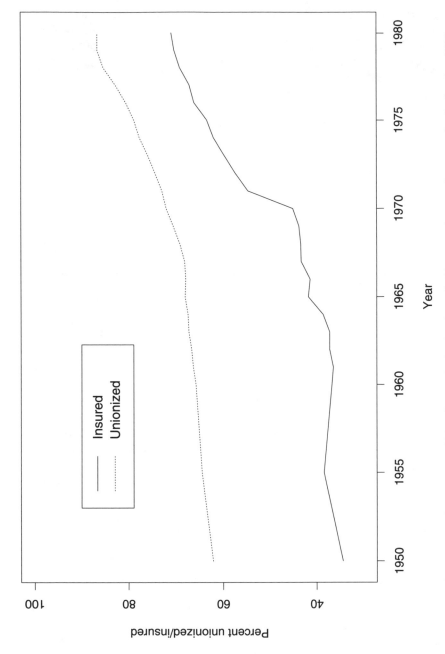

Figure 4.2. Time series of percentage of labor force unionized and enrolled in unemployment insurance funds, Sweden, 1950–1980. Insurance figures are from Olsson (1987, p. 55).

who were most at risk of unemployment, were beyond the reach of the union movement, leaving them uninsured (Harris 1972, 304). The final plan contained in the National Insurance Act established a public insurance fund. In this plan benefits were refused to those losing work because of an industrial dispute, an employer's dismissal, or a voluntary resignation (Whiteside 1987, 215). Opposition to the act was modest because a partial Ghent system was retained. Unions received some state support for their own private insurance funds. Indeed, membership in unions providing benefits increased from about 1 million to more than 4 million between 1916 and 1921 (Whiteside 1987, 216).

However, the institutional ground had been laid, and when unemployment climbed in the early 1920s, the meager union funds were stretched to breaking point. The state Unemployment Fund itself went deeply into debt, prompting the repeal of the residual Ghent system. With union subsidies eliminated and unemployment skyrocketing, union membership declined from 8.3 million in 1920 to 4.4 million in 1932 (Bain and Elsheikh 1976, 135). The unions' institutionalized hold over the labor supply had ended.

While there was consensus among Swedish and British unions about the necessity for some type of unemployment insurance—whether voluntary or compulsory—there was no such agreement within the American labor movement. Although the British scheme of 1911 stimulated debate among academics and social reformers, the major union confederation, the American Federation of Labor (AFL), opposed compulsory unemployment insurance and emphasized preventive measures, as opposed to unemployment relief. As late as 1931, the AFL insisted that American workers "abhor charity and . . . resent the imposition of the dole" (AFL 1931, 17). Although active in its support for public labor exchanges, the confederation insisted that unemployment should be combated through public works, the restriction of immigration, and shortening working time (Nelson 1969, ch. 4; AFL 1931, 17–18; cf. King 1995, 49–50). Influenced by the Webbs' work on unemployment insurance, however, progressive unionists in Illinois and New York pressed for social insurance programs in local elections in 1918 and 1919 (Nelson 1969, 70).

The weak commitment to unemployment insurance by the American union movement is reflected in the poorly developed union-run unemployment insurance funds. Although many unions had offered members temporary relief from unemployment in the first decades of the twentieth century, permanent unemployment insurance funds were rare. The early schemes were divided between local and national unions but were more modest than the extensive policy networks created by the British and Swedish unions. In the state of New York in 1894, for example, less than a fifth of local unions paid benefits. Rising unemployment severely tested the solvency of unemployment funds, and few national plans survived until 1930. Only two years earlier, one estimate counted the total number of trade union members covered by local or national unemployment schemes at 34,700, or just under 1 percent of the entire membership of the AFL (Stewart 1930, 82–91).

Because union-run unemployment insurance schemes were few, the Ghent system was never seriously considered in unemployment policy debates. In Britain, the Ghent system received extensive attention and was written into the 1911 act. In the United States, by contrast, the unions were simply too weak to deliver unemployment benefits on a large scale in a way that was possible in Europe. From a very early point, a British-style compulsory insurance program dominated discussions (Nelson 1969, 11–12).

Public unemployment insurance came to the United States during the 1930s in two stages. First, at the state level, the Wisconsin legislature passed a compulsory insurance bill in 1932. This provided coverage to nonagricultural workers in enterprises with ten or more workers. Workers leaving employment because of a labor dispute were not eligible for benefits. The Wisconsin plan sparked a wave of legislative activity in more than two dozen other states (Haber and Murray 1966, 66–70). Second, at the federal level, the Social Security Act was signed into law by President Roosevelt in 1935. The act established a system of federal subsidies to state unemployment programs. The state unemployment programs typically featured advisory councils designed to advise on unemployment policy and to propose legislation. The advisory councils often contained union representation, and as late as 1952, the Congress of Industrial Organizations (CIO) urged their "activation" (CIO 1952, 76). The AFL and CIO were both represented on the early advisory councils, although the influence of the councils on unemployment legislation and administration was limited to a few states (Becker 1959, 400–409).

Consistent with the marginal role of unions in the development of U.S. unemployment insurance, postwar unemployment insurance in the United States reinforces market inequalities (King 1995). Benefit levels are closely tied to local wage rates and vary substantially across states. Benefits are denied to those involved in industrial disputes or dismissed because of misconduct (OECD 1979b, 263). Labor market deregulation is also enforced through strict job-search provisions. Stringent by OECD standards, these provisions require unemployed workers to make a relatively large number of job inquiries and document these to the labor exchanges (OECD 1991a, 211). Eligibility provisions for American unemployment benefits thus contribute substantially to competition among workers in the labor market.

In sum, there are many historical examples of voluntary unemployment insurance funds administered by trade unions. These examples point to the positive effects of such programs on union membership. From the establishment in 1911 of compulsory unemployment insurance in Britain, however, unemployment relief has increasingly been a state responsibility. Only in Belgium, Denmark, Finland, and Sweden have unions taken a strong role in the administration of unemployment insurance throughout the postwar period. These contemporary Ghent systems provide unions with close institutional control over the labor supply, and unionization in these four countries has steadily grown in the last forty years. A brief review of the experiences of Britain, Sweden, and the United States shows that U.S. union weakness largely excluded organized labor from any role in unemployment policy. In Britain, unions were stronger and had an important formative impact on unemployment insurance. Still, by the start of World War II, the British government had assumed full responsibility for relief from unemployment. In Sweden, where the labor movement was strong both industrially and electorally, a national Ghent system was established in the 1930s and has remained intact as part of a larger set of tripartite institutions for unemployment policy administration.

Five

Political Parties and
Trade Unions

So FAR, we have considered the link between labor movement growth and labor market institutions. In this chapter I extend the story to the state, examining how state institutions can advance or arrest union organizing. The key agents here are working-class political parties. The histories of unions and parties are closely intertwined. Beginning with early struggles over suffrage reform, unions and parties in many countries presented a united working-class organization straddling state and market. The task of this chapter is to disentangle the threads of union and party organization and explain how unionization depends on strong labor parties.

The link between unions and parties is more complicated than it might first appear. The relationship between the two varies enormously across the advanced capitalist democracies (Ebbinghaus 1995). From the Scandinavian perspective, Esping-Andersen (1985, 64) observes emphatically that "from the late 1800s until today, there is little doubt that union power has depended on the success of the party and vice versa." Korpi (1983) and Stephens (1979, 112) make similar observations about the Nordic scene. Still, econometric evidence for the effects of prolabor parties on union growth is often weak (Sharpe 1971; Sheflin, Troy, and Koeller 1981; Booth 1983). Union membership does not appear to increase routinely when social democratic or labor parties win elections. There is thus a puzzling disagreement between the econometricians and the macrosociologists of labor movements.

I examine this puzzle by reviewing some historical evidence for the relationship between unions and political parties in the advanced capitalist countries. My main argument is that political parties enlist the institutional resources of the state in support of union growth but the relationship between parties and unions is cross-nationally variable, lumpy, and simultaneous. This means, first, that some parties have been more helpful to unions than others, depending on the shared history and institutional connections between the organizations. Second, political parties often influence union growth not in a smooth and consistent way but through key events, such as a change in a labor law or an intervention in collective bargaining. Third, the impact of parties on unions suggests that the electoral success of political parties is strongly dependent on union support. Prolabor political parties have done well where unions have grown.

This chapter begins by asking how parties affect union growth. Next, I describe differences in the institutional ties that join parties and unions. This is followed by an examination of how parties have influenced union organizing through the administration of labor law and through collective bargaining. I then investigate two elaborations of partisan explanations of union growth. The first says that support for left parties reflects public opinion, which is really driving unionization. The second says that Christian democratic parties have also been important supporters of union growth.

How Do Unions Influence Parties?

The impact of political parties on union growth depends on how well unions can influence party policy and how successfully parties advance that policy through government. Despite the great variability in party-union relations, one generalization stands out: unions retain an important influence over parties where the parties were originally formed for the parliamentary representation of union members (Beyme 1985, 62). Elsewhere, where parties developed independently of unions or where political leaders gave unions a narrow industrial role in a programmatic division of social movement labor, partisan support of unions has been more tenuous.

Table 5.1 summarizes the institutional ties between parties and unions in the advanced capitalist countries. The oldest of the modern social democratic parties can be found in Scandinavia. In Denmark, Norway, and Sweden, unions were instrumental in founding labor parties in the final decades of the nineteenth century. Parallel developments can be found a little later in all English-speaking countries except the United States and Canada. The earliest moves toward independent political representation came in Australia, when unions of miners and shearers founded the Australian Labor party in 1891 (Maddox 1978). In Britain the Labour party was formed a little later, in 1906, following experiments with representation through the Liberal party (Pelling 1993). A decade later, union conferences in Ireland and New Zealand resulted in the formation of national labor parties.

In all these countries, where political parties were formed to secure the parliamentary representation of the unions, unions were given collective affiliation in the party. Through collective affiliation, the unions were represented in party congresses, and the parties received large financial contributions in return. Union representation within labor parties was strongest in Britain, Australia, and New Zealand, accounting for nearly all labor party membership (Pelling 1993, 205–207; Maddox 1978, 203; Levine 1979, 71). In these countries, national unions can join the labor parties. In contrast, only local unions affiliate collectively with the Swedish and Norwegian parties. Still, leaders of the Swedish and Norwegian LOs are strongly represented in the leadership

TABLE 5.1

Organizational Ties between Unions and Major Working-Class Parties and Left Party Representation in Government, Eighteen OECD Countries

	Party-Union Relationship	*Left Government Index*
High-density countries		
Belgium	Socialist, Catholic, and Liberal confederations each provide candidates for their political parties; some formal organizational links between socialist FGTB and Belgian Socialist party (BSP), but these are not strong in practice	43
Denmark	Unions involved in founding of Danish Social Democratic party (1878); LO has automatic representation in party secretariat, and contributes candidates and financial support	90
Finland	Social Democratic and Communist factions within Central Organization of Finnish Trade Unions (SAK); some Social Democrats split into rival federation, the Finnish Trade Union Federation (SAJ), after war; unions supply candidates to both Social Democrats and Communists	59
Sweden	Unions involved in Swedish Social Democratic party (SAP) founding (1889); high rate of collective affiliation among local unions; high rates of party membership among union members; party leadership typically drawn from unions	112
Middle-density countries		
Australia	Australian Labor party (ALP) founded by unions (1891); unions have collective affiliation with party; ACTU holds ex officio representation in party congress; ALP candidates regularly recruited from unions	34
Austria	ÖGB formally independent of political parties; however, presidents and government ministers commonly recruited from ÖGB leadership, and union has ex officio representation at party conference	49
Canada	Local unions affiliated with party; unions regularly supply NDP candidates	0
Germany	German Confederation of Trade Unions (DGB) formally independent of political parties, but German Social Democratic party (SPD) leadership often drawn from DGB, and union leaders advise SPD governments; Christian Democratic Union (CDU) also has small representation in DGB leadership	35
Ireland	Labour party founded by unions (1912); unions collectively affiliated to parties; union officials have ex officio membership in Labour party branches	0
Italy	Parties created single union confederation at end of war; split in 1948 left three confederations aligned with three major parties; unification of unions in 1970s loosened party ties	0
New Zealand	Labour party formed at union conferences (1916); widespread collective affiliation of unions to Labour party; unions also supply party candidates	60

TABLE 5.1, continued

	Party-Union Relationship	Left Government Index
Norway	Unions involved in founding Norwegian Labor party (DNA) in 1887; local unions are collectively affiliated with the DNA, but this has steadily declined; LO supplies financial support and leading candidates to party	83
United Kingdom	Unions founded Labour party (1906); national unions and TUC have collective affiliation in the party; liaison committees also link the TUC to the party at the national level; unions regularly supply Labour candidates	44
Low-density countries		
France	Three unions—the General Federation of Labor (CGT), the Reformist Federation of Labor (CGT-FO), and the French Federation of Christian Workers (CFTC)—support the French Communist party (PCF), the Socialist party (PS), and the Union for French Democracy (UDF); PCF and CGT are most closely connected, with the CGT general secretary holding a position in the PCF political bureau	9
Japan	Japan Socialist party (JSP) closely tied to major union confederation, Sohyo; during campaigns, confederation provides JSP with organizational help, financial contributions, and candidates	2
Netherlands	Social democratic and Christian union confederations support Labor party (PvdA) and Catholic People's party (KVP, later included in the ecumenical Christian Democratic Appeal [CDA]), although parties and unions are financially and organizationally independent; union leaders typically represented on executive boards of parties	32
Switzerland	Major confederation, SGB, is formally independent but closely tied to Swiss Social Democratic party (SPS); union leaders often contest cantonal elections on the SPS slate; SPS and SGB have collaborated in campaigns for constitutional amendments	12
United States	Unions and Democratic party are formally independent; AFL-CIO and unions financially support Democratic and Republican candidates; AFL-CIO generally endorses Democratic presidential candidates	0

Sources: Armingeon 1982; Lorwin 1975; Horowitz 1968; Esping-Andersen 1985; Suvinanta 1987; Reynaud 1974; Markovits 1986; Treu 1991; Weitz 1975; Richardson and Flanagan 1984; Windmuller 1969; Howells 1982; Berenstein 1993; Goldman 1983. Left government data is from Wallerstein 1989.

Note: The left government index gives a total score for left party representation in cabinet from 1919 to the 1980s. Countries score from 0 to 3 points for each year of leftist participation in government (see Wallerstein [1989, 498] for details).

of the social democratic parties. Denmark is exceptional among the Nordic countries, having abolished collective affiliation at an early stage. Still, the Danish LO exchanges ex officio leaders with the Social Democrats and financially contributes to a range of party activities, including the party newspaper (Esping-Andersen 1985, 65).

On a smaller scale, the Canadian New Democratic party (NDP) also maintains close ties to the union movement through the collective affiliation of local unions. Although unions did not found the NDP's precursor, the Cooperative Commonwealth Federation (CCF), collective affiliation of unions began within six years of the party's establishment in 1932. The earliest collective affiliation, involving a Nova Scotia mineworkers' local, was modeled on the constitutional provisions of the British Labour party. Although the NDP has not enjoyed the national electoral success of the British or Scandinavian parties, it has been influential in government at the provincial level, both in Saskatchewan and British Columbia (Horowitz 1968).

Throughout continental Europe, the relationship between party and union has been complicated by religion and political divisions on the left (Ebbinghaus 1995, 70). Where labor is divided along confessional lines—in Belgium, France, Italy, the Netherlands, and Switzerland—parties took an active role in developing their own union confederations. Unions are formally independent of their parties in all these countries, but are active in supplying candidates for political office. In several cases, the capacity of left parties to support unions has been weakened by coalition government. Switzerland is the extreme case. There, the Socialist party enjoys institutionalized minority representation in a stable grand coalition involving all the major parties. There are also differences across the political spectrum. In general, the socialist and communist union confederations are more closely linked to their political parties than the Christian unions. In Belgium and the Netherlands, union leaders are represented on the executive boards of their socialist parties. The Communist parties of France and Italy also closely monitored the activities of their union confederations and placed union leaders in the executive positions in the party congresses. For the French Communists and the Italians before the 1970s, the unions formed an industrial wing in a division of labor featuring the political leadership of the parties. In Italy, the communist faction of the CGIL acquired greater autonomy as a result of unification of the three union confederations in 1972.

Some thirty years earlier in Germany and Austria, postwar labor movement unification also served to increase the autonomy of unions from parties. While the Germanic social democrats were historically joined to their union movements, the formation of unified confederations embracing liberal and Christian democratic factions at the end of the war forced the formal separation of union and parties. In Germany, this separation was quite thorough, with the DGB prohibited from making campaign donations or actively endorsing candidates in election campaigns. Moreover, Christian Democrats were guaranteed minority representation on the DGB executive committee. In practice, however, ministers in Social Democratic governments were drawn from the DGB, and since 1968 the party-union activities have been coordinated by a liaison committee (Markovits 1986, 24–25). In Austria, the de facto connection between the union and the Socialist party is even closer. Austrian union leaders commonly hold seats in parliament, and often occupy key ministries, including the presidency of the House of Representatives.

In a number of other countries, unions maintain strong ties with left-wing parties, even without collective affiliation and competition from confessional unions and parties. The Finnish central union, as in France and Italy, is split by strong socialist and communist factions. Electorally less successful than either the Finnish Social Democrats or the Finnish Communists, the Japanese Socialist party has relied extensively on the support of the dominant Japanese union confederation, Sohyo.

Not surprisingly perhaps, because the United States has no major labor party, the links between American parties and unions are looser than in the rest of the advanced capitalist world (Greenstone 1977). Unions in the American setting are perhaps less a core constituency than one of a large number of contending interest groups that seek to sway party policy. Unions do not routinely supply candidates, and there are no formal organizational ties between unions and the parties. Still, the Democratic party has consistently received substantial financial support from the U.S. union movement, and the AFL-CIO has endorsed Democratic presidential candidates since 1952 (Galenson 1986, 63).

The electoral strength of left parties is also related to their organizational links to unions. The final column of Table 5.1 shows an index for the representation in cabinets of left parties from 1919 to the late 1970s (Wallerstein 1989). Parties with close ties to unions—in the Nordic countries, and the British Commonwealth—have done well since World War I. Sweden, Denmark, and Norway score highest reflecting long terms of Social Democratic governments from the 1930s. This suggests that not only are the connections in place for unions to press their claims, parties have been in positions of power to support their industrial organizations. Where the labor market and politics is cross-cut by religion—in the Low Countries, France, and Italy—unions occupy a subordinate position in relation to parties. These parties, in turn, have relatively little experience in government. In these contexts, the effects of parties on unionization may be more difficult to find. Considering government experience and organizational ties together, the unitary labor movements seem most likely to benefit from working-class parties.

In sum, the organizational ties between unions and parties vary greatly. Where unions were active in the formation of parties, the parties developed to represent union interests in the parliamentary sphere and this was reflected in their organizational structure. These parties were often successful in the post-war period. Unions were less able to take a leading role in party policy where they were chiefly conceived as the industrial arm of a broader communist or Christian democratic social movement. Even in these settings, however, unions remained well represented in the party executives. The United States does not fit easily into this typology of party-union relations. Organizational ties between the Democratic party and the American labor unions are relatively weak. Still, the AFL-CIO remains a consistent supporter of Democratic presidential candidates and strong financial supporter of Democratic congressional and presidential campaigns.

The Case for Political Parties

In 1935, the first Labour government was elected in New Zealand. A key legislative priority—the Industrial Conciliation and Arbitration Amendment Act—was passed the following year. Among other things, the act made it unlawful for employers to retain any adult workers who were not union members, or who were not willing to become union workers. In effect, the government had legislated a union shop for the entire New Zealand labor market. Between 1935 and 1937, union membership rose from 80,929 to 232,986. After an unsuccessful attempt to amend the legislation in 1951 and a subsequent spell in opposition, the conservative National party won the 1960 election. The following year, the new government introduced a modest qualification to the 1935 law, allowing employers to retain nonunion workers if they were as qualified as unionized ones. This "qualified preference" restriction was strengthened by further National party legislation in 1976 requiring ballots on compulsory unionism (Howells 1982).

A month before the New Zealand National party returned to office in 1960, John F. Kennedy won the U.S. presidential election. Kennedy's election followed a sequence of legislative losses for labor. The Taft-Hartley Act (1947) had been passed over Truman's veto, and the Landrum-Griffin Act was signed into law by Eisenhower in 1959. Both laws sharply curtailed union organizing, legalizing state bans on union shops and limiting sympathy strikes (Goldfield 1987, 184–87). Reversing the tide against U.S. unions, Kennedy formed a task force to report on employee-management cooperation in the federal civil service in 1961. The task force recommended that the government recognize the rights of federal employees to organize. In January 1962, Kennedy issued Executive Order 10988, allowing collective bargaining for federal employees. While the executive order covered only workers in the federal government, state and municipal workers lobbied vigorously for collective bargaining and organizing rights from the early 1960s on (Sharp 1992). By the mid-1980s, teachers' associations and state and local government employee organizations were among the largest U.S. unions. In all, public sector workers in thirty states had won the right to organize and negotiate by 1981 (Goldman 1983, 229).

These examples suggest how political parties influence unionization. First, they illustrate that positive legislative or administrative interventions can effect a one-time change in the union-organizing environment. Neither subsequent Labour governments in New Zealand nor subsequent Democratic administrations in the United States had such dramatic effects on the union growth. Second, while prolabor parties are out of office, unions are vulnerable to legislative or other attacks on their membership by rival political forces. Third, the recognition of collective bargaining rights—particularly for white-collar and public sector workers, as in the postwar period—can substantially increase union membership. How well do these observations generalize beyond the New Zealand and American cases?

Table 5.2 addresses this question by summarizing government-sponsored changes in the collective bargaining environment in the period 1950–1980. The table shows that, in general, labor and social democratic governments have supported legislation that encourages collective bargaining or expands the role of unions in collective bargaining. These effects are clearest in the highly unionized countries and in the upper tier of the moderately unionized countries. In particular, parties of the left have supported collective bargaining by white-collar and public sector workers and have also strengthened workplace representation. Denmark is somewhat exceptional in that public sector bargaining was expanded by a Liberal government in the late 1960s. In the low-density countries, we often see the same relationship, but in a slightly different form. Here, we find that while the left was in opposition, conservative parties have intervened in union negotiations or passed hostile legislation. This tendency for conservative governments to preempt collective bargaining or restrict union rights can also be found in several other countries outside the low-density group. Thus conservative parties in New Zealand and the United Kingdom both sought greater regulation of unionization and collective bargaining at different times before 1980.

Table 5.2 provides a simplified picture of changes in the collective bargaining institutions between 1950 and 1980. In many countries, particularly in Scandinavia and the Low Countries, institutional change is implemented through collective agreement rather than acts of parliament or executive orders. Commonly, political parties have much less influence over this type of institutional change compared to active government intervention. The legislative changes shown in Table 5.2 are also very heterogeneous and we can expect that their effects on union organizing would vary substantially across countries. For instance, the tendency of Conservative governments to intervene in collective bargaining and impose settlements on unions only temporarily suspends the advantages of union membership. The establishment of public

TABLE 5.2

Changes in the Collective Bargaining Environment as a Consequence of Government Intervention, Eighteen OECD Countries, 1950–1980

	Changes in Bargaining Environment
High-density countries	
Belgium	Bargaining for white-collar workers expanded (1968) under government with BSP minority coalition partner; employers reaffirmed recognition of unions in 1971 collective agreement
Denmark	Liberal government passed Civil Servants Act (1969) expanding public sector bargaining; Social Democrats updated mutual recognition of employer associations and unions in 1973
Finland	Shop stewards given protection from arbitrary dismissal, in Employment Contracts Act (1971), while Social Democrats minority coalition partner
Sweden	Social Democrats established Ministry of Civil Affairs for public sector bargaining in 1950, passed laws for civil service bargaining in 1965, and expanded shop floor power of unions in mid-1970s
Middle-density countries	
Australia	State and federal Labor governments intervened before arbitration tribunals in support of union claims; they were also supportive of claims by public sector unions
Austria	Prewar law codified by Socialists in 1974, expanding works council representation and bargaining status of ÖGB
Canada	Public sector workers given bargaining rights in NDP provinces Manitoba and Saskatchewan, as well as Quebec
Germany	Revised collective bargaining and works council legislation (1969 and 1972) under SPD government
Ireland	Several legislative amendments governing union rights while Labour party in opposition; union amalgamation facilitated by Trade Union Act (1975), passed while Labour party minority coalition partner
Italy	Statuto dei Lavoratori, recognizing broad union rights to bargaining and organizing, passed in 1970, while Socialists minority partner in Christian Democratic government
New Zealand	Compulsory arbitration and union shop provisions weakened by National party governments in 1960s and 1970s
Norway	Social Democrats expanded information of bargaining parties in 1956 with establishment of Contact Committee; Conservative government of 1965 took stronger role in collective bargaining
United Kingdom	Little government role in industrial relations until 1970s; Labour government repealed the Conservative Industrial Relations Act; Labour's "social contract" expanded union immunities from legal action

TABLE 5.2, continued

	Changes in Bargaining Environment
Low-density countries	
France	Aroux legislation (1982) passed by Socialist government establishing compulsory workplace collective bargaining
Japan	No major changes in collective bargaining law; Japanese Socialist party in opposition since 1947
Netherlands	Socialists helped establish tripartite Social and Economic Council (1950); government pre-emption of collective bargaining in late 1960s while Social Democrats in opposition
Switzerland	Industrial relations framework regulated mostly by collective agreement rather than by government, although restrictions on union security clauses passed in 1956 while Social Democrats in opposition
United States	Republicans passed Landrum-Griffin Act (1959), restricting strike activity; Kennedy's Executive Order 10988 allowed collective bargaining for federal workers

Sources: Blanpain 1995; Visser 1990a; Flanagan et al. 1983.

sector collective bargaining rights on the other hand, has long-lasting effects on union growth.

The evidence presented so far suggests that unions can and do elicit support from labor parties. Parties and unions share close organizational links, and labor and social democratic parties have strengthened the rights and powers of unions. Parties seem particularly important to unionization in unitary labor movements that are not cross-cut by religious divisions. For precisely these reasons, the electoral success of parties of the left is likely to depend on the extent of union organization. Parties support unions because they can deliver votes and money. This strong interdependence between unions and parties makes good substantive sense, but it causes methodological problems. From a substantive point of view, we can say that the process of class-wide collective action in contemporary capitalist democracies has political and industrial faces that are mutually reinforcing. The reverse would also seem to be true: where class-wide representation has only faint reality in the state and the labor market, class-wide collective action has been in trouble. Methodologically however, it is difficult to unravel the dependence of parties on unions and vice versa. This issue is taken up later on, but for now it is useful to bear in mind that the close association we observe between strong unions and strong social democratic parties is not due entirely to the impact of parties on unions. Strong unions also contribute significantly to the electoral success of parties.

Two More Complications

To this point I have presented some evidence for the idea that working-class parties, when in government, support unions and union organizing. This idea has been developed further in two different directions. One line of research claims that electoral support for working-class parties is really a reflection of a general prounion sentiment. The real mechanism for union growth is not working-class parties, but public opinion. A second argument claims that Christian democratic parties have also supported unions and their effects on unionization should be taken into account.

Elections and Public Opinion

Several studies examining the relationship between political parties and union-ization claim that electoral success is really measuring public opinion. The success of prolabor parties doesn't help unions in a direct way; it just indicates that people are more willing to support unions. This argument is made for the American case by Ashenfelter and Pencavel (1969, 438): "One must recognize . . . that trade union legislation is to a large extent a reflection of the general climate of opinion. A success of union operations is crucially dependent upon the prevailing attitudes within society." They then propose an "index of legis-lative sentiment [House Democratic party representation] that will reflect general attitudes" to predict union membership growth. This argument has motivated the inclusion of political variables in a number of econometric stud-ies of union growth. Certainly, the argument has some intuitive plausibility. As we have seen, most social democratic parties have close organizational ties to parties. Perhaps union support among voters is converted into political sup-port for leftist parties.

Unfortunately, the comparative evidence to study this claim is not very good. Still, relatively long time series of public opinion data on support for unions is available for the United Kingdom and the United States. These two countries provide some helpful institutional variation since parties and unions have close ties in Britain but not in the United States. If the parliamentary representation of left parties were tapping a general prounion sentiment, we would expect the public opinion and political representation series to move together. The British relationship should be stronger than the American one because Labour party voting is more likely to reflect union support.

The British data are taken from annual Gallup polls between 1954 and 1987 (Gallup 1976; Webb 1992, 201). National samples of respondents were asked, "Generally speaking, and thinking of Britain as a whole, do you think that trade unions are a good thing or a bad thing?" A smoothed series of the proportion of respondents answering that unions were a "good thing" between 1954 and 1987 is shown in Figure 5.1. The percentage of seats held by the Labour party in the House of Commons is also shown in the figure. In general, around 60 percent of British respondents approved of unions. Clearly, however, there is no strong positive relationship between union support and Labour party representation. Prounion sentiment generally declined from the 1950s until the late 1970s. Approval of unions fell under Wilson's Labour cabinets of the mid-1960s and 1970s. The low point came during Callaghan's Labour administration, at the time of miners' strike in the winter of 1978. Contrary to expectations, union support increased during the growth of a bitter antiunion legislative campaign following Thatcher's Conservative party victory in 1979.

Gallup poll data are also available for the United States, but here the union approval question has not been asked annually (Lipset 1986, 301). The U.S. data I analyze comes from the General Social Survey (1972–1994) (Davis and Smith 1994). Each year the survey asked respondents about confidence in "people running organized labor," along with their confidence in the leaders of a large number of other fields. With these data I was able to restrict analysis to the workers in the sample, excluding the self-employed and those not in the labor force. Figure 5.2 plots two time series. The first series shows the smoothed trend of the percentage of respondents answering that they had a great deal of confidence in union leaders. This graph indicates that support for unions—or at least union leaders—generally declined in the United States from the early 1970s to the early 1990s (see also Lipset 1986). On average between 10 and 15 percent of U.S. workers declared support for the leaders of organized labor. The second series is a smoothed trend of the percentage of Democrats in the U.S. House of Representatives. There is a modest positive relationship between support for unions and House Democratic representation. Union confidence and Democratic electoral support both fell through the early 1980s, and both recovered slightly through the second term of the Reagan presidency. In the early 1980s, the political series appears to lead public opinion by a year or so, suggesting that political developments shape public opinion, rather than the other way around. American unions suffered several crushing political defeats in this period. The Labor Law Reform Bill was defeated in a Democratically controlled Congress in 1978, and President Reagan raised antiunion sentiment by breaking the air traffic controllers' strike in 1981.

Comparison of the British and U.S. series is speculative because each survey asks different questions and samples from the two countries are not comparable. The striking difference between Britain and the United States in the level of union support, 60 percent compared to 15 percent, may be due entirely to the wording of the question. British respondents were asked about unions in general, while Americans were specifically asked about unions leaders. When U.S. respondents were asked whether they "approved of unions" in Gallup polls, between 55 and 75 percent expressed their approval

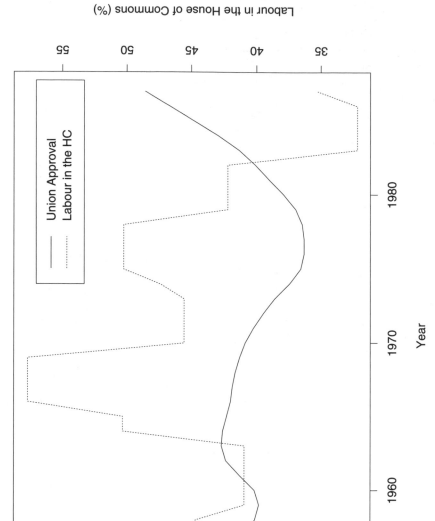

Figure 5.1. Time series of percentage of British respondents reporting that unions are a "good thing" and Labour Party representation in the House of Commons, 1954–1987.

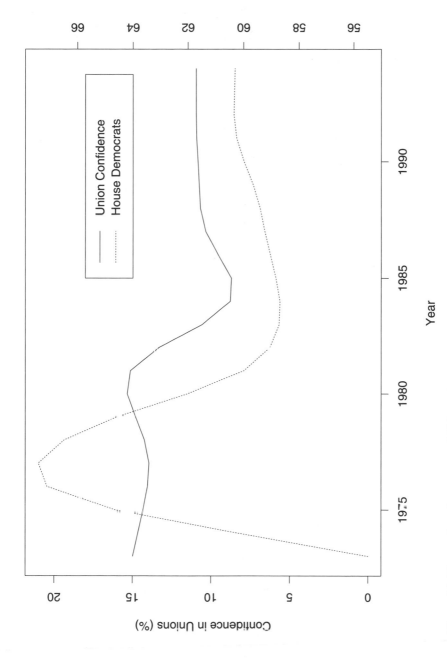

Figure 5.2. Time series of percentage of U.S. workers reporting "a great deal" of confidence in U.S. labor leaders and House Democratic Party representation, 1973–1994.

in postwar surveys. The Gallup survey question in Britain and the United States thus had similar wording, and it elicited similar levels of union approval. In any event, the assumption of the econometric research that political representation is related to public opinion is not supported. No such relationship can be found in Britain, and the correlation we see in the United States is only slightly more promising.

Christian Democracy

Throughout this chapter I have focused on the relationship between unions and social democratic and labor parties. For some countries this is an oversimplification. Originating with the papal encyclical *Rerum Novarum* (1891), Catholic unions and parties emerged throughout Europe in the first decades of the twentieth century. The encyclical warned against the twin dangers of socialism and secularism, and urged Catholic workers to form associations to defend their interests (Irving 1979, 24). Christian union groups were organized shortly afterwards in Austria and Germany to contest the organizations of the left. By the end of World War I, the first national union confederation had been formed in Italy (Visser 1989, 113–14).

Like the political and industrial organizations of the left, the role of Christian democratic parties and unions in the resistance movements helped ensure their survival in the postwar period. In Austria, Belgium, Germany, Italy, the Netherlands, and Switzerland strong Christian democratic parties had established ties to trade unions. In all but the Germanic countries, there are significant Christian democratic union confederations with organizational ties to the confessional parties that resemble the connections in the social democratic camp (Visser 1989; Lorwin 1975). In Austria and Germany, where unitary confederations dominate, the Christian democratic parties are allocated places on the union executive, and trade union members are represented in the party administration (Visser 1990a, 145; Misra and Hicks 1994, 308–9).

The parallel histories and organization of Christian and social democracy, combined with a workerist ethos expressed in encyclicals and party platforms has led some researchers to argue that Christian democratic parties boost union organizations the same way social democratic parties do. Christian democracy has directed "the broad Catholic pro-union values toward unionization by supporting Catholic labor movements and unions more generally" (Misra and Hicks 1994, 309).

In this section, I argue against a strong and general connection between Catholic parties and unions. Instead, I claim that the parallel between Christian and social democracy is overdrawn, and the relationship between Christian democracy and trade unions is weak and uneven. Two pieces of evidence support this claim. First, Christian democratic unions are weakly developed in comparison to their socialist counterparts. Second, Christian democratic parties—unlike traditional class-based parties of the right or the left—try to embrace a range of economic interests. Industrialists, small business, and farmers are also represented in Christian democracy. As a result, worker militancy threatens the organizational unity of union and party in a way that has no parallel on the left.

While unions with links to parties of the left can be found in all the advanced capitalist countries, Christian democratic confederations are found only in a minority of countries in continental Europe. Table 5.3 shows the relative size of Christian democratic and socialist confederations in the six European countries with Christian confederations. In all these countries except Belgium, the socialist confederation is substantially larger than the Christian democratic one. Confessional union confederations are weakest in France and Germany, accounting for less than 5 percent of all union members. Following reforms in 1964, the French Catholic confederation even recast itself as a secular organization, seeking Socialist party support (Ebbinghaus 1993, 96). The Belgian Catholic confederation, the CSC, has grown steadily since the early 1930s, surpassing the membership of the socialist FGTB in 1959 (Lorwin 1975, 250). However, this growth seems unlikely to be related to the power of the Catholic Social Christian party (PSC). As the union more than doubled its membership in the three decades from 1950, the vote share of the PSC declined from 48 percent in 1950 to just under 20 percent by 1981.

In addition to Catholic unions and parties' being numerically small, organizational links between them are often more strained than on the left (Ebbinghaus 1993, 93–96). Secular conservative parties may be more hostile to unions than Christian democrats, but the relationship between the political and industrial arms of Christian democracy has been often tested by union radicalism. In Germany and Italy, Christian Democrats have led the opposition against unions and their affiliated political parties. In Germany, because the main union confederation is formally independent of the parties, it reserves representation for both the Social Democrats and the Christian Democratic Union. Still, the CDU is given only minority representation in the union confederation, and Christian unionists within the CDU remain far less influential than the representatives of industry or small business. As Markovits (1986, 26) writes, the unionists within the CDU are "poor cousins" compared to their Social Democratic counterparts. In Italy, the employers' association, Confindustria, was strongly linked to the Christian Democratic party. As a consequence, the Catholic union confederation, CISL, has had an uneasy relationship with the party. In the twenty years from 1950, bitter anti-communism among the Christian Democrats fueled sharp conflicts between the left-wing and Catholic factions of the union movement. However, the relationship between the CISL and the communist-dominated CGIL was smoothed to some degree by the militancy of the Hot Autumn in 1969. The spirit of solidarity that

TABLE 5.3
Percentage Distribution of Union Members
in the Major Socialist and Christian Union
Confederations, 1985

	Union Affiliation	
	Left Parties	Christian Democrats
Belgium	41	51
France	30	4
Germany	82	3
Italy	52	33
Netherlands	43	18
Switzerland	51	12

Sources: Visser 1989; Vilrokx and van Leemput 1992.

Note: Dutch figures are for 1980, before the merger of the Dutch Confederation of Trade Unions (NVV) and Dutch Catholic Trade Union Confederation (NKV).

animated the labor movement in the early 1970s resulted in a decade-long pact joining the major confederations, distancing the Catholic confederation from the Christian Democrats (Bedani 1995, 193–94).

In the Low Countries, parties and unions have historically been closely connected in the pillars that form the main institutions of Dutch and Belgian society. Despite the outward organizational similarities of the Catholic and socialist pillars, cohesion on the Catholic side faces two ongoing challenges. First, the Catholic unions must compete for support in the party with a wide range of other economic interests. As a result, "unions face much tougher competition for influence on policies and candidacies" than in the Socialist camp (Windmuller 1969, 226–27; Vilrokx and Leemput 1992, 370). Second, growing secularization throughout the postwar period has reduced conflict and competition among the confederations. In Belgium, following the resolution of a dispute about subsidies to Catholic schools, the socialist and Catholic confederations have been highly cooperative and coordinated in collective bargaining. These developments were mirrored in the Netherlands as "de-pillarization" ultimately culminated in a merger of the Catholic, socialist, and liberal confederations between 1975 and 1981 (Visser 1989, 132).

In sum, labor parties use state institutions to help unions grow. Labor parties in Scandinavia and the British Commonwealth were formed partly for this purpose. On the Continent, formal organizational ties between parties and unions are weaker but working-class parties have still been active union supporters. Precisely because of these ties binding unions and parties, strong unions have also contributed significantly to the electoral success of labor parties. This organizational story, however, is patterned by class relations. Although historically connected to Catholic unions, confessional parties are not as responsive to unions as their counterparts on the left. Christian democratic parties express a heterogeneous range of interests and have often been in the vanguard of union opposition. Partisan support may also reflect a diffuse prounion sentiment in the general public, although the evidence for this idea is modest. Survey data from Britain and the United States suggest little more than a weak relationship between union approval and the representation of prolabor parties. The mechanism linking parties to unions thus appears to be essentially institutional. From this viewpoint, public opinion has a secondary role in providing parties with access to state institutions.

This institutional viewpoint has guided the discussion of the last three chapters. The class analysis has been prominent but little has been done to consider the market position of workers, employers, and their representatives. I have also done nothing to weigh the relative effects of the three institutional sources of union growth. The next three chapters address these tasks by estimating the effects of the institutions on unionization and the market forces that influence union organizing.

Part III

ESTIMATING THE INSTITUTIONAL EFFECTS

Six

Cross-Sectional Analysis of Union Density

THIS CHAPTER begins a sustained statistical analysis of unionization. This analysis tries to weigh the institutional effects and study the link between the institutional arguments and rival explanations of union growth. To do so, both this chapter and the next two adopt and expand the main research designs for statistical study of union organization. This chapter applies the cross-sectional design typical of comparative research. The following chapter provides a time series analysis. Chapter 8 examines disaggregated social survey data. Each type of data analysis provides different insights into the institutional effects. Taken together, the three analyses offer a strong test of the institutional account of the development of labor movements.

The first pass through the data uses a very simple design. This involves studying just the cross-sectional relationships between union density on the one hand, and the Ghent system, labor market centralization, and working-class political parties on the other. This design is weak. It generates only a handful of observations, and it sheds no light on the key issues of changing union organization over time, or subnational variation in union strength. These issues are taken up in subsequent chapters.

Still, the simplicity of the design provides a good opportunity for looking at a number of tricky questions that are often ignored in quantitative comparative research. After briefly reporting a conventional regression analysis of the cross-sectional data, I then go on to consider three more issues. First, how can historical evidence for the institutional effects be integrated into the quantitative analysis? Next, complicating the causal picture, how can we can take account of the possibility that not only do labor governments promote unionization, but strong unions also assist the electoral success of labor parties? Finally, what about the sociology of data production? The union density statistics are generated by social processes that introduce bias and noise. If we can make reasonable guesses about the size and direction of these measurement errors, how can we include this information in the analysis?

Model and Data for Regression Analysis

Historical evidence suggests that union movements have grown where unions control unemployment benefits, the labor market is centrally organized, and social democratic parties with close ties to organized labor have been in power. These ideas can be expressed more formally in a regression equation. Union density is the dependent variable that is predicted by the three institutional conditions:

$$d = b_0 + b_1 g + b_2 c + b_3 l + e,$$

where d is union density, g is the Ghent system, c is labor market centralization, l is a measure of left government, e is a random error term, and the bs are coefficients describing the institutional effects.

Data for this analysis are shown in Table 6.1. The dependent variable is the average union density for the eighteen OECD countries for the period 1971–1980. The presence of the Ghent system is indicated by a dummy variable. Labor market centralization is measured by Bruno and Sachs's (1985) index, introduced in Chapter 3. This index captures information about the strength of central union confederations and employer associations, and the development of shop floor organization. Finally, left representation in government is measured by the index used by Wallerstein (1989) in his comparative study of union organization. This index records the representation of left parties in government from 1919 until the late 1970s. To assist interpretation of the coefficients, both the centralization, scores and the left government variables have been rescaled to vary between 0 and 1. This way, regression coefficients describe the difference in union density between countries with greatest and least centralization and greatest and least experience with labor government.

Introducing Qualitative Information

The data set in Table 6.1 is a very abstract summary of the political parties and labor market institutions that we examined in the previous three chapters. A regression analysis using just the information from Table 6.1 would seem to understate what we have learned from our more qualitative and historical look at the institutional sources of union growth. This is a common problem in quantitative comparative research. Much of the historical evidence that motivates statistical analysis guides the specification of regression equations, but is ignored when we try to estimate effects (Western 1994a). What's worse, many of the data sets in comparative work are quite small, and the independent variables are often highly correlated (Western and Jackman 1994). Under these conditions, statistical estimates are usually imprecise. A lot of good—qualitative and historical—information is going to waste in favor of a small quantitative data set. Can we somehow include the nonsample information when estimating the regression coefficients?

One method pools all sorts of information—qualitative historical narrative, weak quantitative data—and estimates a new model from the pooled data. This type of analysis, which mixes sample and nonsample information, is character-

Table 6.1

Cross-Sectional Union Density Data Used for Regression Analysis,
Eighteen OECD Countries

	Union Density	Ghent System	Labor Market Centralization	Left Representation in Government
High-density countries				
Belgium	63	1	0.75	0.39
Denmark	71	1	0.75	0.81
Finland	74	1	0.75	0.53
Sweden	82	1	1.00	1.00
Middle-density countries				
Australia	52	0	0.00	0.30
Austria	59	0	1.00	0.44
Canada	32	0	0.00	0.00
Germany	40	0	1.00	0.32
Ireland	56	0	0.00	0.00
Italy	49	0	0.12	0.00
New Zealand	43	0	0.12	0.54
Norway	59	0	1.00	0.74
United Kingdom	52	0	0.00	0.39
Low-density countries				
France	20	0	0.00	0.08
Japan	33	0	0.38	0.02
Netherlands	39	0	0.50	0.28
Switzerland	34	0	0.25	0.11
United States	23	0	0.00	0.00

Notes: Union density is the national average for 1971–1980. Left representation in government is taken from Wallerstein 1989; the labor market centralization scores are adapted from Bruno and Sachs 1985. Left government and labor market centralization variables were rescaled between 0 and 1.

istic of Bayesian statistics. In the Bayesian approach, the nonsample information, called prior information, represents beliefs about statistical parameters before the quantitative sample data have been observed. The sample data are then used to update the prior beliefs to arrive at posterior inferences about the parameters. Bayesian analysis of the regression model of union density begins by choosing priors for the institutional effects. The qualitative institutional description must be distilled into a prior mean and variance for each regression coefficient. The mean describes our best guess at the magnitude of an institutional effect. The variance reflects our confidence in this guess. We can specify that prior distributions for the coefficients are Normal. Prior variances can then be found from bounds two standard deviations above and below the prior means. These bounds describe the minimum and maximum values we believe the coefficients could possibly take. If prior information is vague, the prior mean is set to zero and the prior variance to some arbitrarily large number.

With this diffuse prior for all coefficients, the sample data dominate, and posterior inference is close to the usual least squares results, which use no prior information at all. Inference is described by posterior distributions that attach a range of coefficient values to a given confidence level. For example, we might conclude that on the basis of the prior and sample information, we are 80 percent sure that the Ghent system raises union density somewhere between 10 and 25 points. (The Appendix and Western [1994a] give more detail about Bayesian regression analysis.)

For many statisticians, the subjective dimension of Bayesian analysis is controversial. The final inference is based partly on priors that are chosen at the researcher's discretion. Because priors are subjective, Efron (1986, 4) argues that Bayesian methods fail to "reassure oneself *and others* that the data have been interpreted fairly" (emphasis in original). Bayesians themselves concede that precise numerical specification of prior opinion is a "preposterous" demand (Leamer 1991). Our ideas about coefficients of the regression equation are simply too vague for exact quantification.

The Bayesian response to this criticism has two parts. First, all data analyses—Bayesian or not—use prior information. In practice, researchers make a large number of decisions in the course of a data analysis with an eye to generating sensible results (Leamer 1983; Western and Jackman 1994). Often the data are analyzed in many different ways before an attractive set of results are generated. This data-mining approach—probably dominant in the social sciences—also involves prior information. With data mining, however, the use of prior information is hidden from the reader. For most real research problems, then, prior information is ubiquitous. The Bayesian approach provides a methodology for its explicit description and coherent incorporation. Second, because Bayesian conclusions depend on subjectively chosen priors that may not be shared, it is important to assess the sensitivity of posteriors to priors. The main idea behind the sensitivity analysis is that strong conclusions should not rely heavily on narrow assumptions.

The Institutional Effects

In the Bayesian approach, we need to describe our prior belief in the size of the regression coefficients (see Table 6.2). Disposing first of the intercept term, I locate a diffuse prior at 0, allowing the sample data to dominate the results here. This reflects vague prior beliefs about the value of the intercept. However, a rich fund of qualitative institutional information provides us with strong prior beliefs about the impact of the Ghent system, labor market centralization, and left governments on the size of a union movement.

For the Ghent effect, strong historical evidence suggests the positive impact of the Ghent system on unionization (see Chapter 4). All countries with post-

TABLE 6.2
Priors for Bayesian Regression Analysis of
Union Density Data

Coefficients	Prior Mean	2 × Standard Error	Prior Variance
Intercept	0	200	10,000
Ghent system	20	20	100
Centralization	20	20	100
Left representation in government	20	20	100
Simultaneity bias	8	20	100

war Ghent systems have high union densities in comparison to countries with public unemployment insurance. Furthermore, we can observe the impact of the Ghent system at subnational levels (in the Dutch construction industry, for instance), and in quasi-experimental contrasts of Belgium and the Netherlands and of Sweden and Norway. How much of the difference in union density can we attribute to the Ghent system? Here, and for the other institutional effects, I adopt the convention of setting the prior to 20. This means that about 20 points of the difference in union density between Ghent and non-Ghent countries depends on this institutional variability. This is in line with the historical record, which places the unionization advantage of Sweden over Norway and Belgium over the Netherlands at between 10 and 30 percentage points. Confidence in this effect is described by the prior variance. The prior variance of 100 indicates that the impact of the Ghent system is unlikely to be negative, but union-run unemployment insurance may add as much as 40 points to union density.

The comparative institutional discussion of Chapter 3 also suggested that the centralization effect is positive. Countries with centrally organized labor markets, such as the Scandinavian ones, tend to have large union movements. On the other hand, decentralized countries, such as France and the United States, have the smallest union densities among the capitalist democracies. Even more compelling, in Italy—the one country to show a strong reversal in union decline—labor market institutions centralized after the Hot Autumn of 1969. As for the Ghent system effect, labor market centralization is specified to contribute 20 points to the level of union organization. In substantive terms, this suggests that about a third of the difference in unionization between the United States and Sweden is due to institutional variation in collective bargaining. A similar level of prior uncertainty is given to this effect as it seems unlikely to be negative, but may add as much as 40 points to a country's union density.

Finally, I also place a positive prior on the left government coefficient (see Chapter 5). This corresponds to the belief that the strongest social democratic parties, in Denmark and Sweden, have added about 20 points to union organization. This historical experience contrasts with the North American experience, where left parties are not represented in national government. As for the other two coefficients, I have a high level of prior certainty in this effect. The prior standard error of 10 means that I doubt that the impact of left governments on union organization is negative. There is also a chance that the strongest left parties have raised union density by no more than 40 points.

Does Left Representation in Government Depend on Union Density?

The model described by the regression equation suggests that union density depends on the institutional variables, but causality doesn't flow in the opposite direction. If union density has a positive effect on the institutional variables, the institutional effects will tend to be overestimated. This is the problem of simultaneity bias. Quantitative comparative research is often charged with ignoring simultaneity bias, providing an unrealistically simple picture of causal relationships.

The problem of simultaneity is most serious for the left government effect. Left parties are often supportive of unions precisely because unions can help them get elected and govern more effectively once elected. Where there is collective affiliation of unions to labor parties, organized labor also makes significant financial contributions to party coffers. For this reason, researchers often remark on the mutual determination of the electoral success of left parties and the organizational strength of union movements (e.g., Wallerstein 1989; Rothstein 1992; Ebbinghaus 1995). The argument is less strong for the labor market institutions, simply because they show much more stability than the periodic fluctuations in party incumbency. The centralization of industrial relations institutions changed relatively little between the 1950s and late 1970s, while union densities changed a great deal. Similarly Ghent systems showed little variation once the postwar configuration of institutions was established by the early 1950s.

A large literature in econometrics is taken up with the problem of simultaneity bias. In the econometric approach, reciprocal causation is typically addressed by augmenting single-equation models with additional equations. Often, however, making statistical models more complicated to take account of simultaneity can make things worse rather than better. More complex models provide greater opportunity for specification errors, introducing another layer of courageous assumptions. Things are worse in small samples because the statistical properties of estimators for simultaneous equation models are unknown except where sample size is large.

Bayesian analysis provides an alternative approach to simultaneity. In the Bayesian approach, instead of adding more layers to the statistical model, we can simply revise our prior to allow for the effects of endogenous variables. Leamer (1991) suggests an ingenious way of doing this that involves specifying a prior for the strength of the feedback relationship. In this approach, the predictors appear in the regression models twice—once to capture the effects of interest, and a second time to account for simultaneity bias. In the current analysis, I work with a relatively large prior for the simultaneity bias. If I say that a 50 point difference in union density accounts for about half the distance between the largest and smallest left government scores, the prior for the feedback coefficient is .5/50 = .01. Uncertainty about the true size of the coefficient, is represented by a standard error equal to the prior coefficient. This prior is used in combination with the prior on the coefficients, to form a prior for the simultaneity bias. As shown in Table 6.2, the prior mean for the simultaneity term is 8, with a standard error of 20. The left government coefficient and the feedback effect are both positive a priori, so the effect of the simultaneity prior is to shrink the posterior for the left government coefficient to 0. This offsets the effect of the simultaneity bias. The Appendix gives more details about this prior.

Regression Results

The starting point for the analysis is the conventional least squares estimates. Regression diagnostics are consistent with the usual least squares assumptions. The residuals are reasonably Normally distributed, there are no large outliers, and there are no strong nonlinearities in the data.

Table 6.3 shows the least squares coefficients from the regressions. In the spirit of Bayesian statistics, we look at confidence intervals rather than p-values to make our statistical inferences. All the coefficients are positive as expected. Consistent with the historical overview of the institutional effects, union density tends to be higher in countries with Ghent systems, where labor markets are highly centralized, and where labor and social democratic parties have a long history of government control. Results are strongest for the Ghent system and left government variables. The estimates show that countries with Ghent systems have union densities about 17 points higher than those that don't, controlling for labor market centralization and the strength of left parties. The coefficient of the left government variable is even larger. Countries with the strongest labor or social democratic parties have union densities more than 25 percent higher than comparable countries with weak left parties. This suggests that nearly half of the difference in the size of the Swedish and U.S.

TABLE 6.3
Regression Analysis of Cross-Sectional Union Density
Data, Eighteen OECD Countries

Predictor	Least Squares	Cross-Validation Bounds
Intercept	35.2	(32.1, 37.6)
	(30.2, 40.3)	
Ghent system	16.7	(14.2, 19.5)
	(6.6, 26.8)	
Centralization	2.5	(−2.1, 6.5)
	(−8.8, 13.8)	
Left representation	26.9	(23.7, 32.6)
in government	(10.0, 43.8)	

Notes: Sample size is 18; R^2 = .72. Eighty percent confidence
intervals are in parentheses.

labor movements is associated with the relative strength of the Swedish Social
Democrats. Confidence intervals for the two coefficients show that with diffuse prior information, we can be quite certain that the effects of both these
variables are positive.

The evidence is much weaker for the impact of labor market centralization
on union density. Although the estimated coefficient is positive, it is quite
small, and the confidence region overlaps 0 by a large margin. While the confidence region estimated from sample data alone suggests that the effect of
labor market centralization may account for as much as 14 points in union
density, the effect may also be negative.

Further insight into the sample data is given by the cross-validation bounds
in the second column of Table 6.3. To obtain these bounds, each observation
is sequentially omitted from the data, and a new set of coefficients is estimated
from the reduced sample of seventeen countries. The cross-validation bounds
are given by the largest and smallest coefficients yielded by this procedure.
The regular behavior of the sample data is shown by the stability of the Ghent
and left government effects. No one country is especially influential for either
of these coefficients. The instability of the labor market centralization effect
on the other hand is indicated by the cross-validation bounds that include 0. In
other words, when some countries are omitted from the data (Austria and New
Zealand), the effect of labor market centralization is estimated to be negative
(although still close to 0).

Table 6.4 shows results based on the informative prior. Bracketing the feedback from unions to parties at first, large and relatively precise posteriors are
obtained for positive institutional effects. The posterior mean of the Ghent
system effect changes little as a result of introducing prior information, but the
precision of the effect increases by about one-third. Prior information increases

TABLE 6.4

Bayesian Regression Analysis of Cross-Sectional Union Density Data, with Informative Priors for Coefficients and Simultaneity Bias, Eighteen OECD Countries

Predictor	Prior Information			
	Informative Prior		Diffuse Prior	
Intercept	34.3	33.3	35.2	36.3
	(29.7, 38.8)	(19.6, 47.1)	(30.2, 40.0)	(−4.9, 79.1)
Ghent system	17.3	17.0	16.9	16.9
	(10.1, 24.4)	(9.6, 24.5)	(7.5, 26.6)	(6.4, 27.3)
Centralization	9.8	9.0	4.7	4.1
	(2.2, 17.5)	(1.2, 16.9)	(−5.7, 15.8)	(−6.9, 15.7)
Left representation	19.8	17.3	24.1	20.7
in government	(10.5, 29.1)	(6.6, 27.9)	(8.0, 39.2)	(−8.1, 50.6)
Simultaneity bias	—	5.4	—	5.1
		(−5.2, 16.0)		(−25.8, 34.9)

Notes: Diffuse priors multiply the informative prior covariance matrices by 10. Eighty percent confidence intervals are in parentheses.

our confidence that the Ghent system raises union density by around 17 points. The left government effect is also more precisely estimated, but the posterior mean has shrunk by about one-fifth. With this prior for the left government coefficient, we have greater confidence in a smaller effect. Finally, the centralization effect is now large and positive once informative priors are used. The posterior shows we can be confident that labor market centralization accounts for about 10 points in the difference in union density between the most and the least centralized countries (say, Sweden and the United States).

The second column of Table 6.4 shows the revised estimates once prior information is provided for the feedback from union density to the electoral success of left parties. Although the simultaneity term is relatively large, the left government effect shrinks only slightly. The posterior confidence region also increases slightly but we can still infer a strong positive left government effect of around 15 points, even when prior information about simultaneity is taken into account.

Because the choice of prior is subjective and different people may prefer different specifications it is useful to see how the posteriors depend on the prior information. The priors can be modified by increasing the prior variances. This effectively reduces the amount of nonsample information in the analysis, allowing the sample data to have greater influence on the final result. Posteriors for these diffuse priors are given in the final two columns of Table 6.4. If simultaneity is ignored for the moment, strong evidence is found for the Ghent and left government effects, as we would expect given the least squares results. The centralization coefficient is now much smaller, but a majority of the posterior probability still supports a positive effect of centralized labor markets on union density. The confidence interval with this more diffuse prior, however, still includes 0. This suggests that a highly confident conclusion about the impact of labor market centralization depends crucially on a strong prior belief in its effect—the quantitative data alone are not strong enough to provide the evidence. With the simultaneity priors, the posterior distribution for the left government effect also now overlaps 0. Although the diffuse prior reflects more uncertainty about the feedback from union density to left government, there is also more uncertainty about the impact of left parties on unions. The net consequence is that considering simultaneity slightly shrinks our best guess at the left government effect, but considerably enlarges our uncertainty. As for the centralization effect, a majority of the posterior probability remains consistent with the story from the historical record.

The Sociology of Data

Empirical researchers are periodically reminded that data are generated by social processes that affect their interpretation. From the diverse perspectives of ethnomethodology and historical sociology, quantitative researchers are cautioned against taking official statistics at face value. These statistics are often the product of organizational procedures in which the interests of the data producers are quite different from the interests of the academics who do the data analysis. "A choice of statistical sources . . . is a choice of social processes" (Starr 1987, 30). More specifically, administrative data are "particularly sensitive to vagaries of bureaucratic policy or procedure unrelated to the external social phenomenon they may be taken to measure" (ibid.). Or, following Harold Garfinkel (1967, ch. 6), there are often good organizational reasons for bad records.

These warnings apply well to information on union density. Unionization statistics are generally taken from one of two sources. In Australia and the United States, union membership data have been collected in a regular way through large national labor force surveys over the last two decades. This information is usually viewed as very accurate. Even here, errors can result from failures to obtain union status from retired and unemployed respondents (Chang and Sorrentino 1991). The vast majority of union density statistics, however, come from reports by the unions themselves. Although a pioneering archivist of U.S. union membership observed that union reports show "every evidence of accuracy and truthfulness" (Wolman 1924, 24), unions often have incentives both to overestimate and to underestimate their membership. Overestimates may result where union representation at confederation or party conferences is linked to membership. In other cases, recordkeeping is simply poor, and many members with unpaid dues are retained on the membership rolls and in the union density statistics. Underestimates can be found where the dues paid by union affiliates to confederations are based on membership (Bain and Price 1980, 5). The centralization of the union movement also influences the quality of union density statistics. Small confederations or small unions are often not required to report to governmental statistical authorities or the major confederations. Additional data from independent unions is often collected, but the possibility of error in this process is still introduced. Underestimates may thus result from extensive independent unionism.

From a methodological point of view, the sociology of data production can be viewed as a special source of measurement error. Unfortunately, this error is highly heterogeneous, characterized by bias in some cases, as well as random perturbation. This type of error falls outside of the uncertainty captured by the usual error term of a linear regression model. To acknowledge the sociology of data production in a regression analysis, I perform a sensitivity analysis where uncertainty about the true value for a union density statistic is described by a probability distribution. This distribution says where we think the true value may lie, but also concedes that it may be higher or lower. To take account of our uncertainty about the union density data, we can just replace the observed density score with a random draw from the probability distribution for that country.

Analysis would then proceed as follows. We allow for two sources of uncertainty. First there is the usual sampling uncertainty, from a frequentist perspective, or perhaps subjective uncertainty about the quality of prediction or unobserved heterogeneity across the countries (see Berk, Western, and Weiss 1995). To account for this uncertainty in our batch of eighteen countries, we randomly draw a set of eighteen cases, sampling with replacement. Sampling with replacement means that some countries may by chosen more than once, while others may not be selected at all. This scheme simulates the process of sampling from a larger population. If we draw many samples of eighteen countries and estimate the regression coefficients from each sample, we can generate a distribution of coefficients akin to a sampling distribution produced by repeated sampling from a population. This simulation procedure is called a bootstrap (Efron and Tibshirani 1993).

The bootstrap, however, does not take account of uncertainty about the data due to variation in the institutional conditions of its production. To allow for this second source of uncertainty, we add another resampling stage. For each country in a given bootstrap sample, we assign a union density score randomly taken from the specified probability distribution that describes uncertainty due to the social process of data generation. With a random sample of countries, and their randomly drawn union density scores, regression coefficients are estimated with least squares. Repeating this procedure many times produces a distribution of coefficients that can be used to assess the sensitivity of the results to measurement error. The resulting distribution of coefficients reflects the different estimates we might have obtained given uncertainty about processes generating the observed data. The additional uncertainty introduced by the measurement error should inflate the standard errors, and may change the coefficient estimates from the least squares results. Although I don't know any strong statistical justification for this procedure, it seems a useful way of including information about a heterogeneous data generation process into the analysis.

Table 6.5 describes the data generation process in the eighteen OECD countries. In some countries (the Scandinavian countries and Austria) union density statistics appear to be quite accurate. Weak independent unionism reduces the chances of an undercount of union members. In other countries, such as Belgium or France, where unions are competitive or membership is simply inefficiently recorded, both bias and error are likely. The Belgian and French figures are both likely to have large errors and overreporting biases.

The analysis based on the resampling methods is reported in Table 6.6. The "No Measurement Error" column reports a conventional bootstrap analysis, where we assume that union density has been accurately observed. As we would expect, these results are similar to, but a little more optimistic than, the least squares results. As before, strong evidence is found for positive Ghent system and left government effects. The results in the "With Measurement Error" column allow for measurement error in the dependent variable. Although the prior assessment of data quality was rather pessimistic—union densities for some countries were allowed to vary by as much 20 points—allowing for measurement error makes little difference to the final conclusions. The Ghent and left government effects show little sensitivity to possible errors in measurement. The means of the sampling distributions are also extremely close to the least squares results even though observations from some countries were thought to show large biases.

In sum, the social conditions of data production vary greatly throughout the OECD. This variation introduces potentially large and heterogeneous measurement errors. Despite our uncertainty about the true level of union density in many countries, the regression results remain very stable. When averaging across countries, patterns in the data remain strong. The Ghent systems are associated with a 15 point rise in union density. Countries with strong social democratic parties, such as those of Scandinavia, organize about 20 percentage points more of their work forces than do countries with weak left parties. Finally, these sample data again provide only weak evidence for the impact of labor market centralization on union organization.

In this chapter, I have investigated how union density depends on the three institutional conditions, using a very simple cross-sectional regression model. The simplicity of the design provided a useful opportunity to explore several hard methodological and substantive issues that are usually ignored in comparative research. First, the weak quantitative data were combined with the rich qualitative historical data through a Bayesian prior distribution. This

TABLE 6.5

Quality of Union Membership Data and Distributions for Measurement Error,
Eighteen OECD Countries

		Distribution for Measurement Error		
	Method of Data Collection	*Minimum*	*Mode*	*Maximum*
Australia	Survey figures exceed union reports by about 10%, but surveys exclude unemployed and retired members. Members with unpaid dues may also be included in membership reports.	40	52	59
Austria	Union reports come from central confederations. Reporting errors should be small because there is no independent unionism and unemployment is low, reducing the inclusion of nonfinancial members.	53	59	65
Belgium	Data are collected from the three major confederations. There is error associated with downward adjustments to take account of likely overreporting by unions.	53	63	73
Canada	Small unions (fewer than 50 members) are not covered in official statistics, although survey data suggest an overcount of several points.	22	32	37
Denmark	Official statistics come from reports of major confederations. Current data also include reports of independent unions, although an undercount is likely.	65	71	80
Finland	Statistics are collected by the major union confederation. An overcount, due to inclusion of the self-employed and students, is likely.	65	74	80
France	Data are from the five major confederations. Interunion competition may inflate the figures, but this is partly offset by missing data for independent unions, perhaps about 5% of French union membership.	8	20	27
Germany	Small independent unions are not included in the figures collected by major confederations, causing an undercount of several points.	34	40	49
Ireland	There are no data on retired and unemployed members, but given the high rate of Irish unemployment it seems likely that they are included. Some error is associated with inclusion of the self-employed.	48	56	64

TABLE 6.5, continued

	Method of Data Collection	Distribution for Measurement Error		
		Minimum	*Mode*	*Maximum*
Italy	There is no coverage of independent unions in the public and financial services sectors, but these grew mostly in the 1980s, after collection of the current data. A significant overcount, due to membership of the self-employed, is also likely.	39	49	59
Japan	Membership data are based on union reports. There are no reported sources of systematic error.	27	33	39
Netherlands	Membership data are taken from government surveys of unions with adjustments for the unemployed and military conscripts. These figures understate union reports by about 5 points.	32	38	50
New Zealand	Government records report only registered unions. An undercount results from the exclusion of some white-collar unions, notably the teachers' union.	36	43	54
Norway	Confederation membership reports are supplemented by statistics from independent unions. Coverage is extensive, so any undercount is likely to be small.	66	63	69
Sweden	Membership reports are collected from major confederations. Figures are likely to be accurate because reports of independent unions are given to the LO. A slight overestimate may result from inclusion of the self-employed.	75	82	89
Switzerland	Membership reports failed to include small independent unions, although the current figures have been adjusted to allow for this.	27	34	41
United Kingdom	Error may result from adjustments to exclude the self-employed and Irish membership of unions based in Britain. Aggregate figures consistently exceed social survey numbers by several points.	42	52	58
United States	Figures are based on membership reports collected by the Bureau of Labor Statistics. This series exceeds survey data figures by between 7 and 15%.	12	23	30

Sources: Visser 1989; Bain and Price 1980; Chang and Sorrentino 1991.

Notes: The three-figure summary of the distribution for measurement error gives the lowest possible union density, the most likely (or modal) value, and the largest possible union density.

TABLE 6.6
Bootstrap Coefficients for Observed Union Density Data, with Additional Results for Resampling with Measurement Error

	Resampling Plan	
Predictor	No Measurement Error	With Measurement Error
Intercept	35.3	35.3
	(29.0, 41.5)	(28.9, 41.7)
Ghent system	17.3	17.4
	(11.4, 24.0)	(10.4, 24.9)
Centralization	2.2	2.3
	(−7.1, 12.0)	(−8.0, 13.0)
Left representation	26.2	26.1
in government	(13.1, 38.5)	(12.1, 40.0)

Notes: Coefficients are the means of bootstrap sampling distributions. Numbers in parentheses are 10th and 90th percentiles of bootstrap sampling distributions.

analysis provided very strong evidence in favor of the three institutional effects. Indeed, the nonsample information was decisive for a confident belief in the positive impact of labor market centralization. Second, prior distributions were also used to take account of the reciprocal effect of large union movements on the electoral success of social democratic parties. Once the causal relationship between parties and unions was allowed to run in both directions, evidence for the dependence of unions on left parties became weaker, although we can still find good support for the positive effects of parties. Finally, I examined how union density statistics are produced in different countries, and performed a sensitivity analysis to allow for the measurement error that might result. The sensitivity analysis showed that sizable biases in the union density data may exist, but the estimates from the model remain stable even in the face of this error.

Seven

The Business Cycle and Union Growth

THE CROSS-SECTIONAL regression analysis of the last chapter has many important limitations. There was no consideration of rival, noninstitutional, explanations of union organization. The static analysis that examines only a slice of the union density statistics also ignores important clues in the pattern of variation over time. At the beginning of the 1950s, our capitalist democracies had similar levels of labor organization, with union density varying between 30 and 50 percent. By 1985, however, over 80 percent of the Swedish labor force was unionized, while less than 20 percent of American workers were union members. Despite the common constraints of capitalist democracy, national labor movements traced vastly different trajectories in the postwar period. This pattern of postwar divergence in union organization suggests something about its causes.

Most research examining the changing trends in union organization emphasizes the impact of the business cycle. The idea that the strength of labor movements depends on prevailing economic conditions can be traced back at least as far as Engels, who observed: "The favorable effects of workers' resistance organization are limited to times of brisk and average trade" (quoted in Draper 1978, 102). An early academic statement of the theory comes from Commons (1918), who argued that workers demand collective representation in times of rising prices to protect the purchasing power of their wages: "[L]abor movements in all countries pursue these [business] cycles" (10). These insights have been faithfully retained in a long line of econometric research that associates fluctuations in union growth with economic cycles.

In this chapter, I place the business cycle and other time series explanations of union growth in the broader context of an institutional theory. The key idea is that the effects of market conditions and organizing effort on unionization are shaped by stable institutional contexts. In the right institutional framework, unions grow even through downturns in the business cycle. Centralized bargaining and the Ghent system insulate unions from surrounding economic conditions. Strong left parties offer another route to collective action that liberates labor movements from their dependence on strong economic performance. Without favorable institutional conditions, unions are vulnerable to cyclical changes in the economy and grow only through extrainstitutional strategies, such as strike action. Divergent trends in unionization are thus distinct products of institutions that either tame or inflame the impact of economic developments.

Time Series Analysis: The Business Cycle and Organizing Effort

Modern approaches to unionization time series originated with early disagreements about the role of market conditions and politics in labor organizing. In his 1954 paper on American union membership growth, Irving Bernstein weighed the comparative merits of the theoretical monism that excluded all accounts except the business cycle and the theoretical pluralism that entertained other forces, such as social upheaval and public policy in wartime. Today, a similar division can be drawn between the business cycle tradition and approaches that emphasize the mobilizing force of workers and unions.

Longitudinal Explanations of Union Growth

Modern business cycle explanations are based on the idea that workers translate market power into collective action in response to fluctuating economic conditions. When times are bad, labor's market power is weak, and competition for jobs increases, along with employers' resistance to unions. A strong economy, on the other hand, improves labor's hand by increasing the benefits of collective action and lowering employer opposition. This reasoning generated a large econometric literature, which found business cycle effects in Australia, Sweden, the United Kingdom, and North America (Hines 1964; Ashenfelter and Pencavel 1969; Sharpe 1971; Swindinsky 1974; see also Bain and Elsheikh 1976, 26–57; Hirsch and Addison 1986, 52–56).

Operationally, the business cycle theory has taken many different forms but the impact of two variables stand out. Union membership is positively related to inflation, but negatively associated with unemployment. The interpretation of both effects is straightforward. When prices rise, workers organize to protect their wages, and employers accede to labor organizing to avoid interruptions in production. For the unemployment effect, employers resist unions when labor markets are slack because the costs of industrial action are small in times of reduced demand. For workers, union membership provides few benefits and is very costly during spells of unemployment. Other measures of the economic cycle, such as wholesale price and wage movements, have also been proposed but the theory remains essentially the same: collective action flows from market power.

The business cycle story takes a thin view of labor movements. The key agents are workers and employers, rather than unions. Instead of taking an active role in mobilizing or defeating collective action in the labor market, the agents are reactive, responding to exogenously shifting market conditions. Unionization doesn't result from organizing effort and the active construction of shared interests. Instead, it follows from the conditions under which the rewards of union membership would be high.

In response, other researchers have focused on the mobilizing efforts of militant workers and unions themselves. The first account in this approach looks at the impact of strikes. The second focuses on the organizing problem of the union. The idea that strikes can serve as points of mobilization was developed and largely abandoned by economists, but rehabilitated by political sociologists. John Dunlop's (1949) work on the early development of U.S. unions associated spurts in labor movement growth with periods of intense militancy. The strike waves of the 1890s and the 1930s were critical moments in this analysis. Bernstein (1954, 309) agreed, noting the importance of social unrest that "calls into question the very foundation of society." In the economic research of the late 1940s and early 1950s, the lessons of U.S. union radicalism in the 1930s were forgotten, but the ideas remained fresh for students of comparative politics. Comparativists noted that unions grew rapidly in the wake of strike waves, not only in the United States of the 1930s, but also in Sweden in the 1910s, in Italy after 1969, and in France for most of the twentieth century (Korpi 1978, 211–12; Regalia, Regini, and Reyneri 1978; Tilly 1986, 369). In general, union density increased throughout Europe following the strike waves of the late 1960s. In this political theory, strike activity raises unionization by mobilizing workers around a collective project. Oftentimes the strikes are explicitly intended to obtain union recognition and rights to collective bargaining (Griffin, McCammon, and Botsko 1990, 179).

The organizing problem of the union has been tackled in work by Michael Wallerstein (1989, 1991). Wallerstein argued that the benefits of unionization depend on the proportion of the work force organized but the cost of organization to the union depends on the absolute number of new union members. As a result, the optimal level of unionization for the union falls as the size of the labor force increases. Although this idea was originally examined in a cross-sectional sample of twenty industrialized democracies, the basic point is readily extended to a time series analysis. The union organizing task is made more difficult when the labor force is growing quickly. In practice, the growth of new jobs challenges unions to organize new workplaces and negotiate with new employers. Maintaining and increasing union density under these conditions is harder than when the employed labor force shows little growth and labor market exit and entry is accounted for by turnover in existing jobs. Employment growth should then be negatively related to unionization.

In sum, a large body of research literature sees longitudinal variation in union organization linked to cyclical movements in the economy. This is not the whole story, however, because it omits the organizing efforts of unions and workers. Thus other researchers claim that strike activity has driven union growth, and that union organizing becomes more costly when the labor force is growing quickly.

The Limits of Longitudinal Explanations

The main shortcoming of the time series theories can be seen from an institutional perspective. If the business cycle and organizing efforts influence union growth, are these effects the same in all contexts, or will they vary? This type of question has been posed frequently in the business cycle research from comparative and historical viewpoints. From the historical point of view, reported business cycle effects were based on analyses of long time series that concealed important structural breaks. For example, American studies reported changes in the coefficients of business cycle variables after the constitutionality of the Wagner Act was upheld by the Supreme Court in 1937 (Sheflin et al. 1981; Fiorito 1982). Other analyses found that business cycle effects had virtually disappeared by the time of the postwar period in many European countries (Neumann et al. 1989). From a comparative viewpoint, the business cycle model neglected cross-nationally variable institutional conditions that influence union organizing. For example, although inflation increases with union membership in Sweden, the United States, and the United Kingdom, this relationship is weak and negative in Ireland because wage indexing maintains wages without renegotiation of union contracts (Roche and Larragy 1990). In Denmark, where unions pay unemployment benefits, unemployment is positively associated with union growth, contrary to business cycle predictions (Pedersen 1990). These examples point to the more general idea that business cycle effects are conditional on institutional context.

Combining Longitudinal and Institutional Accounts

The limited historical and comparative generality of the time series theories suggests an alternative explanation of unionization. Viewed institutionally, time-invariant but cross-nationally variable labor market institutions may shape the relationship between unionization and its temporally variable determinants. The impact of left parties fits less easily into this scheme, but there are good institutional reasons to think their effects will also differ across countries.

Labor Market Centralization

While market conditions and mobilizing effort vary from year to year, we saw earlier that labor market institutions endured for the three decades from 1950 on. Exceptions include Finland, Japan, and Italy. In Finland, centralized industrial relations were largely established relatively late, after the general strike of 1956, when unions began regular wage bargaining (Knoellinger 1960). Japanese labor market institutions crystallized in the late 1950s, following the defeat by employers of industrial unionism and the installation of enterprise organization (Armstrong et al. 1991, 131–35). Institutional change was most radical in Italy. There, the industrial relations framework was overhauled following the Hot Autumn of 1969 (Regalia et al., 1978). Except for these three countries, the basic rules, actors, and patterns of labor market centralization were established in the capitalist democracies by the end of postwar reconstruction. While a few changes in the bargaining institutions can be seen before the 1980s, cross-national variation overshadows change over time.

In the current context, the key issue is whether durable patterns of centralization shape the effects of longitudinal variables. I argue that the impact of strikes and labor force growth can both be understood to depend on labor market centralization. While unified labor organization and corporatist bargaining may influence the level of unionization, Korpi and Shalev (1979) and Hibbs (1987) claimed that these factors also shape the level and consequences of labor militancy. Substantial power resources for class actors are embedded in corporatist bargaining institutions and unified working-class organization, and these provide workers with institutional means for advancing their interests. However, when forums for class conflict and working-class organization are decentralized, workers are compelled to adopt extrainstitutional tactics, principally strikes, to achieve their goals. Snyder's (1976) analysis of strikes in France, Italy, and the United States has a similar flavor. For Snyder, the logic of strike action—its causes and goals—varies with the integration of unions into the institutional framework of the labor market.

Although these ideas are usually used to explain strike activity, they also suggest that the longitudinal relationship between strikes and union growth varies with labor market centralization. With centralized labor markets, the construction of class-wide interests that mobilize workers is efficiently pursued through channels established by the union confederations rather than through industrial action. As a result, the mobilizing impact of strikes is low in corporatist countries. Where there are industrial disputes, strikers usually advance sectional interests, and reject the class representation embedded in centralized bargaining. When unions are decentralized and collective interests have few avenues for institutional expression, strikes can serve as focal points for organization.

The consequences of labor market centralization for the unionization-strike relationship is illustrated by the different effects of the European strike waves of the late 1960s. In Sweden, well-paid and highly unionized miners led wildcat strikes in 1969. Demanding greater wage militancy and pay equity with white-collar workers, the miners effectively repudiated the LO as a class representative (Swenson 1989, 85–87). In Italy, by contrast, the unofficial strike wave of the Hot Autumn of 1969 helped reverse declining union density and provided the basis for organizing southern and migrant workers in industrial unions. A similar but less dramatic picture is given by the consequences of the Events of May 1968 in France (Lange et al. 1982). Fragmented class organization in France and Italy led to strikes that fueled union growth, but unified class organization in northern Europe was divided by militancy, with no effect on the size of the organized working class. In short, labor market centralization dampens the positive effect of strikes on union growth.

The impact of labor force growth on unionization should also be affected by labor market centralization. Wallerstein's empirical analysis of the effects of labor force growth assumes that union organizing costs per worker are the same across countries. This contradicts the idea that centralization lowers the cost of unionization by reducing employer resistance and interunion competition. Because labor market centralization creates low-cost contexts for labor organizing, rapid employment growth should exert a negligible downward pressure on union density where centralization is high. In decentralized labor markets, organizing costs are high and union organizers should find it more difficult to keep pace with an expanding labor force. The negative effect of labor force growth should be large here.

This is illustrated by the contrast between the United States and Germany through the 1950s and early 1960s. Both are large countries, and the labor forces in both grew at about 2 percent a year through the 1950s and 1960s. Union membership growth could not keep pace with employment growth in the United States, and union density dropped continuously from the early 1950s. In Germany, on the other hand, union membership grew with the labor force, and union density remained roughly constant until the late 1970s. The more general conclusion is that labor market centralization should reduce the negative effect of labor force growth on unionization.

The Ghent System

Like collective bargaining institutions, systems of unemployment insurance have provided durable contexts for labor organizing throughout the postwar period. As we saw in Chatper 4, the important institutional variation here is the difference between compulsory unemployment insurance run by the state and union-run insurance plans that operate with public subsidies. During the postwar period, union-run Ghent systems could be found only in Belgium, Denmark, Finland, and Sweden. The Netherlands is a partial exception: it discarded its Ghent system in 1952, in favor of compulsory public unemployment insurance.

While we expect the Ghent system to raise union density, we can also ask the same question that we posed before: will the institutional context influence the effects of longitudinal variables? Here, the Ghent system speaks directly to the logic of business cycle theories of unionization. By integrating those at risk of unemployment into the labor movement, Ghent systems reverse the vulnerability of labor movements to poor economic conditions. Although business cycle theory predicts a negative relationship between unemployment and unionization, workers in Ghent countries retain their union status during recessionary periods. Thus, the Ghent system has a positive influence on the relationship between unemployment and unionization (Pedersen 1990; Freeman 1989; Western 1993).

A similar argument can be made about the effects of employment growth. When the labor force is growing rapidly, there are many new labor market entrants. The risk of unemployment for these new workers is high. But where unions are closely involved with the unemployed, new workers are more likely to hold union membership. In effect, joining a union helps guard against the costs of unemployment in Ghent system countries. The reverse will be the case where the state manages unemployment benefits. Unions have little to offer workers at high risk of unemployment, so union membership will be less attractive to new workers. Rapid labor force growth in these settings should apply strong downward pressure on union density.

Political Parties

Up to this point, the contrast between the institutional and longitudinal accounts of unionization is clear. Labor market institutions don't vary much over time, but are very different across countries. Their influence on the context of labor market competition drives variation in the effects of longitudinal variables. The third prong of the institutional argument—political parties—fits less neatly into this scheme. Although the mobilizing power of the state is enduring, the capacity of parties to activate state institutions varies over time.

Left parties, we have seen, support unionization by sponsoring prounion labor law and by integrating unions into state policymaking bodies. The opportunities for parties to support unionization depend importantly on their representation in government. The paradigmatic Nordic examples suggest that long terms of social democratic government can substantially expand the power of trade unions (Stephens 1979; Korpi 1983; Esping-Andersen 1985). Unions have declined where social democratic or labor parties have spent long periods in opposition, as in Italy until the 1970s, or France for most of the postwar period.

Business cycle researchers have been sensitive to the possible impact of parties, but the econometric results have turned up little support. The first of the modern studies, by Ashenfelter and Pencavel (1969), found that U.S. Democratic party representation in the House of Representatives is significantly associated with union growth between 1900 and 1960. This result, however, is not robust to alternative specifications or time periods. Analysis of a slightly modified model found no Democratic party effect (Bain and Elsheikh 1976, 92). Another study of the post–Wagner Act period, 1937–1975, could not replicate the party effect either (Sheflin et al. 1981). In British research, party effects were similarly weak. Bain and Elsheikh's (1976, 85–86) model of the British series found no significant relationship between Labour party representation in the House of Commons and membership growth. The Labour party effect in Britain was also rejected by Booth (1983).

One problem with these analyses might simply be an issue of measurement. In the research on British and American series, lower house representation of the Democratic or Labour party was used as the indicator of party power. But because legislation and government industrial relations policy have been the chief mechanisms for union support through the state, control of the executive is likely to be much more important. After all, it is the capacity of parties to pass legislation and legitimate unions as economic actors that contributes to labor movement growth. Left party representation in government, rather than representation in the legislature, may be driving the growth of labor movements. Although there are good reasons to think that left government raises union density, we have also seen why this may be hard to detect in a statistical model. In Chapter 5 we saw that left governments do not help unions in a smooth and continuous way. Instead, governments often improve the organizing environment with one-time changes in industrial relations policy and law. In addition, in some countries, many changes to the regulatory framework are implemented through collective agreements, rather than legislation. In sum, left government should increase union density; but consistent with the other institutional arguments, we can expect that the effects of this longitudinal variable will differ across countries.

Model Specification, Estimation, and Data

Longitudinal and cross-national theories of unionization can be combined into a single model. Business cycle researchers typically have used figures on annual change in union membership as the dependent variable. The use of change scores in the dependent variable substantially reduces serial correlation in the series, while still allowing a focus on union growth. In comparative studies in which the size of the dependent labor force varies substantially among countries, union density is used as the dependent variable to adjust for this confounding source of variation (Neumann et al. 1989; Bain and Elsheikh 1976, 58). The current analysis, which capitalizes on cross-national and longitudinal variation, takes the outcome to be explained as the annual change in union density. This approach removes serial correlation but eliminates large cross-national difference in labor force size as a source of variation.

To model the idea that the impact of longitudinal variables depends on relatively stable institutional conditions, I begin by looking at union growth in just one of $j = 1, \ldots, 18$ countries. The longitudinal explanations suggest that the annual change in union density in year t depends on a number of time series variables:

$$\Delta d_{jt} = b_{0j} + b_{1j}\, \dot{p}_{jt} + b_{2j}\, u_{jt} + b_{3j}\, s_{jt} + b_{4j}\, \dot{w}_{jt} + b_{5j}\, l_{jt} + e_{jt}, \qquad (7.1)$$

where d_t is union density and $\Delta d_t = d_t - d_{t-1}$, $\dot{p}$ is the inflation rate, u is unemployment, s is a measure of strike activity, $\dot{w}$ is the percentage growth in the size of the dependent labor force, l is the cabinet representation of labor and social democratic parties, and e is an error term. With this model, diagnostics show that there is little autocorrelation among the errors, so these are treated as independent.

Equation (7.1) looks a lot like many of the models that have been estimated in the econometric literature on union growth. The big difference is that the regression coefficients carry the j subscript, indicating that regression relationships vary across countries. For example, the impact of unemployment on the yearly change in union density is specified to differ cross-nationally. These coefficients do not vary randomly, however. Instead, they vary in a way that depends on the configuration of labor market institutions. This contextualized version of the conventional time series model says that variation in the country-level ("micro") time series regression coefficients can be written as a function of the time-invariant cross-national institutional ("macro") variables, labor market centralization, and the Ghent system:

$$\begin{aligned} b_{0j} &= \gamma_{00} + \gamma_{01}\, C_j + \gamma_{02}\, G_j + \alpha_{0j} \\ &\;\vdots \\ b_{5j} &= \gamma_{50} + \gamma_{51}\, C_j + \gamma_{52}\, G_j + \alpha_{5j}. \end{aligned} \qquad (7.2)$$

In this macro equation, the time series coefficients for each country depend on labor market centralization, C, union-distributed unemployment benefits, G, and the random effects, α. Multilevel models of this type allow for error at the micro and macro levels (Mason, Wong, and Entwistle 1983). An alternative approach could just specify interaction effects, where the institutional variables are used to form product terms in the time series equation (7.1). (The interaction model of Alvarez, Garrett, and Lange [1991] is an example.) That approach assumes that the institutional variables exhaustively explain variation in the time series coefficients. We relax this assumption by adding some random effects, the αs, to the macro equation. These hierarchical models have a Bayesian justification. The random coefficients, α, are treated as draws from a population distribution whose parameters can be estimated by combining data from all the countries and prior information. Combining information in this way yields more accurate coefficient estimates (lower mean squared error) than if each country-level equation were fitted separately (Gelman, Carlin, Stern, and Rubin 1995).

An interesting feature of the union density time series is that they poorly approximate a Normal distribution. In each series, there are a few extreme values, where union density rose or declined sharply in a given year. This can be seen in Figure 7.1, which shows quantile plots of the residuals from a least squares fit for each country. With Normal data, the residuals should fall in a straight line. Here, many of the residual distributions have heavy tails, meaning that outliers occur with greater frequency than we would expect under the Normal distribution. To accommodate this data distribution, I fit a t rather than a Normal distribution to the data. Because the tails of the t distribution are fatter than those of the Normal distribution, it provides a useful model for data with outliers (Lange, Little, and Taylor 1989). The t distribution is indexed by a degrees of freedom parameter. This parameter is like a tuning constant in robust regression that determines the sensitivity of estimates to outlying observations. When the degrees of freedom is set to a small number (say, 1 or 2), the resulting estimates are very resistant to outliers. When the degrees of freedom is large, the t model behaves like the Normal, and the estimates are similar to those from least squares estimation.

The superiority of the t model is shown in Table 7.1, which compares the maximized log likelihoods of both models. These statistics simply provide a way of measuring the fit of both models in a common metric. For these results, the degrees of freedom parameter was set to 4. We can see that the t model has a higher likelihood than the Normal model in twelve out of the eighteen countries. In only three countries—Australia, Finland, and Sweden—does the conventional model clearly perform better than the robust version. Indeed, the strong performance of the t model is precisely what we would expect given the residual diagnostics shown in Figure 7.1. In the remainder of this chapter, I focus on results from the t distribution, although it should be noted that the Normal results are similar. More technical detail about the model and estimation is provided in the Appendix.

Summary statistics for the time series data are presented in Table 7.2. Inflation, $\dot{p}$, and unemployment, u, are annual rates. The low-inflation regimes of Germany and Switzerland are reflected in the data, as are the strong employment records of Sweden and Japan. Labor force growth, $\dot{w}$, is the annual percentage change in the size of the employed labor force. The strong performers here are the North American countries. The representation of prolabor parties, l, is the percentage of cabinet seats held by labor, social democratic,

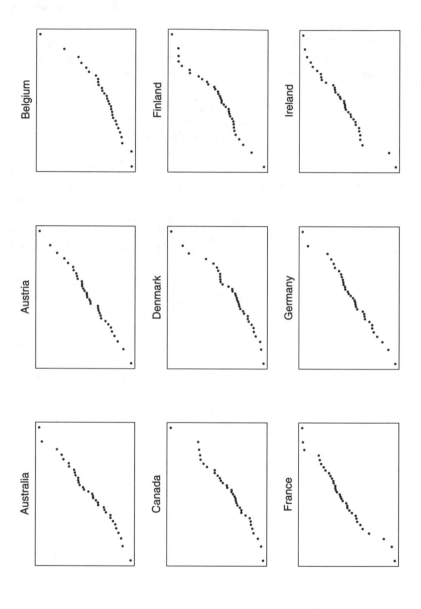

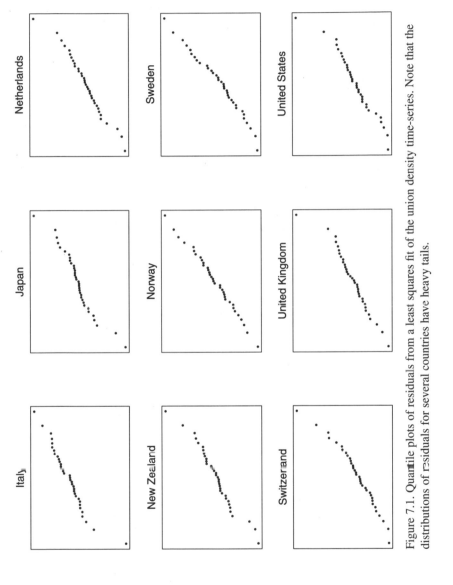

Figure 7.1. Quantile plots of residuals from a least squares fit of the union density time-series. Note that the distributions of residuals for several countries have heavy tails.

TABLE 7.1
Maximized Log Likelihoods from Normal and
t Models of the Union Density Time Series,
Eighteen OECD Countries, 1950–1985

	Log Likelihood	
	Normal	t (4 d.f.)
Australia	−45.3	−46.7
Austria	−16.2	−16.2
Belgium	−41.9	−39.0
Canada	−24.0	−24.9
Denmark	−52.7	−49.3
Finland	−74.9	−75.7
France	−47.6	−45.8
Germany	−30.3	−29.3
Ireland	−41.4	−41.2
Italy	−64.7	−62.3
Japan	−51.6	−47.2
Netherlands	−28.1	−25.5
New Zealand	−43.6	−39.9
Norway	−36.3	−37.0
Sweden	−30.9	−32.0
Switzerland	−19.5	−16.6
United Kingdom	−40.5	−37.7
United States	−32.8	−27.8

socialist, or communist parties. Liberal party and New Democratic party representation in Canada and Democratic party representation in the United States were included because of the relatively prolabor stances of these parties in their particular national political contexts. Following Hibbs (1987, 19–22), strike activity, s, is measured as days lost due to industrial disputes per 1,000 workers. As in most strike statistics, France, Italy, and the English-speaking countries show the highest levels of strike action. This series is logged to restrict the influence of outliers. As before, labor market centralization is measured by the adjusted Bruno and Sachs (1985) index, and the presence of the Ghent system in Belgium, Denmark, Finland, and Sweden is indicated by a dummy variable. (Chapter 6 describes the macro data.)

In the analysis, country-level time series data are centered (mean deviated) within each country. This allows the intercepts of the time series equation (7.1) to be interpreted as the average union density growth in a particular country through the postwar period. In contrast to a single-equation model, centering data in a multilevel model can have unpredictable consequences for statistical inference. However, in this application, the centered and uncentered data yield substantively similar results.

TABLE 7.2
Means of Longitudinal Variables for Time Series Model

	Annual Density Growth (Δd)	Inflation ($\dot{p}$)	Unem- ployment (u)	Strike Volume (s)	Left Representation in Government (l)	Labor Force Growth ($\dot{w}$)
Australia	−0.1	6.6	3.5	327	.2	2.2
Austria	−0.1	5.1	2.5	10	.6	1.0
Belgium	1.0	4.2	3.6	177	.3	1.0
Canada	0.2	4.8	6.0	520	.8	3.2
Denmark	0.7	6.6	5.7	39	.6	1.6
Finland	1.4	7.3	2.6	175	.4	1.9
France	−0.4	6.9	3.2	176	.2	1.3
Germany	0.0	3.3	3.1	15	.3	1.3
Ireland	0.3	8.2	7.8	415	.1	1.0
Italy	0.1	8.0	6.7	845	.2	1.1
Japan	−0.5	5.8	1.6	97	.0	2.4
Netherlands	−0.2	4.8	3.7	13	.2	1.9
New Zealand	−0.2	7.7	1.0	157	.2	1.9
Norway	0.3	6.3	1.4	31	.7	1.5
Sweden	0.8	6.4	2.1	16	.8	1.3
Switzerland	−0.2	3.4	0.3	2	.2	1.7
United Kingdom	0.0	7.1	3.5	234	.3	0.6
United States	−0.3	4.4	5.5	373	.4	2.0

Source: See Appendix.

Results

Table 7.3 shows the institutional effects on the time series coefficients. These results are encouraging but not overwhelming. With a relatively small number of countries, two sources of error at the micro and macro levels, and a very large number of coefficients to estimate, the findings probably admit about as much certainty as these data will bear. Consistent with the hypothesis, the Ghent system is estimated to have a strong positive impact on the average growth of union density. Average growth is nearly 1 point higher in the Ghent system countries compared to non-Ghent countries. This estimate accounts for nearly the entire difference between the Scandinavian pair, Sweden and Norway, and the Low Countries, the Netherlands and Belgium. The centralization effect is not estimated as precisely, but we can be about 70 percent confident that the effect is positive. The estimate indicates that roughly 10 percent of the difference between the Swedish and American growth rates can be explained by differences in labor market centralization. The centralization effect is small,

TABLE 7.3

Effects of Labor Market Institutions on Longitudinal Coefficients

Endogenous Time Series Effects	Institutional Effects		
	Intercept	Centralization	Ghent System
Estimates from 1950–1985 series			
Average growth (b_0)	−.11	.02	.87
	(−.21, −.02)	(−.03, .06)	(.67, 1.07)
Inflation (b_1)	.02	.00	.06
	(.00, .04)	(−.01, .01)	(.00, .11)
Unemployment (b_2)	−.17	.04	.04
	(−.21, −.13)	(.02, .06)	(−.05, .12)
Strike volume (b_3)	.19	−.03	−.02
	(.11, .27)	(−.06, .00)	(−.13, .09)
Left representation in government (b_4)	.33	−.07	−.17
	(.10, .56)	(−.17, .04)	(−.75, .39)
Labor force growth (b_5)	−.12	−.05	.12
	(−.19, −.04)	(−.08, −.02)	(−.08, .32)
Estimates from shortened time series			
Average growth (b_0)	−.08	.01	.90
	(−.19, .03)	(−.05, .06)	(.68, 1.12)
Inflation (b_1)	.01	.00	.06
	(−.01, .04)	(−.01, .02)	(.01, .12)
Unemployment (b_2)	−.18	.04	.01
	(−.22, −.13)	(.02, .06)	(−.09, .10)
Strike volume (b_3)	.19	−.03	−.02
	(.11, .27)	(−.06, .00)	(−.13, .09)
Left representation in government (b_4)	.32	−.07	−.13
	(.06, .55)	(−.17, .04)	(−.71, .42)
Labor force growth (b_5)	−.12	−.05	.07
	(−.19, −.04)	(−.09, −.02)	(−.015, .29)

Note: Numbers in parentheses are 80 percent confidence intervals.

in part, because of the strong relationship between the Ghent and centralization variables. The two variables correlate at greater than .5, so it is difficult to get an accurate idea of their separate effects. An informal idea of the positive relationship between union growth and union centralization is given by Figure 7.2, which shows a scatterplot of country-level intercepts for given values of the centralization variable. The bivariate relationship is fairly strong. On average, centralized labor markets grow about .4 of a point faster than decentralized labor markets.

The argument throughout has been that institutions do not just raise or retard unionization; they also reshape the relations of labor market competi-

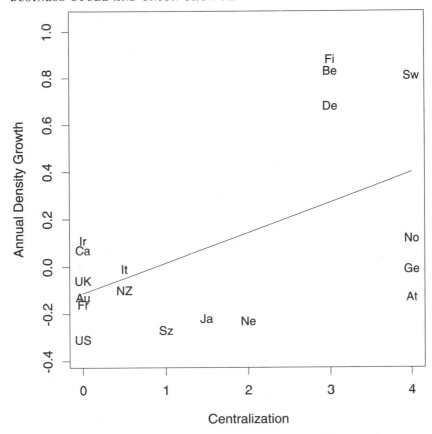

Figure 7.2. Scatterplot of union centralization and country-level intercepts from equation (7.1). A least squares line indicates the trend.

tion. In this analysis, this means that institutions influence the impact of the time series variables. The institutional account of how labor market centralization operates is only partially supported by the data (see Table 7.3). The results for the impact of centralization on the strike effects are very good. As expected, labor market centralization negatively affects the relationship between strikes and unionization. In highly centralized countries, the positive effect of strikes on union growth is much smaller than in decentralized countries. Put another way, the data indicate that strikes are effective tools for mobilization only in countries with decentralized union movements. The impact of centralization on labor force growth is directly contrary to my theory, however. Labor force growth has its strongest negative effect on unionization in centralized labor markets. These negative effects are more modest in decentralized settings. It is difficult to know what substantive interpretation can be placed on this result. One clue may be that the high-density countries have relatively sluggish rates of labor force growth. Work forces in these countries grew by between 1 and 1.5 percent a year. In most of the low-density countries, work forces grew by around 2 percent a year. Declining labor forces in the high-density countries may be making powerful contributions to union density growth.

Ghent systems also condition the union-organizing environment, turning shifting market and demographic conditions to the unions' advantage. The Ghent coefficients in the last column of Table 7.3 show that the effect of unemployment tends to be close to 0 in the Ghent system countries, but negative elsewhere. Although the confidence interval overlaps 0, we can be about 75 percent certain of a positive Ghent system effect. This result can be placed in the historical context of the 1970s recession. While unemployment increased sharply in the Netherlands, Belgium, and Denmark through the 1970s, labor movements grew only in Belgium and Denmark. In the Netherlands, where the Ghent system was abandoned in 1952, union density dropped by one-fourth, from 40 percent to 30 percent, between 1975 and 1985, while unemployment climbed from 6 to about 13 percent.

Unlike the centralization estimate, the impact of the Ghent system on labor force growth is consistent with the theoretical expectations. The results show that the negative effect of labor force growth is close to 0 where unions manage unemployment insurance funds. In most countries, strong labor force growth exerts strong downward pressure on union density, but the impact of labor force growth is relatively small in the Ghent countries. Compare the Norwegian and Swedish results, for example. Norwegian density growth falls by almost 1 point in response to a 2 percent increase in labor force size. In Sweden, new labor market entrants are converted into union members more effectively. A similar increase in the size of the Swedish labor force is estimated to reduce union growth by only a third of a point.

Results from the macro-level equation may rely heavily on the assumption of time-invariant institutions in each country for the period 1950–1985. Although qualitative historical and quantitative evidence suggest that variation over time in labor market institutions is small compared to cross-sectional variation, significant institutional change is suggested in several cases. For example, enterprise unionism did not emerge in Japan until the late 1950s. Institutional change may affect relationships among the time series variables. Time series for Finland (1957–1985), Japan (1958–1985), Italy (1970–1985), and the Netherlands (1953–1985) were truncated because of the late crystallization of labor market institutions in these countries. The shortened time series estimates shown in Table 7.3 indicate that the effects of the Ghent system and union centralization are generally robust for these shorter, more "historical" series. The estimated effect of the Ghent system on the unemployment parameter is much smaller, however, and has a large variance.

TABLE 7.4

Posterior Time Series Coefficients for the Longitudinal Predictors of Union Density Growth

	Annual Density Growth (b_0)	Inflation (b_1)	Unemployment (b_2)	Strike Volume (b_3)	Left Representation in Government (b_4)	Labor Force Growth (b_5)
High-density countries						
Belgium	.85	.12	−.02	.09	−.22	−.17
Denmark	.68	.08	.01	.09	−.14	−.16
Finland	.86	.06	−.02	.09	.00	−.17
Sweden	.81	.09	.03	.00	.14	−.18
Middle-density countries						
Australia	−.13	.02	−.15	.20	.52	−.16
Austria	−.13	.01	.03	.03	−.03	−.30
Canada	.09	.05	−.14	.18	.37	−.06
Germany	−.01	.04	−.01	.10	.02	−.30
Ireland	.10	−.02	−.23	.21	.31	−.18
Italy	−.01	.04	−.18	.21	.30	−.09
New Zealand	−.10	.05	−.17	.15	.20	−.06
Norway	.12	.06	−.01	.08	.08	−.39
United Kingdom	−.06	.03	−.18	.21	.49	−.15
Low-density countries						
France	−.16	.03	−.15	.20	.38	−.07
Japan	−.22	.02	−.12	.11	.23	−.13
Netherlands	−.23	−.02	−.11	.13	.56	−.29
Switzerland	−.27	.02	−.13	.16	−.15	−.25
United States	−.31	.01	−.16	.15	.21	−.15

Finally, the longitudinal component of the institutional theory—claiming the importance of left governments—also receives strong support (see Table 7.4). The effect is positive in most countries. Particularly large effects are found in Australia, the Netherlands, and the United Kingdom. Both Australia and the United Kingdom share very tight organizational links between parties and unions, and labor governments in both countries have actively supported unions through labor law and industrial relations policy. In the Netherlands, the socialist PvdA has cultivated the influence of unions through tripartite policy boards. The most unusual result is found for Denmark. The negative left government coefficient for Denmark is difficult to reconcile with the Danish LO's close relationship to the Social Democrats. Several substantive explanations can be offered. In contrast to Sweden, the Danish unions do not collectively affiliate with the Social Democratic party. This may loosen the link between parties and unions in the Danish case. Also the opposition parties may be less hostile to unions. The Danish bourgeois parties have supported trade unionism; for example, a Liberal government expanded civil service bargaining rights in 1969. More likely, the estimate reflects more stochastic sources of variation. Despite the negative coefficient, the Social Democrats presided over the Danish union movement's strongest membership gains through the late 1970s.

The other time series coefficients are also shown in Table 7.4. The business cycle explanation gets mixed support from the data. The inflation effects are generally positive as expected, but in many cases these effects are quite small. These results agree with other findings of weak business cycle effects in the postwar period (Sheflin et al. 1981; Neumann et al. 1989). The effect of unemployment is more consistent with the business cycle theory. It is negative everywhere except in two of the Ghent system countries and Austria. The effects are particularly large in Ireland and the United Kingdom, two countries in which unemployment rose sharply in the 1970s. These estimates suggest that a 10-point rise in the unemployment rate—not unprecedented in the recession of the 1970s—can reduce union growth by about 2 points a year. Strong union growth could thus be turned into labor movement decline by high unemployment in these two countries.

Explanations focusing on the union's role in organizing are strongly supported. Strike effects are positive everywhere, in accord with the idea that worker militancy can stimulate more lasting collective action. As the historical cases suggested, the impact of strikes on unionization is large in France and Italy, but much smaller in Scandinavia. Wallerstein's argument that union organizing is more difficult when the labor force is growing quickly also receives compelling support from time series data. All the labor force growth effects are negative, as Wallerstein's theory would expect. In many cases—in Norway, Austria, the Netherlands, and Switzerland—the effects are quite large. The moderate U.S. coefficient can be interpreted in light of the tremendous labor force growth that the American job machine has generated since the 1960s. Nearly 9 percentage points of the 15-point postwar American union decline can be explained by the 2 percent annual growth rate of the American labor force.

In sum, this chapter has tried to place time series explanations of union growth in an institutional context. This involved studying how the effects of time series variables depend on enduring patterns of labor market centralization and systems of unemployment insurance. The data analysis provided encouraging evidence that institutions can assist the growth of labor movements in good times and bad. Where unions manage unemployment insurance funds, rising joblessness has not threatened union membership rolls. Rapid labor force growth, a danger to unionization in most countries, can also be absorbed in Ghent system countries. The state provides additional resources for unions outside the marketplace. Density growth is strong where prolabor political parties have held government in the postwar period. Finally, strong union growth is found only in countries with centralized labor markets. Where class-wide representation in industrial relations is undeveloped, however, strikes can serve as points of mobilization for lasting collective action. Still, the institutions are not the whole story. Tight labor markets in Austria and Norway have helped maintain union representation. The long dole queues in Britain, Ireland, and the Netherlands, on the other hand, have severely undermined labor organization, particularly since the early 1970s. Lastly, rapid labor force growth has presented the non-European labor movements with an uncommonly difficult organizing task, which was largely unknown on the Continent.

Eight

The Structure of Labor Markets

THE TIME SERIES analysis of the last chapter constitutes just one of the two major research traditions in studies of unionization. The second major approach disaggregates the national union density figures to examine how opportunities for organizing unions vary across industries, occupations, and demographic groups. For this research, the structure of employment exerts a significant influence on union growth. The power of structural effects is indicated by high union membership in manufacturing industries and blue-collar occupations, but low membership in service jobs and among young workers and women. Like the time series theories of union growth, structural explanations pay little attention to institutional variation in labor markets. Comparative researchers often argue in response that long-run structural trends, such as manufacturing decline or work force aging, are too similar across countries to account for the great cross-national variability in union organization; instead, institutional variation provides a better explanation (Freeman 1989; Visser 1991; Rothstein 1989; Griffin, Botsko, Wahl, and Isaac 1991; Western 1994a).

Research on structural effects and research on institutional effects both employ research designs that favor their hypotheses. Economic studies of the impact of industry or demography on unionization typically analyze social survey data from individual countries. In this approach, national institutions are held constant by design. This is usually justified by theories whose chief implications concern subnational variation in unionization across labor market sectors. Comparative research, on the other hand, usually analyzes highly aggregated national union density statistics. Strong evidence for structural effects with these data rests on the tacit hope that subnational variation is sufficiently large to observe at the national level.

In this chapter I try to synthesize both streams of research by presenting an analysis of social survey data from a large number of countries. This analysis examines variation in unionization within countries, along industrial, occupational, and demographic lines. As for the time series analysis, I try to avoid contriving a horse race between institutional and structural variables. Instead, the analysis in this chapter investigates how the relationship between unionization and the structural features of labor markets depends on the institutional context.

Structural Theories of Unionization

As for the business cycle explanations of union growth, market power is the underlying mechanism for collective action in the labor market in theories of structural effects. The industrial structure of an economy is linked to union organizing by the elasticity of the demand for labor. The costs of unionism to employers tend to be small where the demand for labor is largely independent of the wage bill. In capital-intensive industries, where labor costs are a small fraction of total production costs, and in concentrated industries, where firms can pass on wage rises to consumers without reducing sales (Farkas, England, and Barton 1984, 97–100), employers are more tolerant of organized labor. Inelastic labor demand also spurs union growth because the union wage premium is potentially high and because the big shops of concentrated industries yield large membership gains. By contrast, the costs of unionism are high for employers in industries with high labor costs or unskilled (and highly substitutable) workers. Here, resistance to unions is likely to be higher, and unionization lower.

This argument is used to explain differences in unionization across industries. The large workplaces and high levels of industrial concentration in basic manufacturing, transport, and utilities lower the costs of union organizing and reduce employer opposition. The service sector—with smaller workplaces, a larger wage bill, and more unskilled workers—provides a setting for intense employer resistance. The same argument applies to the public sector. For state employees, the level of employment is not closely connected to the level of wages. Public sector union density has thus been high in all the advanced capitalist countries, at least since the early 1970s (Visser 1991, 117).

In the structural explanations of unionization, the cost-benefit calculus for union membership is also influenced by occupation, age, and sex. Researchers observe high rates of union membership among production workers compared to those of white-collar workers. Manual workers, it is argued, are relatively cheap to organize because they are less likely to identify with management and more likely to hold homogeneous preferences that facilitate union representation (Hirsch and Addison 1986, 59). Demand for unions is also claimed to be low among white-collar workers because they enjoy higher pay, greater job autonomy, and more job security than their blue-collar counterparts. Well-developed internal labor markets for white-collar workers may also make individualistic strategies more attractive than collective action (Freeman and Medoff 1984, 32).

The effects of occupation on union membership are also seen in the gender gap in unionization. Women frequently hold nonunion, part-time jobs, often in poorly organized sales and clerical occupations. Because of this occupational

124   CHAPTER EIGHT

segregation, women are less unionized than men throughout the OECD (Visser 1991, 115–17). Although a large part of the gender gap results from labor market segregation, some studies show that residual differences in unionization remain even when the effects of detailed occupational categories are controlled (Antos, Chandler, and Mellow 1980; Freeman and Medoff 1984, 28). It is sometimes argued that rewards to seniority provided by union contracts may be less appealing to women because they have weaker attachments to the labor market (Flanagan, Smith, and Ehrenberg 1984, 355).

The advantages of seniority are also small for young workers. As a result, unionization is higher among middle-aged and older workers. Although low unionization is widely observed for young workers, the functional form of the relationship between age and unionization is not well understood. Several analyses show a curvilinear relationship between age and union status (Hirsch and Berger 1984; Duncan and Stafford 1980). This suggests that older workers are less likely to be union members because unions flatten the relationship between work experience and wages. It is countered, however, that nonwage benefits gained through seniority should result in higher incentives for union membership among the oldest workers so the likelihood of union membership should increase with age (Hirsch and Addison 1986, 58).

In sum, the structural accounts of labor organizing describe conditions that influence the costs and benefits of unionization for unions, employers, and workers. In this approach, the institutional context for union-employer relations is taken to be fixed and labor markets are treated as generic forums for wage-labor exchanges. Labor markets share industrial, occupational, and demographic cleavages that structure union organizing costs in an undifferentiated way regardless of institutional setting. Parallel to the time series studies, the assumption of the primacy of structural conditions is supported by a research design that restricts analysis to individual countries.

Some Aggregate Evidence for Structural Effects

Several of the broad empirical claims of the structural theories of union organizing are supported by data showing that union density varies across industries. Table 8.1 summarizes this information for the eighteen OECD countries in 1985. As the structural theory would predict, union density in manufacturing industries is generally higher than the national average. Unionization in services is generally lower. Perplexing for the structural theory, the relationship between industry and unionization varies a lot across countries. In a few countries, manufacturing sector union density is actually less than the national average. France is the extreme case, with virtually no union members in the traditional industry sector. A similar but more modest cross-national variation is found in the service sector. Unions in most countries organize less than 20

TABLE 8.1

Union Density by Sector and Sex, Eighteen OECD Countries, 1985

			Union Density			
	National	Manufacturing	Private Services	Public Sector	Women	Men
High-density countries						
Belgium	54	90	37	—	—	—
Denmark	76	100	47	75	72	78
Finland	71	80	49	86	75	69
Sweden	84	100	50	88	86	83
Middle-density countries						
Australia	46	51	9	71	45	63
Austria	49	56	23	61	37	57
Canada	36	45	11	63	30	39
Germany	37	50	14	50	22	47
Ireland	56	—	—	—	47	60
Italy	49	49	18	56	—	—
New Zealand	54	58	53	—	—	—
Norway	56	85	13	77	—	—
United Kingdom	45	58	10	69	37	55
Low-density countries						
France	16	Below 5	—	35	11	21
Japan	29	33	21	62	22	32
Netherlands	29	34	8	49	13	37
Switzerland	29	33	11	71	13	39
United States	18	25	8	36	13	22

Source: Visser 1991.

Notes: National density includes only the employed membership as a proportion of all wage and salary earners. Belgian density is low compared to gross density figures, which include unemployed members. Private services includes wholesale and retail trades, restaurants, and hotels. Other details are given in the notes to Table 2.1.

percent of workers involved in trades, hospitality, and food industries. Still, about half of all private service industry workers in Denmark, Finland, and Sweden are union members. This type of variation seems unlikely to be due to differences in industrial concentration or similar factors that affect the elasticity of labor demand. Norway, which is structurally similar to other Scandinavian countries, shows dramatically lower organization among its service industry workers.

Indeed, cross-national variation is typical for other divisions in the labor market. The data in Table 8.1 also show that public sector workers are generally more unionized than average, but rates of public sector unionization differ a great deal. There is more going on than similar patterns of variation around a national average, however. Countries with widely differing national union densities exhibit similar levels of public sector unionization. Australian union density was nearly twice as high as Swiss union density in 1985, but public sector union density in both countries was the same—around 70 percent. On this dimension, the United States compares favorably to Scandinavia. In the United States, public sector union density is 36 percent, compared to 18 percent nationwide. In Denmark, public sector union density, 75 percent, is just slightly lower than the national average.

The gender gap in unionization also varies across countries. In all the countries for which data are available, unionization is higher among men than among women, except in Sweden and Finland. The exceptional rate of unionization among Scandinavian women is related to their high representation in well-organized social service occupations in the public sector. Unlike the sectoral figures, gender patterns are related to national union densities. Gender differences in union organization are small in the highly organized countries but larger elsewhere. Denmark and France illustrate the contrast. In Denmark, union density among men, 78 percent, exceeds women's union density by only 6 points. French men, on the other hand are almost twice as likely to be unionized as women, reflecting a 10-point gender gap in union organization. Switzerland provides the extreme case among the low-density countries. Swiss men are three times more likely to be union members than women, and male union density exceeds female union density by 25 points.

This brief review of the aggregate statistics of union organization across different sectors of the labor market suggests a conclusion and a question. We can conclude that the effects of industry and gender vary across countries. In some countries, union membership is strongly patterned according to these labor market divisions. In other countries, the level of union organization appears to depend little on the industrial and demographic structure of the labor market. This type of cross-national variability is difficult to explain with structural theories. As I argue below, cross-national variability in structural effects can be understood once the structural theories of unionization are placed in an institutional context.

The question remaining from the aggregate statistics is, How do we know the industry effects we observe are not artifacts of, say, sex segregation in the labor market? If men are more likely to be union members than women and men dominate employment in manufacturing, high union density in manufacturing may be due to the overrepresentation of men in this industry, rather than to any industry effect. Gender differences themselves may be due to differences in age profiles of male and female workers. In short, there is only so much that can be gained from the aggregated tables presented so far. To sift out the separate effects of industry, sex, and other structural variables, we need to examine more disaggregated figures. This allows us to take account of the relationships among the structural variables.

In the following analysis, I examine cross-national variation in unionization and the effects of structural variables with disaggregated data. Using social survey data from a number of different countries, I provide a systematic institutional explanation of the relationship between labor market structure and labor market institutions. This analysis is based on a mixture of structural explanations, which usually ignore cross-national variation, and institutional explanations, which usually neglect subnational variation.

Combining Structural and Institutional Explanations

The implications of nationally specific structural accounts and comparative institutional explanations of unionization are quite different. The predictors of unionization are viewed as general features of labor markets in studies of structural effects. Cross-national variability in the process of unionization is ruled out by design, as data analyses use information from just one country. Research findings tend to conform to a pattern regardless of national setting. Manufactures are more highly unionized than services, men more unionized than women, and so on. In comparative research, trade union membership depends on cross-nationally variable institutions that shield unions from the market forces that increase competition among workers. Contrasting these two approaches raises a question neglected in the nationally specific accounts of unionization: do the industrial, occupational, and demographic causes of unionization vary with the national institutional context? In the remainder of this chapter, I present a data analysis that investigates this question.

In contrast to earlier chapters, I focus here just on the effects of the labor market institutions—centralized labor markets and the Ghent system. The effects of the labor market institutions on the structural sources of unionization are clear; this is less true in the case of political parties. Many labor law reforms that lower organizing costs, for instance, are more likely to operate across the board rather than to systematically drive union growth in specific sectors. Accordingly, research shows that left governments raise the overall likelihood of union membership but do not influence the effects of industry, age, and sex (Western 1994b). The current analysis uses data from just ten countries, lowering the precision of statistical estimates as the number of institutional predictors increases. Without strong theoretical reasons for studying the effects of parties in this context, there seems little need to risk loss of statistical precision for the other institutional effects. None of this is to claim that political parties, and left governments in particular, are uninvolved with the structural sources of unionization. My only point here is that these effects are difficult to detect with the current research design.

Labor Market Centralization

I argue that centrally organized labor markets and Ghent systems are closely tied to how the industrial and demographic structure of labor markets affects unionization. In centralized labor markets, opposition to unions is low and central union confederations are actively involved in organizing. Centralized bargaining is also a redistributive institution in the process of national union organization, working to equalize organizing costs across the labor market. On the employer side, the inclusiveness of wage bargains tends to homogenize organizing costs across industries because employers share similar incentives to acquiesce to unionism. On the union side, centralized coordination of unionization involves the transfer of organizing expenditures from those industries and occupations that are inexpensive to organize to those that are costly. Interunion cooperation further assists economy-wide coordination of organizing. In effect, with highly centralized industrial relations, the entire national labor market becomes the constituency of the union movement (Stephens 1991). Thus, not only does labor market centralization foster high union densities; it should also be associated with small variability in union membership across industries and occupations. If organizing costs are similar across sectors, union membership will not depend greatly on employment in the traditional industrial strongholds.

These institutional arguments are supported by historical evidence. Recall the comparative account of labor market centralization (Chapter 3). In Sweden, relations among the unions have been cooperative, and organizing efforts have historically been coordinated at the national level. In the postwar period, Swedish public sector and white-collar unions have enjoyed the greatest growth. The expansion of union membership in these two sectors was actively supported by the blue-collar union confederation, the LO. In particular, the LO contributed organizing expertise at an early stage and helped negotiate jurisdictional disputes at the highest level with the white-collar confederation. In this instance, then, centralized union organization assisted unionization across occupational categories. In the decentralized U.S. labor market, interunion competition is built into the machinery of the certification election. Unions run election campaigns against one another for exclusive representation rights in an authorized bargaining unit. Weak unions outside of the public sector and traditional manufacturing receive little support from the AFL-CIO or other unions. In short, there is no centralized coordination of the organizing effort, and gaining union membership strongly depends on working in certain industries.

The Ghent System

A similar argument can be made for union-run unemployment insurance. Union administration of unemployment insurance contributes to the general level of unionization, because all workers face some risk of unemployment. Still, some groups are more at risk than others. Young workers and women both have high risks of unemployment, which are reflected in high unemployment rates (OECD 1994, 43). These workers are thus likely to face particularly extensive exposure to unions where union officials staff labor exchanges and administer unemployment benefits. As a result, in countries with Ghent systems, we would expect high overall levels of unionization and comparatively high union organization among young and female workers, for whom the risk of unemployment is particularly severe. Without the Ghent system, workers at the margins of the labor market are less likely to have access to union representation. Countries with public unemployment insurance should thus have relatively low rates of unionization among young workers and women.

The comparative discussion of unemployment insurance in Chapter 4 provides historical evidence for the Ghent effects. In Sweden, unions were closely involved in the development of a national Ghent system in 1934. This institutional innovation had long-lasting effects, as the great growth in unemployment insurance and unionization in the 1960s was among women and salaried workers. Contrast the United States, where unemployment insurance received only mixed support from the labor movement in its formative period. The resulting unemployment program reinforced the division between those with little power in the labor market and the union movement. Access to benefits now depends on rigorous job searches, which push workers to the low-wage and least-organized corners of the job market. This system of unemployment insurance contributes to a model of labor market deregulation in which unions have colonized only monopoly sectors. The time series analysis also supports this picture, indicating that labor force growth and rising unemployment widely erode union growth (Chapter 7). However, this pattern is reversed in the Ghent system countries. The increasing risk of unemployment thus depletes labor movements except where the unemployed are integrated into unions through the system of unemployment insurance.

Model Specification and Estimation

The argument developed so far suggests that the propensity of workers to join trade unions is related to industry, occupational, and demographic variables. However, the effects of these variables differ across countries in ways that depend on the institutional setting. Labor market institutions also directly influence unionization. Centralized bargaining and the Ghent system raise the general level of union organization. Following the approach of the pooled time series analysis in the last chapter, this argument can be expressed as two sets of regression equations. First, the probability that a worker will be a union member can be written as a function of occupational, industry, and demographic characteristics. Separate regressions can be specified for each country, indicating that structural effects vary across countries. Coefficients of these country-level equations can be treated as dependent variables in a regression using institutional characteristics as independent variables. This specification captures the idea that the effects of industry, occupation, and demographics on unionization are contingent on the institutional context.

Specifically, the country-level equations for the structural effects can be written as logistic regressions. The log odds of union membership for the ith worker in the jth of $j = 1, \ldots, J$ countries being analyzed can be written as:

$$\text{logit} (u_{ij}) = b_{0j} + b_{1j}\, s_{ij} + b_{2j}\, o_{ij} + b_{3j}\, p_{ij}, \tag{8.1}$$

where u is the probability of union membership, s, o, and p measure sectoral, occupational, and demographic characteristics, and the bs are regression coefficients. In equation (8.1), the coefficients carry the subscript j, indicating that the relationship between unionization and the structural variables differs across countries. I have argued that the relationship between unionization and the structural features of labor markets depends on the institutional variables of centralization, C, and union-run unemployment insurance, G. The impact of the macro-level labor market institutions on the micro-level structural effects can then be specified in another set of regressions:

$$b_{0j} = \gamma_{00} + \gamma_{01}\, C_j + \gamma_{02}\, G_j + \alpha_{0j}$$
$$\vdots \tag{8.2}$$
$$b_{3j} = \gamma_{30} + \gamma_{31}\, C_j + \gamma_{32}\, G_j + \alpha_{3j}.$$

The relationship between the institutional variables and the country-level coefficients is expressed by the γ coefficients, which are fixed across all countries. Equations (8.1) and (8.2) form a Bayesian hierarchical model that is characterized by two sources of uncertainty. First, uncertainty is generated by the usual binomial sampling of the logistic regression in equation (8.1). The random component of this equation is in the probability that forms the dependent variable, in contrast to the usual trailing error term in a linear regression. As in the time series analysis in the previous chapter, uncertainty also arises at the cross-national level, expressed by the α's. This means that the institutional variables do not exhaustively explain variation in the country-level coefficients. As in the time series analysis, an alternative spe-

TABLE 8.2
Sample Union Density, Aggregate Union Density, and Institutional Variables,
Ten OECD Countries, Various Years

	Survey Year	Sample Size	Sample Density	Aggregate Density	Union Centralization	Ghent System
Australia	1986	610	45	50	0.0	0
Canada	1982	1,408	44	37	0.0	0
Denmark	1985	939	84	86	3.0	1
Finland	1981	558	77	74	3.0	1
Germany	1985	1,319	32	35	4.0	0
Japan	1987	370	34	28	1.5	0
Norway	1982	1,183	66	57	4.0	0
Sweden	1980	1,007	80	80	4.0	1
United Kingdom	1984	1,019	46	48	0.0	0
United States	1980	1,321	18	22	0.0	0

Sources: All aggregate densities are from Visser 1992a, except that of Canada which is based on OECD 1991b wage- and salary-earner figures and on Visser's 1992a gross union membership figures. Sample densities are based on Wright 1990.

Notes: Aggregate density is measured in the survey year. For comparability with the survey data, aggregate density excludes the retired as a percentage of all employees.

cification might write the institutional variables as interaction effects with the country-level variables in equation (8.1). That model, however, relies on the unrealistic assumption that the institutions explain all variation in the country-level structural effects, with no possibility of stochastic variation at the cross-national level.

The Data

To investigate cross-national variability in structural effects, I analyze social survey data from a large number of advanced capitalist countries. To minimize the effects of differences in survey design, the data were taken from Wright's (1990) study of class structure and class consciousness. For each survey, a comparable core instrument was administered in ten countries. Despite efforts to maintain common survey methodologies across countries, sampling methods, survey instruments, and data collection techniques showed cross-national variation. These data limitations are addressed in two ways. First, respondents' occupation and industry were coded coarsely to maintain common codes across countries. Second, I try to capture unobserved heterogeneity due to differences in research design with the random effects equations (8.2). The structure of the survey data is described in Table 8.2. The data include all

TABLE 8.3
Description of Industry, Occupation, Age, and Sex Variables from the Pooled Social
Survey Data, Ten OECD Countries

Variable	Description
Industry	A four-category code distinguishing workers in manufacturing industries, those in other secondary industries (including construction, transportation, and utilities), private services (including trades, hospitality, and finance), and social and community services; dummy coding was used with manufacturing workers in the reference category
Occupation	Respondents are divided into manual and nonmanual occupational categories; a dummy variable indicates nonmanual workers
Age	A three-category code distinguishing young workers (18–35), middle-aged workers (36–50), and older workers (over 50); dummy coding was used with middle-aged workers in the reference category
Sex	Males are in the reference category

respondents in paid work, aged 18–65. All the data are based on national samples except those for Japan, which are from a Tokyo sample.

The middle two columns of Table 8.2 provide an informal check on data quality. Union density in the sample is compared to aggregate union density statistics. Union density is generally accurately measured by the social surveys, differing from aggregate statistics in most cases by less than 10 percent. There appear to be no systematic biases; union densities found in the social surveys are larger than the aggregate figures in some countries but smaller in others. The biggest discrepancies are found in Norway and Canada, where the survey figures exceed the aggregate statistics by about 15 percent. Aggregate statistics may underestimate Canadian union membership because workers in firms with fewer than fifty employees are not counted in the government tallies. Norwegian aggregate statistics are generally quite accurate, so sampling variability seems the most likely explanation of disagreement between the two figures here.

Table 8.3 describes the variables taken from the social survey data. Exploratory analysis showed marked nonlinear relationships between age and union membership, which varied across countries. Age is coded as three categories to detect nonlinearities. In the regression analysis, manufacturing industries, manual occupations, age group 36–50, and males are the omitted categories. With this coding, country-level intercept terms express the log odds of union membership in manufacturing industries among male manual workers, aged 36–50. Because workers falling into this category form the traditional constituency for union movements, the intercept terms in the regression provide a good sense of the general level of unionization in a country.

TABLE 8.4
Effects of Labor Market Institutions on the Structural Determinants of Unionization, Ten OECD Countries

Endogenous Structural Effects	Institutional Effects		
	Intercept	Centralization	Ghent System
Intercept (b_0)	0.09	0.03	1.91
	(−0.31, 0.49)	(−0.14, 0.20)	(1.27, 2.57)
Nonmanual (b_1)	−0.78	0.19	−0.22
	(−0.98, −0.57)	(0.10, 0.28)	(−0.59, 0.14)
Other industry (b_2)	0.20	−0.10	−0.18
	(0.00, 0.38)	(−0.18, −0.01)	(−0.52, 0.15)
Private services (b_3)	−1.01	0.21	−0.48
	(−1.45, −0.55)	(−0.00, 0.40)	(−1.24, 0.29)
Social services (b_4)	0.68	−0.08	−0.03
	(0.37, 0.97)	(−0.22, 0.05)	(−0.59, 0.52)
Female (b_5)	−0.35	−0.07	0.06
	(−0.49, −0.22)	(−0.13, −0.02)	(−0.17, 0.31)
Under 36 years old (b_6)	−0.15	−0.01	0.20
	(−0.39, 0.09)	(−0.12, 0.09)	(−0.23, 0.62)
Over 50 years old (b_7)	−0.002	0.01	−0.02
	(−0.18, 0.18)	(−0.05, 0.08)	(−0.29, 0.23)

Note: Numbers in parentheses are 80 percent confidence intervals.

Results

Table 8.4 reports summaries of the institutional effects. The country-level intercepts represent the log odds of union membership among middle-aged men in the traditional working class. These intercepts correlate at greater than .9 with both the sample union density and the series of aggregate union densities shown in Table 8.3. Consequently, the effects of the institutions on the country-level intercepts can be interpreted as the impact of the institutions on the general level of unionization in a country. The first row of Table 8.4 reports the institutional effects. The Ghent system effect is extremely large and precisely estimated. The coefficients indicate that union-run unemployment insurance funds raise the odds of union membership among manufacturing sector workers by $e^{1.9} \approx 6$ times.

Evidence for the effect of labor market centralization on the general level of union organization is more modest. The estimated effect is small and the 80 percent confidence interval overlaps 0. Still, the sign of the coefficient is positive, as expected. This means that the chances of union membership in the traditional manufacturing sector tends to be higher in countries with

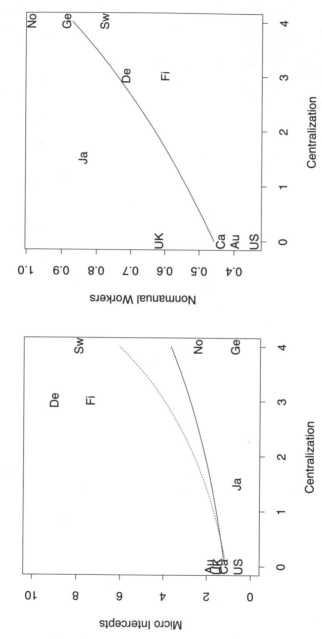

Figure 8.1. Scatterplots of centralization scores against country-level intercepts and nonmanual coefficients, 10 OECD countries. Regression lines indicate the trend. The dashed line in the left-hand panel shows the regression line with Germany omitted.

highly centralized labor markets. A more detailed picture is given in Figure 8.1, which shows a scatterplot of the labor market centralization variable against the exponentiated intercepts from each country. Plotted on this scale, the intercepts can be interpreted as the odds of unionization for blue-collar middle-aged men in manufacturing jobs. The solid regression line, showing the trend, indicates that the odds of union membership is about four times higher in the most corporatist country compared to the least (say, Sweden and France). The German case is a large outlier for these data, and is largely driving the small centralization effect. German union density is unusually low given Germany's level of labor market centralization. We can see the pattern in the rest of the data from the dashed regression line, which is fitted to the reduced sample. If we exclude the German case, unionization strongly increases with labor market centralization. In sum, evidence is reasonably strong with these data that both institutional conditions are positively associated with unionization.

Centralized labor markets and the Ghent system do not just influence the general level of union organization. They also structure the pattern of unionization across labor market segments. Labor market centralization reduces the organization gap across industries and occupations. The Ghent system of union-run unemployment funds reduces age and gender gaps in unionization. Evidence for the by-products of centralized labor markets is given by the institutional effects on the country-level coefficients for occupation and industry. Here the theory is strongly supported. Occupational and industry effects are small in countries with highly centralized labor markets. The positive centralization effect for nonmanual workers is especially large. Nonmanual workers are generally less organized than manual workers, but as centralization increases, the gap in unionization between white- and blue-collar workers shrinks substantially. This centralization effect is illustrated in the right-hand panel of Figure 8.1. The points on the graph are the exponentiated effects for nonmanual workers from each country plotted against the labor market centralization scores. With decentralized labor markets, as in the United States, holding a nonmanual occupation roughly halves the odds of union membership. In countries with strong corporatist bargaining, such as the Scandinavian countries, holding a nonmanual job reduces the odds of union membership by only about a fifth. Norway provides the extreme example, as occupational differences in unionization have almost been eliminated there. These figures underline the high levels of white-collar unionism in the corporatist countries. The United Kingdom and Japan are somewhat exceptional according to the survey estimates. White-collar workers in both these countries are unionized at very high rates given the level of labor market centralization. Evidence for the impact of labor market centralization in equalizing unionization across the industrial structure is equally strong. The positive effect of centralization on private service coefficients suggests that corporatist institutions level unionization rates across secondary and tertiary sectors of the labor market. As labor markets become more centrally organized, the difference in unionization rates between service and manufacturing workers narrows. Estimates indicate that the unionization gap between services and manufacturing sectors is about 25 percent smaller in the highly corporatist countries (say, Germany or Sweden) compared to the countries with more decentralized labor market institutions (Britain or the United States).

Some unexpected estimates are found for the other-industry coefficient and for the female worker coefficient. Figure 8.2 plots both sets of exponentiated coefficients against the labor market centralization scores. Workers in manufacturing industries are less organized than those in transport, construction, and utilities in the more decentralized countries. The reverse is true in countries with highly developed corporatist institutions. For instance, the odds of union membership among Danish workers with manufacturing jobs are about a third higher than those for workers in other secondary industries. In Australia, on the other hand, working outside the core manufacturing industries, that is, in transport, construction, or utilities, raises the odds of union membership by about half compared to those for manufacturing sector workers. Unions in corporatist countries have thus maintained their organizational strength in the traditional core of manufacturing industries.

The right-hand panel of Figure 8.2 shows the gender gap in union membership. Here, the exponentiated gender effects are plotted against the labor market centralization scores. These effects express the gap in union representation between men and women in each country, controlled for age, occupation, and industry. Note that the gender effects are less than 1 in all countries. This means that even when age and job characteristics are controlled, women are less likely to be union members than men. The gender gap in union organization grows with labor market centralization. When Germany is omitted, the relationship between centralization and the gender gap remains negative, but is much flatter.

These results can be placed in the context of the labor market attachments of women in the highly centralized countries. In the Nordic countries, rates of female participation in part-time work and occupational gender segregation are extremely high (Treiman and Roos 1983; Cook 1984; Scriven 1984). In Germany, female labor force participation rates decline sharply with age and marriage. Women's risk of unemployment in Germany is also high compared to that in other European countries (Norris 1987, 58; Meulders, Plasman, and Stricht 1993, 153; see also Windolf and Haas 1989). Perhaps women in these countries are holding unusually segregated and unorganized jobs that are not captured by the coarse industry and occupation codes. Sex, net of other factors, may be identifying feminized secondary occupations that unions have not reached (but cf. Rosenfeld and Kalleberg 1991).

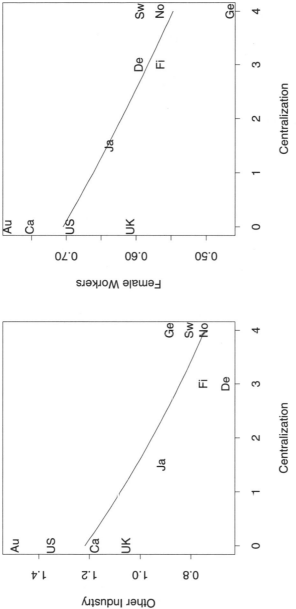

Figure 8.2. Scatterplots of centralization scores against country-level other industry and female coefficients, 10 OECD countries. A regression line in plots, indicates the trend.

This interpretation is supported by other research. I have found similar patterns in a slightly larger batch of countries, including the Netherlands (Western 1994b). In that analysis, both German and Dutch women were found to have unusually low chances of union organization. The gender gap in earnings, participation rates in part-time work, and risks of unemployment for women are high in the Netherlands. As in the German case, this raises the possibility of feminized secondary sectors of the Dutch labor market that remain unorganized (Treiman and Roos 1983; United Nations 1985). Here, the implication seems to be that where differences in market power are reinforced by gender differences in social power, the capacity of class institutions to secure solidaristic patterns of organization is limited. Or to put it another way, class-wide organization in unions is undermined where market inequalities are reinforced by nonclass divisions, such as gender. At a minimum, the strong relationship between the gender gap in unionization and labor market centralization indicates that unified union organization has failed to overcome an important nonclass divisions in the labor market.

Evidence that the Ghent effect increases unionization among those facing a high risk of unemployment is shown by the macro Ghent system coefficients for those aged 18–35 years and females. As predicted, the Ghent effects are positive in both cases (see Table 8.4), but the effect of a Ghent system on the gender gap in unionization is quite small. The positive sign of the Ghent effect on the age coefficient indicates that the difference in unionization between young and middle-aged workers is smaller in countries where unions manage unemployment funds. While the Ghent effect here is reasonably large, it is not estimated very precisely.

Table 8.5 gives more detail, showing the youth and female coefficients for the ten countries. Recall that the coefficients describe the difference in unionization between men and women and between young workers and middle-aged ones. The data in this table show that the smallness of the positive effect of the Ghent system on gender differences in union membership is due almost entirely to the outlying case of Germany. Germany—with a very large gap in unionization between men and women—has no system of union-managed unemployment insurance funds. For the age coefficients, young workers are generally less unionized than the middle-aged; seven out of ten coefficients for young workers are negative. In the Ghent system countries, however, there is virtually no unionization gap between young workers and the middle-aged. These results support the idea that union-managed unemployment benefits produce union members by attracting workers who face a high risk of unemployment. In sum, the evidence for the institutional effects of unemployment insurance schemes is reasonably strong for young workers but much weaker for women.

It may be objected that the equalization of unionization rates across industries, occupations, and demographic characteristics in highly corporatist coun-

TABLE 8.5
Sex and Age Effects on Unionization, Ten OECD Countries

	Unionization Gap	
	Females (b_5)	Aged under 36 (b_6)
Ghent system countries		
Denmark	−.51	.06
	(−.69, −.34)	(−.17, .30)
Finland	−.56	.18
	(−.76, −.36)	(−.11, .47)
Sweden	−.52	−.19
	(−.70, −.34)	(−.40, .02)
Non–Ghent system countries		
Australia	−.25	−.36
	(−.42, −.06)	(−.57, −.15)
Canada	−.29	−.19
	(−.43, −.15)	(−.35, −.02)
Germany	−.76	−.41
	(−.93, −.58)	(−.58, −.24)
Japan	−.45	.51
	(−.62, −.28)	(.13, .84)
Norway	−.54	−.23
	(−.70, −.39)	(−.39, −.06)
United Kingdom	−.49	−.32
	(−.68, −.33)	(−.50, −.13)
United States	−.37	−.18
	(−.52, −.22)	(−.37, .01)

Note: Numbers in parentheses are 80 percent confidence intervals.

tries results from a "saturation effect"—that is, as union density increases, large differences in unionization will not be observed across the labor market, simply because nearly every organizable worker is already in the union. Similar arguments have been made by researchers linking the effects of the business cycle to unionization (e.g., Bain and Elsheikh 1976, 67–68). Following the business cycle literature, I addressed this objection by reestimating the model using union density as a predictor. The institutional effects remained generally robust to this respecification.

In this chapter I have tried to synthesize structural explanations of unionization with the institutional account. I claimed that labor market centralization and the Ghent system increase the general level of union organization and shape patterns of unionization across the labor market sectors. The analysis showed that centralization is associated with a high general level of union organization and that unionization varies little across industrial and occupational lines in centrally organized countries. There is also evidence that Ghent systems of union-run unemployment insurance raise labor organization among those acutely at risk of unemployment—young workers—as well as increasing the general level of organization. In short, both institutional conditions yield a solidaristic type of union organization. Not only are workers very likely to be union members where unions secure some institutionalized control over labor market competition; the unions have successfully reached beyond their traditional constituencies, weakening the impact of industry, occupation, and demographics on the chances of union membership. There is also evidence for a major exception, however. Gender differences are large in the centralized countries. This is particularly true in Germany. If the labor market institutions are equalizing the chances of unionization, the evidence here shows that gender divisions have so far remained more intractable.

Part IV

THE TURBULENT 1980s

Nine

Introducing the Decline of Unions
in the 1980s

THE INSTITUTIONAL story to this point has associated the main paths of union growth with three stable institutional contexts. Large union movements developed in centralized labor markets, with strong labor parties, and with union control over unemployment insurance. Where these institutional conditions were only partly satisfied, unions steadily organized between two-fifths and two-thirds of the labor force. In contrast, postwar labor organization was constrained by decentralized labor markets, weak labor parties, and unions uninvolved in social welfare. The punchline: stable institutional differences produced divergent trajectories of labor movement development.

This story works well into the 1970s, but the 1980s marked the beginning of a new phase for trade unions. Instead of extending the widening gap between the most and least unionized countries, the 1980s saw a widespread fall in union density. While union density grew by nearly half a point annually on average in the 1970s, this growth was nearly halved in the 1980s. By the end of the decade, union density was falling even in the social democratic strongholds of Scandinavia. Convergence was thus replacing divergence. This stylized fact of general union decline fundamentally challenges the institutional account of labor movement growth. If institutional variability is enlisted to explain divergent trends, how can the novel and universal decline of unions in the 1980s be explained?

In this chapter I examine the pattern of union density decline in the eighteen OECD countries and consider two leading explanations. The first extrapolates from Chapter 7 to examine the predictive performance of the time series analysis for the 1970s and 1980s. As we shall see, the time series estimates based on business cycle, political, and institutional variables do a poor job of forecasting the large union density declines that we find in such countries as France, the Netherlands, and the United Kingdom. Extending the analysis of Chapter 8, the modest forecasting results lead us to consider perhaps the most common explanation of union decline—that the emergence of the postindustrial economic structure and the decline of manufacturing industries in particular has weakened the class basis of trade unionism.

Union Decline in the 1980s

Table 9.1 summarizes union density trends in the eighteen OECD countries in the two decades from 1970. The pattern of declining unionization is clear. Through the 1970s, union density fell in only a few countries. The United States was the big loser in this period: union membership as a percentage of the dependent labor force dropped by a fifth, from 26 percent to 20 percent. This fall in labor organization was unparalleled in the advanced capitalist countries. In fact, the 1970s were generally a buoyant period for unions: density increased in all but five of the eighteen countries. In the high-density countries of Scandinavia, the membership gains approached 20 percentage points.

This period of growth was sharply reversed in the 1980s. By the end of the later decade, union organization was widely shrinking. The low-density countries suffered small organizational losses in the 1970s, but decline accelerated in the following ten years. In France and the Netherlands, between a third and a fifth of total membership was lost between 1980 and 1989 (Visser 1992a). Generally, union decline in the middle-density countries was more limited. Even here, however, the drop in density often reversed a ten-year pattern of union growth. In the four high-density countries, Belgium, Denmark, Finland, and Sweden, union density grew very little. Compared to the membership gains of the 1970s, the slowdown in growth of the 1980s is remarkable. The fall in the growth rate from 1 to 2 points a year to almost 0 represents an even larger change in trend than in the low-density countries.

While the broad pattern of union decline is striking, the exceptional stories of deunionization are found in Ireland and Britain. Unions in both countries grew strongly in the 1970s. Irish union density approached Nordic levels, and British unions for the first time organized more than half the labor force. The 1980s by comparison were disastrous. Irish and British union density time series for the postwar period are shown in Figure 9.1. Irish union membership had grown steadily for thirty years before the 1980s decline of more than 10 percentage points, or about one-quarter of the organized labor force. In the United Kingdom, the drop in union membership from about 55 percent to 45 percent of the labor force more than erased the growth of the previous decade. In both countries, nearly all the organizational gains of the entire postwar period were lost between 1979 and 1988.

The Irish and British cases suggest alternative paths to working-class disorganization. In Ireland, the decline of unions seems to have been driven by economic forces. An extraordinary increase in unemployment had left nearly 20 percent of the labor force out of work by the beginning of the 1990s. This feeble labor market performance, like the large fall in unionization,

TABLE 9.1

Change in Union Density, Eighteen OECD Countries, 1970–1979 and 1980–1989

	Change in Union Density		
	1970–1979	*1980–1989*	*Union Density in 1970*
High-density countries			
Belgium	14.9	0.2	52
Denmark	17.8	0.1[a]	62
Finland	22.4	5.8[a]	57
Sweden	13.8	6.0	73
Middle-density countries			
Australia	3.2	−3.7	49
Austria	−4.1	−2.3	62
Canada	4.3	−0.5	29
Germany	3.9	−3.1	38
Ireland	3.6	−12.0[b]	54
Italy	16.0	0.1	38
New Zealand	5.3	−5.2[c]	40
Norway	4.0	−0.1	57
United Kingdom	5.9	−11.2[d]	49
Low-density countries			
France	−2.9	−7.4	22
Japan	−3.8	−5.4	35
Netherlands	−2.5	−8.1	40
Switzerland	3.5	−4.4	49
United States	−5.0	−5.4	26

[a] 1980–1988
[b] 1980–1987
[c] 1980–1985
[d] 1980–1987

was unmatched in Western Europe. In Britain, the unions felt the brunt of a political offensive led by Thatcher's Conservative government. This dislodged them from an institutionalized position in the British labor market and limited their options for industrial action. While the Tory backlash often assumed sensational proportions, other researchers pointed to a more silent process, maintaining that the decline of British unions was due to deindustrialization and the massive decline of manufacturing in Britain through the 1970s and 1980s (Waddington 1992). In the rest of this chapter, I investigate each of these explanations in the broader, comparative context of the OECD.

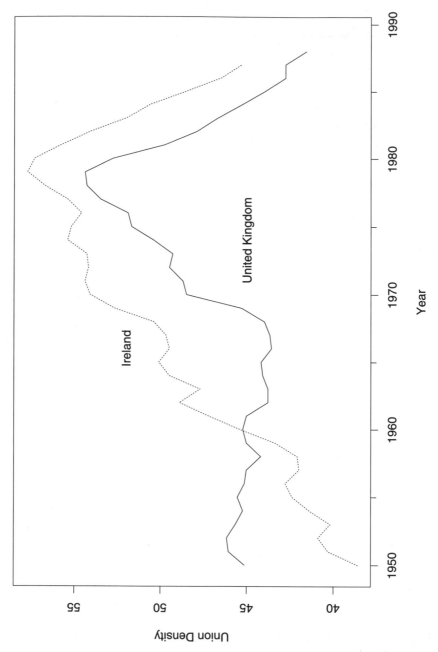

Figure 9.1. Time series of British and Irish union densities, 1950–1988.

Forecasting Union Density, 1974–1989

Some of the explanations for union decline outlined for Britain and Ireland are reminiscent of the longitudinal analysis of union growth in Chapter 7. That analysis tried to put the longitudinal explanations of unionization in an institutional context. This involved developing a two-part model. First, the annual change in union density was specified to depend on several business cycle and other variables—inflation, unemployment, labor force growth, strikes, and the representation of left parties in government. Next, the effects of these variables were related to two durable institutional conditions that were invariant over time—labor market centralization and the Ghent system. This model produced a number of promising institutional effects that suggested that labor market institutions did indeed influence the logic of union organizing. Can this model predict the widespread downturn in unionization through the 1970s and 1980s?

To answer this question, I fitted the time series model to the union density data for the period 1951 to 1973. The resulting coefficients can be combined with information about the independent variables to predict the direction of union growth in the post-oil shock period. These out-of-sample predictions test the idea that the underlying relationships of the union-organizing process have lasted into the 1980s. In this scenario, union decline results from changing economic and political conditions, rather than changes in the effects of those conditions. For instance, unemployment may generally reduce union membership in non-Ghent countries, but now we have a novel set of economic conditions in which unemployment is very high throughout Europe. The effect of unemployment on union growth may not have changed; instead, the unemployment rate has changed.

The out-of-sample predictions from the institutional time series model for 1974–1988 are shown in Figure 9.2. The observed time series for each of the eighteen countries is given by the solid line. A large negative spike or a sequence of negative values indicates a downturn in unionization. The predicted series is represented with a broken line. The results of this prediction effort reveal an interesting pattern. In some countries where union decline has been modest—as in Austria, Canada, Norway, and Sweden—the predictions track the observed data fairly well. Canadian union density, for instance, grew until the early 1980s, when a modest fall in union density began. The model predictions tell a similar story of growth and modest decline. The performance of the model for the healthier labor movements suggests a continuity in the statistical regime of union growth from the 1960s to the post-oil shock period. Unexpectedly, perhaps, the model provides good predictions of the U.S. pattern of continuous decline through the twenty years from 1970.

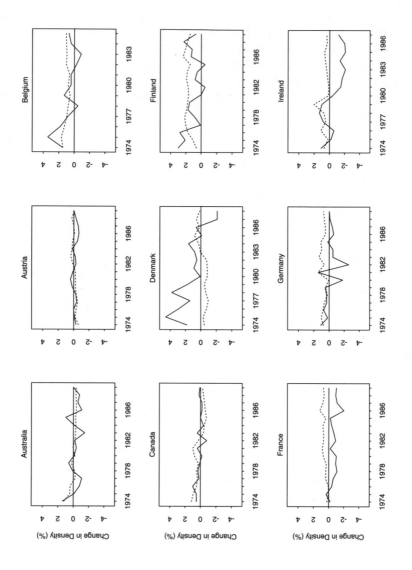

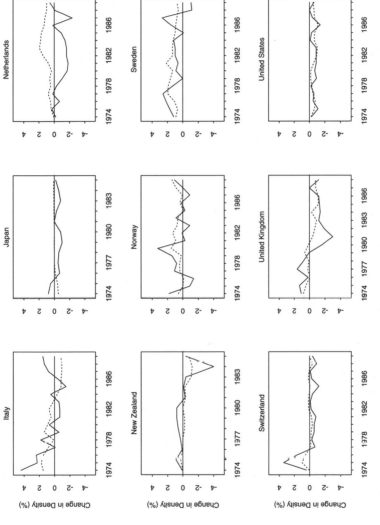

Figure 9.2 Observed and out-of-sample predictions of union density growth, 18 OECD countries, 1974–1989.

However, using information from the 1950s and 1960s provides us with little leverage on the major falls in union density of the 1980s. Where declines in unionization were large (as in the Netherlands and France) or dramatic (as in the United Kingdom and Ireland), the model fares poorly. The limitations of the model fit are particularly clear in the French and Dutch cases. Labor movements in these countries lost between a third and a half of their organizational strength in the 1980s. The model predictions, however, suggest that, given the economic and political conditions of the 1980s, union density should have grown slowly in both countries. Where the model can predict union decline—as in Australia and New Zealand—it tends to underpredict the magnitude of decline and fails to detect the timing of the largest falls in union organization. In short, the conventional pooled cross-sectional model provides a poor fit in the qualitative sense: it fails to capture prominent features of the data that we would want the model to explain. We should thus look beyond the institutional time series model for the causes of declining unionization in the 1980s.

Structural Change and Union Decline

An important limitation of the time series analysis is its neglect of the massive structural shifts in employment that have affected all capitalist democracies increasingly since the 1960s. These structural changes consist of two major trends: the rapid fall in the employment share of manufacturing industries, and the enormous growth of the service sector. Between 1970 and 1990, employment in secondary industries throughout the OECD fell by about one-fifth, from 37 percent to less than 30 percent of the civilian labor force. In the same period, the service sector of the OECD area expanded from 49 percent to 63 percent of all workers. These percentages reflect the addition of some 90 million new service jobs since 1970 (OECD 1995). These trends have been widely followed by sociologists of postindustrialism and postcapitalism (e.g., Bell 1973; Dahrendorf 1959; Lash and Urry 1987; Block 1990). For these writers, structural changes in contemporary economies have undermined the traditional class-based organizations that shaped economic and political life. In this story, unions are just one of many casualties of the erosion of traditional class cleavages; the list also includes labor parties, the mass-production factory, and urban centers of industry.

For the students of postindustrialism, the loss of manufacturing jobs shrinks the traditional constituency of the labor movement (Bell 1973, 137–142; Griffin et al. 1990; Lash and Urry 1987). Wholesale shutdowns, such as the U.S. plant closings of the 1970s or the British pit closures of the 1980s showcase the most spectacular blows to organized labor (Bluestone and Harrison 1982; Winterton and Winterton 1989, ch. 1). The expansion of the service sector also contributes to union decline. The service industries consist of small, spatially dispersed, owner-operated businesses, often employing young, part-time, or female workers. These sectors thus present a more difficult organizing task than do the homogeneous work forces of traditional manufacturing industries (Troy 1986). The growth of services also created immense structural mobility. Sociologists have argued that this mobility weakens class attachments, which undermines union membership (Dahrendorf 1959, 278; Lipset and Gordon 1953). Evidence relating structural change to union decline in North America and Western Europe is reported by Troy (1990). In his analysis, private sector unionism was hit hard by the decline of manufacturing. The shift to services widely eroded union membership in the 1970s and 1980s, but union losses were smaller in Canada and Western Europe because structural change lagged behind that in the United States. Structural change in the postwar economies thus seems a persuasive account of labor movement decline, closely connected to the broad contours of postwar capitalist development.

Although the structural change theory of deunionization is a long-standing conventional wisdom in the social sciences, three pieces of evidence challenge the idea. First, the pattern of structural change provides a poor fit to the data on changing union organization. Second, some structural changes have actually assisted union growth. Third, declining union organization within traditional industry sectors has been a key site of union decline.

Table 9.2 shows structural changes in the advanced capitalist labor markets for three industry sectors. Looking first at the median growth rates across the entire OECD, we see that the employment share of secondary industries declined at about the same rate in the 1970s as in the 1980s. On average, traditional industry sectors lost about half a percentage point each year. Structural trends in the service industries were also similar in the 1970s and 1980s. Here, annual growth in employment share was about a third of a point. So while unions generally did well in the 1970s and poorly in the 1980s, the same trends dominated both decades: manufacturing shrank, and services grew. Looking at particular cases, we see that the decline of traditional industries was largest in several of the countries with the most resilient labor movements. In Italy, Belgium, and Norway, the structural shift from manufacturing was quite rapid in the 1980s, but this was not reflected in extensive deunionization. On the other hand, the United Kingdom fits the theory well, as rapid deindustrialization accompanied British deunionization. In general, however, regression analysis shows that only 10 percent of the variance in union density decline in the eighteen countries can be explained by falling employment in secondary industries.

Results for the two service industry categories are even weaker. Consumer services include employment in hospitality and financial services industries, where union organization is very low. In this sector, employment growth was stronger in the high-density countries than in the low-density countries. Struc-

TABLE 9.2

Annual Growth Rate of the Employment Share of Industry Sectors, Eighteen
OECD Countries, 1970s and 1980s

	Secondary Industry		Consumer Services		Social Services	
	1970s	1980s	1970s	1980s	1970s	1980s
High-density countries						
Belgium	−.71	−.62	.13	.36	.69	.37
Denmark[a]	−.53	−.30	.00	.34	.69	−.03
Finland[b]	.01	−.36	.13	.54	.54	.47
Sweden	−.59	−.28	.08	.30	.74	.22
Middle-density countries						
Australia	−.54	−.45	.43	.34	.23	.24
Austria	−.09	−.33	.45	.19	.38	.32
Canada	−.20	−.28	.97	.26	−.57	.22
Germany	−.51	−.39	.10	.32	.56	.24
Ireland[b]	.24	−.41	.21	.30	.32	.34
Italy[c]	−.17	−.55	.11	.43	.12	.67
New Zealand[b]	−.58	−.83	.01	.68	.39	.45
Norway[a]	−.70	−.44	.48	.34	.55	.43
United Kingdom[e]	−.60	−.83	.45	.46	.27	.41
Low-density countries						
France	−.29	−.58	.24	.34	.47	.45
Japan	−.08	−.10	.56	.24	.14	.16
Netherlands	−.64	−.50	.18	.05	.58	.40
Switzerland[d]	−.63	−.30	.27	.45	.45	.14
United States	−.31	−.38	.26	.35	.17	.14
MEDIAN GROWTH	−.52	−.40	.23	.34	.42	.33

Sources: All data are from OECD 1992b, except 1970s figures for Germany and the
Netherlands, which are taken from ILO 1977, 1991.

Notes: Data are for 1970–1979 and 1980–1989 unless otherwise noted. Secondary industry employment includes mining, manufacturing, utilities, and construction; consumer
services include wholesale and retail trades, restaurants, hotels, finance, and business services; and social services include community, social, and personal services.

[a] Data are for 1972–1981 and 1981–1990.
[b] Data are for 1971–1980 and 1981–1990.
[c] Data are for 1977–1980 and 1981–1990.
[d] Data are for 1970–1979 and 1979–1988.
[e] Data are for 1970–1979 and 1980–1987.

tural change is often enlisted to explain American union decline (Troy 1986;
Farber 1990), but employment in consumer services grew about as fast in the
United States as it did in Denmark and Sweden through the 1980s. Of course,
union density plummeted only in the United States. The Dutch union movement shrank by about a quarter through the 1980s, but employment in trading,

hospitality and financial services grew more slowly there than in the rest of the OECD. Across all eighteen countries, the growth of employment in consumer services industries explains only about 2 percent of the change in union density from 1980 to 1989.

In addition to the poor fit between structural trends and patterns of union decline, not all changes in industrial structure have retarded union growth. The final two columns of Table 9.2 show the 1970s and 1980s growth rates for employment in social and community services, an industry sector character- ized by public sector employment and high unionization. This sector has ex- panded through periods of both union growth (in the 1970s) and union decline (in the 1980s). As in consumer services, structural change in social and com- munity services has been similar in the high- and low-density countries through the 1980s. Indeed, in Denmark, where union density remained con- stant through the 1980s, social services employment declined, while social services continued to grow through the 1980s in all the low-density countries despite falling unionization. In France and the Netherlands, the employment share of social services grew at about half a point a year in the face of large declines in union density. While the growth of social services might support unionization, the statistical relationship is extremely weak. Changing social service employment in the 1980s is virtually uncorrelated with changes in union density. These figures may be interpreted in light of the analysis of labor market structure in Chapter 8, which indicated that the impact of the industrial composition of the labor market on unionization varies across countries. This suggests that similar structural trends can have widely different effects on unionization depending on the institutional context. Evidence for the structural change theory may provide a poor fit to the data on deunionization because the theory wrongly discounts the impact of institutions.

Disaggregated union density statistics provide further evidence against the structural change theory of union decline. These figures show that structural changes have not been large enough to account for the density declines of the 1970s and 1980s. One way of summarizing this information is with a shift-share analysis. With this analysis we ask how much of the union decline can be explained by shifting employment across industries, assuming the unionization rates within industries remain constant. Visser (1991) reports a shift-share analysis for eleven OECD countries for which industry data are available. His analysis shows that estimated changes due to structural shifts poorly fit the observed changes in union density (see Table 9.3). In five of the eleven countries, the predicted change in union density due to structural change is in the opposite direction to the observed change. In most other coun- tries, the estimated change is only a small fraction of the observed change. Only structural change in Britain fits the observed data somewhat well. Even in this case, however, the big decline of the 1980s is much larger than the possible effects of manufacturing decline and service industry growth. While

TABLE 9.3

Shift-Share Analysis of Industrial Structure Change and Union Density Growth, Eleven OECD Countries, 1970–1989

	Years	Observed Density Change	Estimated Density Change	Manufacturing Density Change
Australia	1976–1988	−9.0	−1.6	−6[a]
Austria	1970–1988	−12.2	−3.4	−15
Canada	1975–1988	1.3	−2.2	−8
Germany	1970–1986	3.6	−0.1	12
Italy	1977–1988	−9.7	−3.5	−10[b]
Japan	1979–1988	−4.9	0.6	−3[b]
Netherlands	1975–1988	−10.0	−1.8	−17[b]
Norway	1972–1988	4.5	−2.8	20[c]
Sweden	1970–1988	17.6	−2.5	16
United Kingdom	1970–1989	−5.7	−3.9	−23
United States	1980–1988	−8.6	−1.5	−13

Sources: Visser 1991; Bain and Price 1980.

Note: Estimated changes were calculated from employment and union density shifts in 1-digit industries.

[a] 1982–1988.

[b] 1980–1988.

[c] 1970–1988.

British union density fell by more than 12 points in the 1980s, only a fifth of this loss is attributable to structural shifts in employment. In Britain, a large part of union decline through the 1980s was due to the massive decline of unionization within industries. Union representation in manufacturing, for example, fell from 64 percent to 41 percent between 1980 and 1988 (see also Waddington 1992). This pattern was common, as the big losses in union density are associated with large declines in manufacturing sector unionization (see Table 9.3). The 12-point drop in union density in Austria, for example, is associated with a 15-point fall in manufacturing sector unionization, and the Netherlands' 10-point drop is associated with a 17-point drop for the manufacturing sector. Only where unionization in manufacturing has grown—in Sweden, Norway, and Germany—do we see rises in national union density over the 1970s and 1980s.

These results have two implications for explaining union decline in the 1980s. First, union decline is driven less by changes in employment across industries and more by changes in unionization within industries. Second, explanations of union decline must thus address why union support has fallen so dramatically within traditional industry sectors. Neither the institutional time series analysis nor the postindustrial theory of deunionization has successfully come to grips with this explanatory challenge.

This chapter has reviewed the trend of declining unionization that affected all eighteen of our OECD countries in the 1980s. After three decades of organizational divergence, we observe a common trend to union decline in the advanced capitalist countries. The union density losses were especially large and came particularly early in the low-density countries. In the high-density countries, union growth was halted, reversing a thirty-year pattern of labor movement expansion. Estimates from the time series model introduced in Chapter 7 failed to provide accurate predictions of union decline. The model fared worst where unions lost the most ground, in France, the Netherlands, and the British Isles. The structural analysis of Chapter 8 motivates the leading rival explanation of union decline. This explanation—favored by students of postindustrialism—claims that recent structural changes in capitalist economies have undermined the class basis of trade unionism. Changes in the employment structure, however, provide little help in explaining union decline. Similar structural trends of manufacturing decline and services sector growth dominate the 1970s and the 1980s, yet unions grew strongly in the earlier decade and stumbled only in the latter. Although time series forecasts and evidence of structural trends in employment cannot explain recent declines in unionization, more disaggregated data indicate the importance of falling unionization within traditional industries. I pursue this finding in the next chapter, which examines changes in the institutional context for union organizing.

Ten

Power, Efficiency, and Institutional Change

THE PREVIOUS chapter described the extent of declining unionization in the 1980s, but provided more questions than answers. The forecasting exercise that assumed the durability of labor market institutions through the two decades from 1970 was, in important ways, unsuccessful. There was also little evidence that union decline was rooted in the growth of the postindustrial employment structure. Taken together, these findings suggest that we need a more historically specific explanation of union decline, emphasizing the effects of the recent institutional changes that eroded union support in traditional industry sectors. This chapter takes a step in this direction by investigating changes in the pattern of labor market centralization that shaped unionization in the twenty years following postwar reconstruction.

Widespread institutional reform shifted the ground of industrial relations in the advanced capitalist countries during the 1980s. After a long period of institutional continuity, labor markets were widely deregulated. In the corporatist paradigm of Sweden, divisions within the labor movement widened, while employers dismantled their central bargaining unit. Meanwhile, in the basement of the house of labor, American private sector unions largely abandoned coordinated bargaining strategies under growing pressure for enterprise contracts and wage concessions (Katz 1993). Although this trend to more decentralized labor market regulation was widespread, it was not universal. In Austria, Germany, and Norway, centralized, or industry, bargaining continued through the 1980s (Lange et al. 1995). In less centralized countries, such as Canada and Japan, multiemployer and coordinated bargaining also remained stable. Before studying the effects of institutional change on the level of unionization, this chapter asks the prior question: why did labor markets become more decentralized in some countries but not in others?

For many researchers, the decentralization of labor market institutions was propelled by the novel uncertainty and competitiveness of the contemporary world economy. Centralized negotiations failed to provide employers with the labor market flexibility required by new conditions of intensified global economic competition (Freeman and Gibbons 1993; Katz 1993; Pontusson and Swenson 1992). Wage growth was hard to restrain, and wage leveling under broad collective agreements reduced firms' competitiveness by severing the link between pay and productivity. Where central unions lacked the authority to enforce wage restraint, employers in high-wage industries often faced wildcat strikes. For workers, rising unemployment from the early 1970s created incentives to abandon centralized representation in favor of firm-level productivity coalitions with employers.

Besides suggesting the institutional origins of union decline in the 1980s, the link between world market conditions and the decentralization of labor markets raises a key issue for institutional approaches to economic sociology. Does institutional change result from efficient adaptation to changing market conditions, or is it the product of a political process of institution building by powerful actors? Decentralization appears to provide a clear-cut case of efficient institutional adaptation. Centralized bargaining was simply too rigid for speedy and flexible responses to volatile and competitive global markets.

In contrast to this view, I argue that power and efficiency explanations can be seen as complementary rather than competing accounts of institutional change. From the viewpoint of my institutional sociology of the labor market, we should take of account of the institutional context when we examine the effects of market forces. Given increasing competitive pressures and slack labor markets, employers and unions both wanted to decentralize bargaining through the 1980s. The form of this decentralization, however, depended on the institutional resources of employers, unions, and, in particular, the local representatives of unions. This suggests that the contest between power and efficiency theories of institutional change is off the mark. In many cases, the institutional response to competitive pressures will not be uniquely determined. Instead, there may be a family of institutional solutions, disputed by rival political forces. For the analysis of this chapter, market conditions might establish the pressures and broad range of options for institutional change, but prior institutional conditions decisively shape the final outcome.

Labor Market Institutions in Three Countries

Institutional developments in Sweden, the United States, and Germany illustrate several patterns that are general to the process of bargaining decentralization throughout the advanced capitalist countries.

From 1956 to 1981, Swedish collective bargaining was shaped by centralized wage talks between the blue-collar union confederation, the LO, and the national employer association, SAF. These centralized negotiations resulted in frame agreements that established the terms for industry contracts. From the 1960s on, the LO aggressively pursued a solidaristic wages policy, which minimized wage differences across and later, within industries (Swenson 1989, 135). Although wage differentials were substantially reduced, the policy was offset by locally negotiated wage drift that supplemented the central agreements. In 1983, the engineering employer association split from the centralized framework and bargained independently with its counterpart union. The following year, bargaining was decentralized at the industry level without central coordination by LO or SAF. National-level negotiations resumed in some sectors, beginning in 1985, but no-strike clauses ceased to bind the industry-level affiliates (Lange et al. 1995). The abandonment of the Swedish model of centralized bargaining was completed in 1990, when SAF dismantled its bargaining unit, foreclosing the possibility of further economy-wide wage-setting (Thelen 1993, 29).

The commitment of Swedish employers to centralized bargaining was originally secured by the prospect of wage moderation and industrial peace (Swenson 1989, 42–60). The dynamic of wage drift combined with solidaristic bargaining played out through the 1970s, creating a wage spiral and growing industrial unrest in the public sector (Ahlén 1989; Pontusson 1992a). Wage drift would raise the pay of skilled workers in the export sector. In the following bargaining round, centrally negotiated wage solidarity would then raise the general level of wages to keep pace with the wage leaders and reduce wage differentials (Thelen 1993, 28). The combination of solidaristic bargaining and wage drift created two sorts of labor market rigidities. Wages were downwardly inflexible, and wage differentials within and across firms were narrow. Employers in the engineering industry, who faced increasingly volatile global markets, avoided these rigidities by opting out of the central agreements altogether.

As we have seen, U.S. collective bargaining was much more decentralized than in Sweden. Although most collective agreements were concluded at the firm or plant level, multiemployer contracts characterized industrial relations in several key industries, such as steel, coal, and trucking. As in other countries where local bargaining predominates, pattern bargaining in the United States provided the chief mechanism for coordinated wage-setting. Throughout most of the postwar period, wage rounds in industries such as auto, rubber, and meat-packing were shaped by pattern-setting negotiations in a leading firm. The terms of this firm-level agreement were then followed in subsequent wage talks in other firms in the industry.

Deep in the recession following the second oil shock, the American blend of industry agreements and pattern bargaining quickly dissolved. The watershed year of 1982 marked the "transformation of American industrial relations" (Kochan, Katz, and McKersie 1986). Labor market decentralization consisted of two developments. First, pattern bargaining was disrupted by concessionary wage reductions. Uncoordinated wage talks in the auto industry were initiated in the context of growing foreign competition, record unemployment, and the threat of plant closures. Under these conditions, the uniformity of pattern bargaining was discarded as employers negotiated independently for real wage reductions (Kochan et al. 1986, 115). Second, industry-level agreements also came under pressure. In the steel industry, the United Steelworkers' wage policy distinguished new bargaining goals for "distressed" and "healthy" industries. Coverage of the industry-level Basic Steel Agreement was reduced from eight companies to just six. These developments represent a durable change in collective bargaining, not simply a temporary adjustment to recessionary conditions. By the time of the economic recovery of the mid-1980s, the Basic Steel Agreement had been completely abandoned (Katz 1993, 11). In the auto industry, collective agreements in the Big Three auto manufacturers began to show greater uniformity, but earnings across companies varied substantially because of the divergent effects of new profit-sharing schemes (Katz, Kochan, and McKersie 1990, 197). As in Sweden, bargaining decentralization in the United States was initiated by employers to obtain a more flexible allocation of wages and working time under increasingly competitive economic conditions. In contrast to the Swedish experience, the threat of unemployment in the United States secured union cooperation with the more decentralized and concessionary bargaining arrangements.

The German institutional developments differed from those in Sweden and the United States. German industrial relations are dominated by industry negotiations led by the metalworkers' union, IG Metall. Compared to the Swedish LO, the main German union confederation, the DGB, has only a weak role in collective bargaining. As a consequence, there is no strong system of solidaristic bargaining as in Sweden. The unions maintain some commitment to reducing wage differentials within industries, but there is no mechanism to reduce wage inequality across industries. Industry bargaining in Germany is accompanied by a statutory system of labor representation in works councils. The works councils are endowed with a set of "codetermination rights," which are used to regulate personnel policy. In the coal and steel industries, codetermination extends to worker involvement in decisions about investment and technological change (Thelen 1991, 15). Although legally independent of the unions, unlike Swedish workplace representation, the works councils became increasingly dominated by union representatives through the 1950s and 1960s.

During the 1980s in Germany, working time rather than wages emerged as the central issue in collective bargaining. From 1984, IG Metall pursued a 35-hour week in anticipation of work reductions due to industrial restructuring (Swenson 1989, 216–22). Following a six-week strike that year, employers ultimately exchanged a 1.5-hour reduction for the flexible implementation of the new agreement (Thelen 1993, 30). The arrangement was negotiated in enterprise agreements between individual employers and the works councils. Subsequent bargaining rounds in 1987 and 1990 followed a similar pattern, with further reductions in working time. Throughout this period, the works councils also assumed an increasing role in the implementation of industry-level agreements on wages and technological change (Turner 1991). In contrast to trends in Sweden and the United States, the top level of collective bargaining remained intact in Germany during the 1980s. Industry bargaining shaped the terms of industrial relations, but responsibility for local implementation was increasingly assumed by the works councils.

A comparison of these three cases suggests four general ideas about the process of collective bargaining:

- Decentralization can be found in countries with economy-wide collective bargaining (Sweden) or local bargaining (the United States), but decentralization is not universal (Germany).

- The decentralization of labor market institutions arrives in the form of a clear discontinuity—a turning point—that is not subsequently reversed. This turning point marks a process of decentralization that devolves industrial relations to a lower level.

- The impetus for bargaining decentralization comes from employers who demand greater labor market flexibility (typically, wage cuts) under conditions of recession and intensified global competition.

- Works councils provide a safety valve for the pressure for decentralized industrial relations. Where works councils take a role in bargaining over wages and conditions, employers have fewer incentives to abandon the top level of collective bargaining and workers have a preexisting forum to advance their local interests.

The Swedish, American, and German cases motivate empirical and theoretical claims. Empirically, the trend toward the decentralization of collective bargaining seems general, but not universal, in the advanced capitalist countries. This is addressed in the following data analysis. Theoretically, this institutional change is not simply efficient adaptation to fluctuating market conditions. Change also depends on preexisting institutions, which influence responses to the new market conditions.

Labor Market Institutions in the 1970s and 1980s

This section describes labor market developments in eighteen OECD countries. Trends towards bargaining decentralization are summarized in Table 10.1. In countries such as Sweden, where national bargaining was replaced by industry agreements, decentralization involved employers' withdrawal of support for centralized wage talks. In Denmark, the reversion to industry bargaining in 1981 followed the failure of national talks in the previous three bargaining rounds and the threat of government intervention (EIRR 1991a, 1995). Industry bargaining appeared to crystallize in the 1990s, with the cartelization of the industry-level employer associations. This restructuring effectively devolved authority from the national level to the sector. The Danish

TABLE 10.1

Bargaining Decentralization Trends in the 1980s, Eighteen OECD Countries

	Bargaining Trends
Australia	Centralization in 1983 with the tripartite Prices and Incomes Accord but reversion to two-tier bargaining by 1988
Austria	Stable regional and industry bargaining coordinated by national union confederation
Belgium	Suspension of national bargaining from 1975 to 1986; rapid growth in local bargaining through the late 1970s and 1980s
Canada	Slight increase in local bargaining, but no institutional change
Denmark	Industry bargaining from 1981, following the breakdown of central negotiations in 1975, 1977, and 1979
Finland	Failed attempts at central bargains common through the 1970s and 1980s
France	Aroux legislation establishes compulsory local negotiations in 1982
Germany	Institutional stability accompanies growth of local bargaining in works councils through the late 1970s and early 1980s
Italy	Communists split from the joint confederation in 1984 in dispute over wage indexation
Ireland	Breakdown of centralized bargaining experiments in 1981, following locally organized strike activity
Japan	No institutional change; wage bargaining continues to be strongly patterned by the Shunto
Netherlands	Industry bargaining continues through the 1980s, accompanied by strengthened works council legislation
New Zealand	Bargaining centralized in 1984 by Labour party, but significant de-regulation following passage of the National government's 1991 Employment Contracts Act
Norway	Stability of centralized bargaining despite employer pressure for industry talks
Sweden	Centralized bargaining breaks down in 1983, when metalworkers negotiate independent industry agreement
Switzerland	Stable local bargaining over wages and hours continues through the 1980s
United Kingdom	Rapid bargaining decentralization from 1980, following labor law reforms and Thatcher's policy of reversing corporatist negotiations
United States	Increasing decentralization, with the erosion of pattern bargaining, although no formal institutional change

case was similar to the Belgian one: failed central talks foreshadowed industry bargaining and the rapid diffusion of enterprise negotiations. Central talks structuring industry wage negotiations in Belgium were suspended between 1975 and 1986. Although centralized negotiations resumed in the late 1980s, the number of local agreements had increased by fifty times during the hiatus in national-level negotiations (Spineux 1990; EIRR 1989a, 1989b).

While centralized bargaining had deep roots in Scandinavia and Belgium, institutional change in Ireland and Italy repudiated corporatist experiments of the 1970s. In both countries, the employer associations refused national bargaining when the union confederations failed to ensure wage restraint and industrial discipline from their affiliates. Italian bargaining decentralization was fueled by a split between the Communist and Christian Democratic wings of the union movement over wage indexation. In the late 1980s, industry and firm bargaining were reestablished as the chief methods for wage-setting (Baglioni 1991; Negrelli and Santi 1990, 180). In Ireland, as in Italy, tripartite bargaining was attempted through the 1970s. Industrial unrest increased, in 1981 the employer association withdrew from centralized negotiations, and collective bargaining returned to the industry level through most of the 1980s (Hardimann 1988, ch. 8; cf. Teague 1995).

In several countries, the initiative for decentralization came from governments, rather than from employers. In Britain the Thatcher government's Employment Acts limited coordination among unions in strike activity as the government generally set about reversing the country's corporatist foray under Labour. In its role as an employer, the Conservative party government also decentralized bargaining by contracting out public services (Marsh 1992). In New Zealand, the National party government repealed long-standing legislative guarantees of collective bargaining and compulsory unionism. The new government discarded Labour's Tripartite Wage Conference and abandoned mechanisms for national consultation with the union confederation in the New Zealand Employment Contracts Act of 1991 (Hince and Vranken 1991).

In Australia and France, labor—not conservative—governments led the institutional reforms. French labor legislation, passed by the Socialist assembly in 1982, established compulsory enterprise bargaining over wages, working conditions, and technological change. In Australia, the central union confederation endorsed a "structural efficiency principle" in 1988. This idea, outlined by the quasi-judicial Industrial Relations Commission, established guidelines for enterprise bargaining over productivity payments and work restructuring (Katz 1993, 6).

In all these countries—Australia, Belgium, Denmark, Italy, New Zealand, Sweden, the United Kingdom, and the United States—an institutional break can be identified that devolved industrial relations one level, from national to industry bargaining or from industry to local bargaining. In each country, the key actors cited world economic conditions to justify their moves for institutional change. In Sweden, defection from centralized agreements was led by engineering industry employers in the export sector (Pontusson and Swenson 1992). In Belgium, bargaining decentralization was urged by employers to restore the competitiveness of the Belgian economy (Hancke 1991, 469). Italian employers and local unions resisted national agreements through the

1980s because these obstructed flexible industrial reorganization (Locke 1991, 356). In both Australia and France, labor governments wanted to reshape industrial relations policy to enhance flexibility and boost export industries (Howell 1992, 171; Hancock and Isaac 1992, 220–21).

National or industry bargaining institutions remained intact in Germany, as we have seen, and also in Norway, Finland, Austria, and the Netherlands. Wage bargaining continues in all these countries, much as it did in the 1970s. Indeed, in the Norwegian case, the routinely failed national negotiations of the 1970s were replaced by a more stable pattern of central agreements through the 1980s. The continuity of centralized bargaining in Norway is matched by the growing importance of local negotiations as wage drift accounts for a growing majority of the wage bill. National and industry wage negotiations also continue in Finland and the Netherlands. In Austria, centrally coordinated industry agreements remained the stable mechanism for wage-setting throughout the 1970s and 1980s (Lange et al. 1995).

In less centralized settings, where unions coordinate through pattern bargaining, there is similar institutional continuity. In Canada, the proportion of multiemployer agreements has declined slightly, although unevenly, from the early 1970s, while the institutional framework for collective bargaining remains unchanged (Golden, Lange, and Wallerstein 1993). In Japan, wage bargaining continues to be coordinated in annual wage rounds through the Shunto (Tokuichi 1993, 39–46). Watchmakers in the Swiss metalworkers union have also continued to lead wage negotiations through the 1980s (Aubert 1989).

Bargaining decentralization is thus widespread but not universal. In just over half of the eighteen countries surveyed, the highest level of collective bargaining was effectively dismantled. Where bargaining institutions endured, there appears to be more local negotiations over wages and work time. Thus in Germany and Norway, for example, local bargaining plays an increasing role in wage-setting, but the parameters for local bargaining are established by industry and national agreements.

Market Conditions and Decentralization

Comparative researchers widely claim that pressures for bargaining decentralization stem from basic changes in the world economy over the last twenty-five years (Piore and Sabel 1984; Turner 1991; Katz 1993). Throughout the 1970s, the world economy was reshaped by the growth of trade, deregulation of exchange rates, the oil price shocks, and growing export competition from Asian manufacturing industries. Faced with the pressure of making labor markets more flexible, employers pushed for more uncoordinated industrial relations.

The Economic Context

The development of trading institutions in the 1950s and 1960s laid the ground for massive growth in the global economy. Following the creation of the European Coal and Steel Community in 1952 and the European Economic Community (EEC) in 1957, trade in raw materials, intermediate goods, and agricultural products expanded among France, Germany, Italy, and the Benelux countries. Trade was again liberalized in 1973, when Britain, Denmark, and Ireland gained EEC membership. Tariffs elsewhere in Europe were lowered through the European Free Trade Agreement. Beyond Europe, trade barriers dropped after the Kennedy round of trade talks in 1967 (Keohane 1984, 20). As a result of these developments, the volume of world trade in manufactured goods more than tripled between 1951 and 1971, while the volume of overall output less than doubled. Manufacturing exports grew by nearly five times in the seven largest OECD countries (Armstrong et al. 1991, 153).

The effects of trade liberalization became highly uncertain when the Bretton Woods system of fixed exchange rates was dismantled in 1971. Before 1971, the exchange rates of foreign currencies were pegged to the U.S. dollar, which could, in principle, be exchanged for gold at a fixed rate. The system was abandoned in two steps, with the dollar decoupling from the gold standard in 1971, and European currencies, led by the Deutschemark, floating from 1973. Exchange rates fluctuated widely in the following period in response to shifting demand for foreign currencies (Piore and Sable 1984, 173–74; Scharpf 1987, 258). Central banks' attempts to stabilize currencies were largely unsuccessful (Dornbusch 1980), resulting in large and unpredictable shifts in world prices in the 1970s and 1980s.

Recession was added to the rising global interdependence and uncertainty when the oil shocks of 1973–1974 and 1979 triggered rapid inflation and unemployment growth. The first price shock resulted from an embargo on oil sales imposed by the OPEC countries in response to Western support of Israel in the Arab-Israeli war. The real commodity price of oil jumped 44 percent between 1973 and 1975, in contrast to the 7 percent rise of the previous period. During the second oil shock, following the Iranian revolution, oil prices increased by 36 percent (Bruno and Sachs 1985, 164). The two price shocks contributed to worldwide recession in the mid-1970s and early 1980s. In the OECD as a whole, the rate of economic growth between 1973 and 1981 was less than half that between 1960 and 1973 (Bruno and Sachs 1985, 155).

The impact of the recession on the advanced capitalist countries was aggravated by the export success of the newly industrializing countries of East and Southeast Asia. South Korea, Taiwan, Hong Kong, and Singapore maintained high rates of investment and export growth in the two decades after

1970. Their initial exports to Europe and North America capitalized on low wages in labor-intensive industries, such as textiles and leather goods. Export income increased quickly with expanding production in high-technology sectors, such as computers, other electronics, heavy industry, and shipbuilding. By 1988 the "Asian tigers" had accumulated a $50 billion trade surplus on manufactures, underwritten largely by Japanese capital goods (Armstrong et al. 1991, 289). In the newly industrializing countries as a whole, manufacturing exports to the advanced capitalist countries had grown at about 15 percent annually in real terms between 1950 and 1989. By 1990, manufacturing exports from outside the OECD to the OECD totaled $250 billion (Wood 1994, 1–2, 138–140).

In sum, the early 1970s marked the beginning of a period in which more economic activity was subject to the influences of the world market than ever before. The world market itself had become increasingly turbulent and unpredictable. Under these conditions firms faced increasing competitive pressures as demand contracted during a protracted recession and Asian exporters expanded their market share.

The Effects of Uncertainty and Recession

Why did the newly competitive and volatile global economy create pressures for the reassertion of the forces of supply and demand in national labor markets? After all, corporatist bargaining is often regarded as an effective institutional tool for wage restraint, industrial peace, and economic management (Flanagan et al. 1983; Bruno and Sachs 1985; Katzenstein 1985). All these advantages would seem to make centralized bargaining the preferred institutional option under conditions of intense international competition. Certainly, this was the assessment for the recessionary 1970s, when centrally negotiated wage restraint was associated with superior economic growth.

Researchers argue that centralized bargaining failed to deliver the labor market flexibility that was required for successful economic performance under these novel conditions of international economic volatility and competitiveness (Katz 1993, Pontusson 1992a). Employers' moves for labor market flexibility involved limiting two types of collective action. On the wage front, they sought wage restraint and a tighter link between enterprise productivity and pay scales. They also moved to limit strikes. In Sweden, local negotiations under a solidaristic bargaining policy contributed to the overall level of wages and deprived employers of control over wage incentives within firms. Employers in export industries—facing the most intense competitive pressures— abandoned centralized bargaining. In more decentralized settings, such as the United States, employers rejected wage indexation and sought real wage cuts. In the U.S. auto industries, the Big Three manufacturers each demanded concessions tailored to their own particular straits. Similar developments can be found in Italy, where the central employer association, Confindustria, opposed the *scala mobile* throughout the 1980s (Negrelli and Santi 1990, 186–87). These three examples suggest that employers respond to shifts in nominal wages because these shifts drive price increases under conditions of contracting demand. In short, nominal wage growth increases the chance of bargaining decentralization.

In this explanation, employers operate under a "money illusion," in which they fail to distinguish real and nominal movements in production costs. It may be more realistic to claim that employers try to decentralize bargaining in response to real wage movements. Under centralized bargaining, real wages are too downwardly inflexible to allow pay cuts. In this modified explanation, rising real wages increase the probability of bargaining decentralization. Whether real or nominal wages are more closely associated with bargaining decentralization is addressed in the data analysis below.

In the experimental corporatisms of Britain and Ireland, mechanisms for wage drift were less developed. In those countries, union confederations lacked the political authority to impose wage restraint on their affiliates (Regini 1984; Hardimann 1988). Local unions rejected central authority by striking. In both these countries, centralized agreements in the 1970s were followed by wildcat strikes. In response, employer associations withdrew from central bargains in Ireland. In Britain, the incoming Conservative government used the industrial disputes of the Winter of Discontent (1978–1979) to justify a new industrial relations policy restricting collective bargaining and the role of trade unions (Marsh 1992, 59–81). More generally, this suggests that under the contemporary conditions of intensified global competition, strike activity can raise the likelihood of bargaining decentralization.

Streeck (1984) argues that economic recession also gives workers incentives for labor market deregulation. When labor markets are slack, workers' interests become closely tied to those of their firms. "Under crisis conditions," Streeck (1984, 297) writes, "the rule of the market asserts itself not just over the behavior of firms but also over workers' definitions of their interests—with the interests in the economic survival of 'their' employer becoming so intense that they escape union control." This idea seems to fit the facts of the American case, where threats of plant closures preceded the pattern-breaking concessionary bargains in the auto industry. Union locals, fearing mass layoffs in the context of rising unemployment and stiffening foreign competition, cast their lot with the Big Three. Concession bargaining effectively engaged workers in local productivity coalitions as central coordination was replaced by enterprise-level exchanges of wages for employment guarantees.

The explanations linking wage growth, strike activity, and unemployment to bargaining decentralization share a similar logic. Of key importance to each explanation is the uniformity imposed on wages and conditions by the central agreements. In a volatile and competitive economic environment, employers will prefer a more decentralized allocation, in which the wage structure and working conditions are more closely connected to the productivity and performance of the firm. For workers, slack labor markets redirect their affiliations from the class to the firm.

Institutional Origins of Decentralization

These explanations can be sharpened by considering the institutional conditions of bargaining decentralization. Some researchers have suggested that works councils reduce incentives to abandon the highest level of collective bargaining (Thelen 1991). In this argument, works councils provide an institutional source of labor market flexibility, which reduces employer opposition to centralized bargaining. Workers are also less likely to abandon the centralized framework if their local representation is institutionally guaranteed. These arguments are illustrated by the contrasting examples of Germany and Italy.

In Germany, enterprises with more than five workers can elect works councils. Works council legislation guarantees two types of representation. First, management is obliged to consult with the works council on issues relating to plant personnel and the production process. Second, in some areas, management must reach an agreement with the works council before acting on plant policy. Thus works councils in the German steel industry were actively involved in the rationalization of industry and the introduction of high-technology production processes. Both management and labor (represented by the works councils) jointly planned to meet the competitive challenge of low-cost steel from Japan and the newly industrializing countries (Thelen 1991, 15, 132–35; see also Turner 1991). In this case, the bargaining strength of the union-dominated works councils was underwritten by IG Metall. The metalworkers' union supported the works councils' strategy and negotiated the broad direction of restructuring through industry-level agreements on working time and technical change.

Italy provides a contrast. The workplace role of Italian local unions was historically more tenuous than in Germany. New labor legislation in 1972 guaranteed the rights of union delegates in plants with more than one hundred workers. Unlike the German codetermination legislation, the Italian Statuto dei lavoratori tied workplace representation to the unions, and representation was legally sanctioned only in the large plants. Weak local unionism in Italy created two pressures for institutional change. First, the organizational weakness of local unions compelled militancy, which in turn stimulated aggressive employer opposition to labor. For example, strikes at Fiat over industrial restructuring in 1980 resulted in employer retaliation and a backlash by skilled workers and foremen against the union, which culminated in a major defeat for the local union leadership. Subsequent microeconomic reform at Fiat's Turin plant involved the reestablishment of workplace hierarchies, the expulsion of union activists, and large work force reductions (Locke 1991, 356–58). Second, the national unions were increasingly bypassed and sometimes replaced by autonomous forms of local organization (Locke 1992, 257–58). Without a strong institutional basis for local representation, employers moved to enhance labor market flexibility by decentralizing the top level of collective bargaining. Confindustria initiated fundamental revision of the *scala mobile*, distributing indexation unevenly across industrial sectors for the first time in the mid-1980s (Regalia 1995, 223–24).

The Italian and German cases suggest how works councils contribute to institutional continuity. As pressures mounted on employers to restructure production and shift the level of labor negotiations to firms and plants, works councils provided a ready-made mechanism, and consequently labor was given an institutionally secure stake in the developments. In particular, works councils were an institutional mechanism for the flexible reorganization of work and wages (cf. Streeck 1995, 331–333, 345). This reorganization closed the gap between pay and productivity in a period of intensified competition. Reform of pay schedules and working conditions within firms was compatible with employers' collective goal of wage restraint across the national labor market. Where labor's shop floor presence was weakly institutionalized, moves by employers for firm-level restructuring were difficult to accommodate by union confederations and national industry unions in centralized bargaining frameworks. In response, employers withdrew from centralized forums and unilaterally attempted to impose labor market flexibility.

Table 10.2 shows the relationship between bargaining decentralization and workplace representation. The second column of the table describes institutions for workplace representation. The third column indicates countries with statutory systems of works councils representation. In countries without bargaining decentralization, workers generally retained statutory rights to local representation, independent of unions. Works councils in these countries were empowered to obtain financial information about the firms and consult with management on work-related matters. In the exceptional Canadian and Japanese cases, collective bargaining is focused at a more decentralized level than in Europe. In countries where collective bargaining was decentralized, statutory works councils can be found only in Belgium. Local representation is also strong in Denmark and Sweden, but here the presence of works councils depends on union representation. Elsewhere, in France, Italy, and the English-speaking countries, forums for worker-management negotiation also depend on union representation, but union density is much lower. This comparative evidence is mostly consistent with the idea that works councils are associated with institutional continuity in industrial relations.

TABLE 10.2

Plant Level Labor Representation and the Decentralization of Collective Bargaining, Eighteen OECD Countries, 1974–1991

	Workplace Institutions	*Statutory Works Councils*
Countries with bargaining decentralization		
Australia	Shop stewards in unionized workplaces	No
Belgium	Mandatory works council elections in firms with at least one hundred workers; council rights to information and consultation	Yes
Denmark	"Cooperation committees" established by central union agreement in firms with at least fifty workers	No
France	Works council elections in firms with at least fifty workers, but elections are often ignored in practice; moderate council rights to consultation	No
Ireland	Shop stewards in unionized workplaces	No
Italy	Union delegates in large firms	No
New Zealand	Shop stewards in unionized workplaces	No
Sweden	Consultation and codetermination controlled by local unions	No
United Kingdom	Shop stewards in unionized workplaces	No
United States	Local representatives in unionized workplaces	No
Countries with institutional continuity		
Austria	Works councils in firms with at least five workers; council rights to information, consultation, and codetermination	Yes
Canada	Local representatives in unionized workplaces	No
Finland	Local representation committees in large unionized firms	No
Germany	Works councils in firms with at least five workers; council rights to information, consultation, and codetermination	Yes
Japan	Joint consultation committees in large unionized firms	No
Netherlands	Mandatory works councils in firms with at least one hundred workers; council rights to consultation in small firms	Yes
Norway	Mandatory works councils in firms with at least one hundred workers; council rights to information and consultation	Yes
Switzerland	Works councils elected under terms of some collective agreements	No

Sources: Institutional description is drawn from Ferner and Hyman 1992; Rogers and Streeck 1994; Inagami 1986; EIRR 1981, 1986; and Tsiganou 1991, ch. 2.

Model Specification and Data

We can explore these ideas further in a simple statistical model of bargaining decentralization. One approach could treat the dependent variable as several ordered categories distinguishing, say, national-, industry- and local-level bargaining systems. Preliminary data analysis shows that cross-national variation dominates the dependent variable in this specification and the model fails to capture the current focus on institutional change.

Rather than model the level of collective bargaining, I focus on institutional change as a discrete turning point that begins a process of bargaining decentralization. In this process, bargaining devolves one level, from the national to the industry level, as in Sweden, or from the industry to the local level, as in the United States. Unfortunately, there are no time series of bargaining centralization for all eighteen countries being analyzed. To remedy this, I quantify the earlier qualitative discussion of collective bargaining trends. Although this strategy may yield measurement error in the bargaining decentralization variable, there are no alternative data, and the issue of measurement error is addressed to some degree by examining regression diagnostics.

The probability of institutional change in a given year can be written as a function of time and a number of covariates, which may vary over time or across countries. Observations on the countries begin in 1974, after the turning point year in institutional developments in the world economy. Annual data are used for each country until the point of bargaining decentralization or until the time series data run out in 1991. For the variable measuring bargaining decentralization, countries score 0 in each year, except the year of institutional change, in which they score 1. Countries without significant institutional change are censored, scoring 0 in all years. A logistic regression on the binary decentralization variable yields estimates of the probability of bargaining decentralization given that it has not already occurred (Allison 1982).

The historical evidence above suggests that the likelihood of bargaining decentralization increases when wages are growing quickly. Under these circumstances, employers try to replace the political authority of the central union with market discipline. A similar argument can be made for strike activity: high levels of strike activity stimulate employers' withdrawal from central agreements. When labor markets are slack and unemployment is high, workers will endorse local bargaining over central bargaining (Streeck 1984). Finally, the probability of bargaining decentralization also depends on the institutional starting point. In countries with works councils, the likelihood of bargaining decentralization should be lower than in countries without statutory guarantees for local representation.

Summary statistics for the data analysis are reported in Table 10.3. Centralization survival times—defined as the number of years after 1974 to the date of bargaining decentralization—are shown in the first column of the table.

TABLE 10.3
Centralization Survival Times and Means of Independent Variables for Discrete-Time Hazard Rate
Model of Bargaining Decentralization, Eighteen OECD Countries, 1974–1991

	Centralization Survival Time	Nominal Wage Growth	Inflation	Real Wage Growth	Strike Volume	Unemploy- ment Rate
Australia	15	10.6	10.0	0.6	502.1	6.6
Austria	—	6.9	4.9	2.0	2.9	2.9
Belgium	2	19.6	12.8	6.2	189.6	3.4
Canada	—	7.8	7.3	0.6	661.7	8.6
Denmark	8	13.3	11.1	2.2	115.4	6.6
Finland	—	9.8	8.9	1.9	407.6	4.8
France	9	14.9	11.5	3.1	154.4	5.5
Germany	—	5.4	3.5	1.8	33.2	5.2
Ireland	8	19.3	16.1	2.8	776.8	7.9
Italy	11	21.9	16.2	4.9	1,217.2	7.5
Japan	—	6.7	5.2	1.5	43.2	2.3
Netherlands	—	5.4	4.3	1.0	18.4	8.2
New Zealand	18	10.6	11.6	−0.8	372.0	3.8
Norway	—	10.0	8.0	1.9	80.6	2.7
Sweden	10	5.3	4.3	1.0	137.5	2.2
Switzerland	—	9.0	8.3	0.7	1.1	0.9
United Kingdom	7	16.9	16.0	0.8	530.0	4.4
United States	9	8.5	9.0	−0.5	287.2	7.1

Sources: Wage, inflation, and unemployment data are taken from OECD 1982, 1989, 1992a, 1993. Gaps in the wage series for Austria, Finland, and New Zealand were filled with data from OECD 1988c. Strike data are from ILO (various years). The denominator for the strike volume variable—the number of wage- and salary-earners—is taken from OECD 1987, 1990, 1992b.

Notes: Dashes indicate censored observations. Strike volume is days lost through industrial disputes per 1,000 workers.

Eight of the eighteen countries had experienced no decentralization by 1991. Summing the survival times and adding the lengths of time series for censored countries provides the 241 nation-years used for the analysis. Consistent with alternative interpretations of the wage effects, nominal and real wage series are included for analysis.

Results

Estimates from an initial specification, shown in the first column of results in Table 10.4, provide strong evidence for the wage, unemployment, and works council effects. Among the economic variables, the wage growth and unemployment effects are signed consistently with the theory. The coefficients indicate that a 10 percent jump in wage growth (not unheard of in countries,

TABLE 10.4

Results from a Hazard Rate Model of Bargaining Decentralization,
Eighteen OECD Countries 1973–1991

Predictor	Nominal Wage Model	Real Wage Model	Real wage Model with Inflation
Intercept	−7.96	−4.99	−9.30
	(3.79)	(4.19)	(3.73)
Time	0.14	0.01	0.19
	(1.40)	(0.13)	(1.58)
Nominal wages	0.17		
	(2.13)		
Real wages		0.05	0.13
		(0.38)	(1.00)
Inflation			0.26
			(2.36)
Strikes	−0.03	−0.02	−0.04
	(1.50)	(2.00)	(2.00)
Unemployment	0.50	0.43	0.52
	(3.33)	(3.07)	(3.47)
Works council	−2.41	−2.61	−2.11
	(1.90)	(2.07)	(1.59)
LOG LIKELIHOOD	−31.48	−33.55	−30.36

Notes: The strike effect has been multiplied by 10. Numbers in parentheses are Absolute *t* statistics.

such as Italy, with strong wage indexation provisions) roughly doubles the odds of institutional change. This estimate is also consistent with the Swedish story. Solidaristic bargaining combined with wage drift in Sweden increased labor costs through the late 1970s and the early 1980s prompting institutional change in 1983. In the low-inflation regimes—Austria, Germany, Japan, and Switzerland—where nominal wage growth was comparatively slow, institutional continuity marked collective bargaining trends. Consistent with Streeck's (1984) idea that workers support decentralized bargaining when labor markets are slack, a large unemployment effect is also estimated with these data. According to the estimate, a 2 percentage point increase in the unemployment rate more than doubles the odds of labor market decentralization. The impact of local institutions is indicated by a strong negative relationship between works councils and bargaining decentralization. Other things being equal, countries with works councils were less than a fifth as likely to experience bargaining decentralization as countries with less institutionalized forms of workplace representation. This result supports the idea that works councils release the pressure of local demands within a centralized framework.

In contrast to the wage, unemployment, and works council estimates, the strike effect is negatively signed, rather than positively as expected. Strike volume was low in years of bargaining decentralization. This effect may be an artifact of the very high levels of strike activity of the early 1970s, before the wave of bargaining decentralization that swept through the 1980s. Strike activity commonly declined through the 1980s under the pressure of recession and high unemployment (Shalev 1992), so this trend may offset the pattern of industrial action and employer-sponsored decentralization. Although the strike effect may not be detectable with the fine-grained time series analysis, some evidence is provided by gross patterns of cross-national variation (see Table 10.3). Of the countries with the most strike-prone unions, institutional continuity can be found in only one, Canada. Italy, Britain, Ireland, and Australia all experienced high strike rates, and collective bargaining was decentralized in all through the 1980s. At the other end of the spectrum, the low-strike countries of Switzerland, Austria, Germany, and the Netherlands did not decentralize bargaining.

To investigate the possibility that employers respond to real rather than nominal wage shifts, I also estimate two additional models. The first replaces the nominal wage variable with real wage growth. The second augments the real wage model with a variable measuring the annual inflation rate. This model is intended to capture the effects of movements in prices that are partly expressed in the nominal wage model but are uncontrolled in the model with real growth alone. Movements in real wages are not strongly associated with bargaining decentralization, but inflation is strongly and positively related to the probability of bargaining decentralization. It seems likely that employers were responding to a mixture of signals from nominal wages and prices because bargaining decentralization was often adopted, as in Italy and the United States, as a way of avoiding wage indexation provisions in times of high inflation.

It might be objected that the historical record fails to unambiguously indicate the timing of bargaining decentralization. For example, 1982 was chosen as the year of bargaining decentralization in the United States. The move from industry to local bargaining was signaled then by concession bargaining in the auto industry, the reduction in scope of the Basic Steel Agreement, and the erosion of pattern bargaining in other industries. Still, bargaining decentralization might be dated from as early as 1977 (when Chrysler requested wage concessions and a federal government bailout), or as late as 1986, when the Basic Steel Agreement was finally discarded. Alternative times for bargaining decentralization might also be given for other countries in the sample. With uncertainty about the precise timing of institutional change, it is useful to assess the sensitivity of the results to observations from individual countries. A set of cross-validation coefficients can be obtained by applying the analysis to subsets of the data in which observations from each country are omitted.

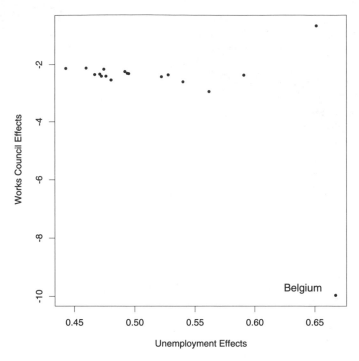

Figure 10.1. Scatterplot of works council and unemployment cross-validation coefficients. Observations from Belgium are highly influential for both effects.

This procedure yields eighteen sets of regression coefficients for each model. Estimates are highly sensitive to data from particular countries if the cross-validation coefficients show substantial variation.

In general, the cross-validation coefficients show that the results are quite robust to slight changes in the data. However, observations from Belgium are influential for a few estimates. This can be seen from Figure 10.1, which shows a scatterplot of cross-validation coefficients from the unemployment and works councils effects. The scatterplot indicates that when Belgium is removed from the analysis, the works council and unemployment effects become much larger. The Belgian observations are suppressing the size of estimates for both coefficients. What is the substantive significance of this?

A closer look at the Belgian case suggests that it is somewhat unusual. The mid-1970s were a volatile period in Belgian industrial relations. Early in the decade, during a period of rapid economic restructuring, the "unions developed a hostile attitude to technological innovation" (Vilrokx and Van Leemput 1992). Strikes, factory occupations, and unemployment all rose rapidly, culminating in the dissolution of national bargaining in 1976 (Hancke 1991). The works councils failed to provide the sort of productivity coalitions that developed in Germany and Austria, largely, it seems, because consultation and codetermination powers were weaker. Only in the 1980s have works councils been integrated into the process of technological change and work reorganization (Vilrokx and Van Leemput 1992). Belgium thus emerges as an outlier because its formal institutional features were similar to those in other countries, but in practice these institutions operated in a more limited way. As a result Belgium showed in the mid-1970s a more conflictual style of industrial relations and institutional development, reminiscent of the Romance countries, France and Italy.

In sum, after a lengthy period of institutional continuity, industrial relations were widely changing through the 1980s. Centralized patterns of collective bargaining were increasingly deregulated. Given the importance of trading blocs, exchange rate regimes, and oil cartels for these global economic developments, the entire story of bargaining decentralization is institutionally circumscribed. Still, these conditions did not uniquely determine just one pathway through the thickets of recession, uncertainty, and intensified global competition. Where there was no institutional change, adaptation to the new market conditions was accommodated by workers' plant-level representation in works councils. Market pressures for decentralization, signaled by rapid wage growth and high unemployment, were also weaker on average. Where the highest level of collective bargaining was dismantled, the existing institutional framework prevented workers and employers from advancing their firm-level interests. Swedish solidaristic bargaining, for example, prevented high-wage workers in export industries from maintaining their wage advantage over public sector workers. In the United States, employers rejected pattern bargaining under the pressure of foreign competition. Motivated by the threat of plant closures, U.S. unions followed the move to the decentralized framework. The direct threat to workers' individual interests undermined their collective interest in the solidaristic contracts generated by pattern bargaining. As we will see in the following chapter, this fragmentation of interests had severe consequences for unions' organizational strength.

Eleven

Globalization, Institutional Change, and Union Decline in the 1980s

ONE OF THE KEY historical conditions for union growth—labor market centralization—was undermined in many countries in the 1980s. The decentralization of labor markets that we find in about half of our OECD countries was not an isolated institutional change. Instead, decentralization was part of a broader current among the contemporary capitalist democracies in which global economic developments increasingly constrained domestic politics and labor markets. In this chapter, I try to estimate the effects of decentralization on union decline. In addition, I place the deunionization of the 1980s in the context of the wide-ranging political and economic changes of the recent period. The guiding idea is that nationally anchored institutions are losing their grip on national labor movements. In short, "globalization threatens workers' rights" (Tilly 1995). I begin by examining the economic explanations that emphasized the impact of recession and changes in the world economy. Next, I build on the institutional explanation of unionization to deal with the conditions of the 1980s. This more historically specific institutional theory underlines the role of political forces, which are reshaping the playing field of industrial relations to the disadvantage of organized labor.

Recession and Union-Organizing Resources

The oil shocks ushered in a period of protracted recession in the capitalist democracies. Inflation rose to double digits in many countries, only to fall again by the early 1980s. Unemployment proved more lasting, jumping to over 10 percent throughout continental Europe and remaining high for the following two decades. Recession hurt the unions. Sharply rising unemployment bit into union membership rolls in Ireland, the Netherlands, and the United Kingdom. Employers responded to slack economic conditions by intensifying their opposition to unions in an effort to control labor costs and reassert control over work. In one formulation, worldwide stagflation created a "crisis of unionism" in the OECD (Freeman 1989). This argument, frequently used to explain union decline in the United States (Freeman and Medoff 1984; Goldfield 1987), is developed in a comparative direction by Richard Freeman. In Freeman's studies of Britain, Japan, and the United States, he concluded that union decline results from employer resistance to organized labor in diverse institutional settings (Freeman 1986b; Freeman and Pelletier 1989; Freeman and Rebick 1989). U.S. employers mounted aggressive antiunion campaigns during certification elections by delaying representation ballots and escalating unfair labor practices. In Britain, antiunion activity by employers was permitted by new labor legislation through the 1980s. In Japan, where employers had long been expected to consent to unionization, this informal requirement was progressively withdrawn under the pressure of the new economic climate.

In the previous chapter we saw that employers and governments cited the pressure of world markets in their opposition to centralized bargaining. International economic competition may also be directly associated with deunionization. Competition from low-wage exporters in Asia and South America may undercut union labor in the wealthy OECD countries. Even within Europe, workers in the southern countries—Greece, Portugal, and Spain—receive significantly lower benefits and wages than those of their counterparts to the north (Reder and Ulman 1993). The high productivity of the unionized work forces in the rich countries erase some of the effects of the North-South wage differential, but residual competitive advantages for the South may remain. This seems most likely in relation to the highly unionized but low-skilled workers of traditional manufacturing industries (Wood 1994). Under these market conditions, unprofitable unionized firms in the traditional industry sector of the old core economies may be forced offshore or out of business in response to the growing global economy.

In addition to this economic argument, some researchers claim that the pressure of the world economy forced wholesale changes in the organization of work. In this story, the low-trust environment of the mass production factory was replaced by small autonomous groups staffed by workers with generally defined responsibilities (Piore and Sabel 1984; Sabel 1987, 34–36). Small work groups were also organized to maintain continuous quality control and incremental innovation in the production process. In this system, status differences among workers and between workers and supervisors were small (Cole 1989, ch. 2). Although typified by the industrial districts of northern and central Italy and Japan, the emergence of flexible work organization has been documented in Europe and North America in the 1970s and 1980s (Piore and Sabel 1984; Cole 1989; Turner 1991; Oliver and Wilkinson 1989; Kanawaty, Gladstone, Propenko, and Rodgers 1989).

Flexible work organization may have hampered union organizing. Workers no longer gathered in large groups under a single factory roof. The standardized working conditions and interests around which unions could mobilize were disappearing (Regini 1987). Because workers took on planning and administrative functions, traditionally conflictual relationships on the shop floor were also blurred. Workers increasingly shared management concerns, and unions were consigned to representing interests that were no longer grounded in the organization of work (Heckscher 1988, ch. 5; Thomas and Kochan 1992; Kochan et al. 1986, ch. 8).

Other researchers claim that flexible organization has, in some places, strengthened labor's hand. The analysis of the previous chapter suggests that this is most likely in countries with powerful union organizations at the national and local levels. The German metalworkers' union, IG Metall, provides a key example (Thelen 1991; Turner 1991). The metalworkers developed policies for technological change and flexible working hours, preempting production reforms that employers in other countries were introducing. These policies were developed by the IG Metall leadership but implemented locally through the works councils. During this period, IG Metall's membership expanded while union densities were declining in other OECD countries (Visser 1991, 109). Whether the German pattern is sufficiently common in the advanced capitalist countries to nullify any positive relationship between union decline and flexible work organization is an empirical question, addressed by the data analysis in this chapter.

Parallel to the time series theories of union organization, some researchers claim that unions could resist the negative effects of market conditions or technological change where they actively maintained mobilizing efforts. Preexisting levels of unionization and industrial militancy are emphasized in this account. Indeed, there is a strong empirical association between the size and timing of union decline and union density (Griffin et al. 1990, 90). In northern Europe, labor's flagging fortunes for the most of the 1980s took the form of a slowdown in union growth rather than an outright decline. In France or the United States, by contrast, union density fell by a large amount quite early in the post-oil shock period. This suggests that unions could forestall or avoid density losses where they had sufficient organizational resources. Unions that were organizationally weak were especially vulnerable to deteriorating economic conditions.

Similarly, union movements maintained organization where strike activity increased in the first half of the 1980s (Griffin et al. 1990, 179; Griffin, Botsko, Wahl, and Isaac 1991, 123). The time series analysis suggested that strikes boost union membership when they are deliberately organized to expand organization. Strikes may also have the unintended consequence of rallying workers behind a collective project. Estimates indicate that the large increases in strike activity in Sweden and Denmark between 1979 and 1985 contributed to 4 or 5 percentage points of union density growth, while unionization fell elsewhere (Griffin et al. 1990). "The lesson appears to be that radically intensified class struggle at the point of production can stimulate workers' self-organization" (Griffin et al, 1990, 189). This finding also fits the historical context of growing labor passivity through the 1980s. Internationally, union declines in the last decade have coincided with "the resurgence of labor quiescence" (Shalev 1992). Nearly all OECD countries had fewer industrial disputes in the 1980s than in the 1970s. Only in Scandinavia, where unions historically eschewed the strike in favor of institutional avenues for action, did industrial conflict delay union decline.

The idea that strikes in the post-oil shock period measure worker militancy should be treated with some caution, however. Increasingly through the 1970s and 1980s, industrial disputes may have reflected employer or state actions. Data on industrial disputes do not distinguish between strikes and lockouts, so employer militancy may be captured directly by the data, particularly in this period of intensified employer opposition. Because recent strike activity is framed by an increasingly fragmented institutional context, interunion strife and unilateral strikes by high-wage workers also color industrial relations. Soskice's (1978, 231) warning that strike activity may be "neither a necessary nor sufficient condition for worker militancy" may therefore be especially relevant.

Evidence for the negative effects of strike activity on union decline—driven chiefly by Scandinavian countries—can be viewed in this light (Griffin et al. 1990). For example, Sweden experienced massive strike activity in 1985 compared to the late 1970s while resisting the union density declines that were common throughout the OECD. The working days lost to industrial disputes in Sweden in 1985 largely reflects the May lockout of 80,000 public-sector workers (mostly teachers) in a dispute concerning differences between public and private sector pay levels (*The Economist* 1985; Peterson 1987). The Swedish public-sector workers protested their wage decline in relation to private sector workers, who benefited from wage drift. Swedish industrial militancy in the 1980s thus received its impetus from employers rather than from workers. Instead of generating working class solidarity, militancy reflected wage competition between state and private sector workers. Although worker militancy may boost union organization, this example illustrates the problems of using strike activity to gauge militancy. In interpreting strike data and the effects of strikes on union decline in the 1980s, it is important to examine the historical significance of specific cases.

Explanations of union decline emphasizing world economic conditions and strike activity focus on union-organizing processes at the enterprise or plant level. The institutional argument suggests a different perspective. From the institutional viewpoint, the decentralization of collective bargaining and the declining success of labor parties have been key causes of union decline. Instead of affecting organization at the enterprise or plant level, these institutional changes have reduced unions' capacity to coordinate and advance organizing efforts at the national level.

Changing Labor Market and State Institutions

Between 1950 and 1980, stable institutional variation produced divergent paths of labor movement development. From the late 1970s on, however, institutional continuity was broken. Labor's place in the framework of the capitalist democracies became more marginal as its class-wide representation crumbled in state and labor market institutions. In the labor market, centralized negotiations between top-level representatives of capital and labor broke down in some countries. Within the state, the power of parties to support unions declined as conservative parties widely assumed power through the 1980s.

The Decentralization of Labor Markets

The previous chapter showed that trends toward decentralized labor market relations were widespread in the 1970s and 1980s. Labor market institutions became more decentralized in Australia, Belgium, Denmark, Italy, New Zealand, Sweden, the United Kingdom, and the United States. Just as centralized labor markets provide an institutional mechanism for union growth, labor market decentralization can drive union decline. When collective bargaining is uncoordinated, competition among workers in the labor market sharpens, and the development of broad collective interests and actions becomes difficult. This can be seen in four mechanisms that connect union decline to the decentralization of labor market institutions.

First, centralized labor markets reduce employer opposition to unions. In centralized settings, unions have often secured employer recognition at the national level. With bargaining decentralization, local industrial relations become more important for setting wages and other terms of employment. Under these conditions, the costs of unionism fall mostly on the firm, increasing employer resistance to organized labor. In these circumstances, unions are particularly vulnerable if market pressures reduce militancy. The historical evidence suggests that the effects of employer opposition seem largest when local unions adopt conciliatory stances in bargaining and workplace control (Clegg 1976). In the United States, for example, the union wage premium rose through the 1970s, and decentralized bargaining and union concessions emerged in the early 1980s. These developments set the stage for intensified employer opposition to unions, which accelerated decline in union density in the early 1980s (Freeman and Medoff 1984; Kochan et al. 1986; Freeman 1986b).

Second, because the benefits of union membership accruing from enterprise contracts are focused at the firm level, enlightened employers can reduce the demand for unions by providing wages and conditions competitive with collective agreements. There will be little demand for unions if employers can persuade workers that they would be no better off with union representation. This is a common union avoidance strategy in the United States (Kochan et al. 1986; Trowbridge 1986, 414–17), and there is evidence of its use in France, Germany, and Britain (Rojot 1986; Verma 1990, 178–80). American multinationals, such as IBM, have also exported this strategy of union avoidance to Europe (Crouch 1990, 361).

Third, because decentralization weakens the authority of central union confederations, they have less influence over economic policy. They are less equipped to pursue full-employment policies or to protect unionized jobs. Consequently, unions are placed in a more passive position in the face of shifting economic conditions with unpredictable consequences for union membership. Thus, Crouch (1992, 183) found that the "employer dominated" corporatist regimes of Germany, the Netherlands, and Switzerland controlled inflation at the cost of increasing unemployment in the 1980s, immediately before the large declines in union density in the mid-1980s (see also Scharpf 1987; Visser 1992b, 25). Compare Norway, where the unions retained some role in tripartite policymaking forums through the 1980s. Norwegian unemployment was kept relatively low, and falls in union membership due to job loss were kept to a minimum.

Finally, with labor market decentralization, interunion rivalry sharpens, organizing becomes more uncoordinated, and resources are increasingly spent on jurisdictional disputes. For instance, jurisdictional disputes were historically rare and resolved at the national level in Sweden. Labor market decentralization, however, was accompanied by increased competition between the blue-collar and white-collar confederations. Jurisdictional disputes also arose over the organization of skilled workers (Ahlén 1989) immediately before the declines of the late 1980s.

The Decline of Social Democracy

Several writers relate the economic conditions of the early 1970s to the declining success of social democratic parties and the growing popularity of conservative or center parties (Pontusson 1992b; Scharpf 1987). Economic developments in the 1970s placed increasing stress on the Keynesian policy packages of European social democracy. Wage restraint could not control unemployment, and high inflation made wage restraint hard to implement. Recession combined with growing competition from newly industrializing countries led Esping-Andersen (1985, 289) to conclude that a "real incompatibility" exists in Scandinavia between social democrats' welfare goals and continued economic vitality. The strains the world economy placed on social democratic policies seemed ultimately overwhelming following the second oil shock of

1979–1980, when renewed recession resulted in an electoral backlash against many social democratic and labor governments of the 1970s.

While the victories of Thatcher, Reagan, and Kohl were the most visible, similar political trends can be found in Scandinavia, where traditional bourgeois parties and newly formed tax revolt movements achieved unprecedented electoral success (Andersen and Bjørkland 1990). After forty-four years of continuous incumbency, the Swedish Social Democrats lost office between 1976 and 1982 and again in 1991; the Danish Social Democrats sat in the opposition benches for most of the 1980s; and the Finnish Social Democrats were unseated in 1991 for the first time in twenty-five years. In countries where social democrats historically had been less successful, such as Belgium and the Netherlands, parties of the left were excluded from governing coalitions for most of the 1980s. More generally, in five out of nine OECD countries surveyed by Pontusson (1992b), the social democratic vote declined in the 1980s compared to in the 1970s. Where social democrats retained a share of government, traditional expansionary economic and social policies were often abandoned (see also Kitschelt 1994).

This sea change in parliamentary politics reduced unions' capacity for organization (Hyman 1992, 156–57). In the past, labor movements with close links to governing leftist parties could influence state policy to protect unionized jobs and secure legislative or administrative protection from employers. Union influence over state policy declined with the rise of nonlabor parties throughout the 1980s. In Belgium, Martens's Christian Social coalition of 1980 preempted collective bargaining by instituting incomes policies without union consultation (Spineux 1990, 49–50). Similar developments followed the defeat of the Social Democrats in Denmark in 1982, leading Amoroso (1990) to predict that "the outcome [of Conservative government] should be a weakened trade union movement bargaining with a strengthened employers organization within an economic framework dictated by the government" (77). Where social democratic parties remained in government, as in Germany in the late 1970s and Sweden in the late 1980s, austerity policies were proposed that involved cuts in welfare benefits and public employment (Scharpf 1987; Pontusson 1992c). Under these conditions, governments had less to gain from political exchange with the unions and less to offer in return. At a minimum, then, the decline of social democracy removed unions from the corridors of state power.

In a few countries, notably Britain and the United States, incoming conservative parties actively opposed labor organization. In Britain, following the Conservative party victory of 1979, the first of five Employment Acts that radically restricted the rights of unions was passed. By 1990, all legal protections had been removed for the closed shop. Union activists were also subject to a variety of new legal penalties, and sympathy strikes were outlawed. The new legal framework was combined with an antiunion policy in the public sector. On this front, collective bargaining for state employees was restricted and decentralized, and unionized workers were replaced with unorganized contractors (Marsh 1992). The Conservative resolve to oppose unions was also demonstrated in several clashes with striking workers, most prominently in the miner's strike of 1984–1985 (Adeney and Lloyd 1986).

A similar antiunion offensive emerged in the United States under the Reagan administration. The Republican approach to unionism was announced during the air traffic controllers' strike of 1981, which culminated in mass firings, hiring of nonunion employees, and decertification of the air traffic controllers' union, the Professional Air Traffic Controllers Association (PATCO). Although PATCO was small numerically, the dispute was symbolically important for U.S. industrial relations in the early 1980s (Northrup and Thornton 1988, 127). The administration's victory over the strikers helped establish the "union-free" environment as a legitimate goal for employers. The PATCO strike also demonstrated the feasibility of hiring permanent replacements to break strikes and unions. In addition, the Reagan administration implemented more concrete measures, including the appointment of antiunion commissioners to the National Labor Relations Board. Under the first Reagan-appointed chairman, Donald Dotson, more than forty of the Labor Board's doctrines were overturned, contributing to an "active regulatory constraint" on unionism in the 1980s (Weiler 1990, 19). In one line of decisions by the Reagan Labor Board, unfair labor practices—the dismissal of union members, or intimidation of prounion workers—no longer imposed an obligation on employers to recognize the unions (Gould 1993, 21). These rulings coincided with the rapid escalation of unfair labor practice violations through the early 1980s (Freeman 1988, 80).

In sum, where prolabor parties lost power, unions' organizing capacity weakened. Union influence on economic policy was often restricted when leftist parties lost office and unions could no longer protect employment in sectors that were highly organized or organizable. Incumbent social democrats were also less supportive of union goals. Finally, in several instances, unions faced hostile conservative governments that actively resisted unionization and encouraged employer opposition to unions.

A Statistical Model of Union Decline

In the remainder of this chapter, I investigate a model that focuses specifically on the downturns in unionization. Here, I try to explain the negative change in the unionization trajectory of a particular country. Instead of assuming that the causes of deunionization are simply the reverse of the causes of union growth, this model views downturns as qualitatively new developments in the trajectories of labor movements. The cost of this specification is a loss of information in the dependent variable. Instead of being treated as continuous, the union density series are dichotomized; key events in the series—sharp negative shifts in unionization trends—are marked by discrete indicators.

The Union Decline Variable

Union declines can be identified by examining first and second differences in the union density time series. The first difference is defined as the annual change in union density; the second difference is the annual change in the first difference. Formally, if d_t is a country's union density in year t, the first difference is given by $\Delta d_t = d_t - d_{t-1}$, and the second difference is given by $\Delta^2 d_t = \Delta d_t - \Delta d_{t-1}$. The two series of differences, Δd and $\Delta^2 d$, give the unionization trend and the change in trend for each year. Accelerating union decline is indicated by negative first and second differences. Working with differences of the smoothed union density series usefully eliminates the effects of several small spikes in a series. The robust smoother used here is based on the means of running medians (Goodall 1990). The smoothed series effectively distinguishes the trend and rough components of the raw series so that the second difference of the smoothed series provides a clear indication of changes in trend. The point of union decline is then defined on the smoothed series as the year of the smallest second difference, given that the first difference is also negative. The year of union decline is described by the set

$$T = \{t; \min (\Delta^2 d_t), \Delta d_t < 0\}. \qquad (11.1)$$

In other words, union decline occurs at the point of most rapidly accelerating deunionization. The year of union decline identifies inflection points in the union density series. Substantively, this definition of union decline as a point of accelerating deunionization includes a range of shifts in unionization trends. Downturns include small declines in unionization after a period of growth, as in Belgium and Denmark in the mid-1980s; they also include accelerated declines, as in France and the United States in the late 1970s and early 1980s. (The robustness of results to this measurement strategy is discussed in Western [1995b].)

Table 11.1 reports the year of union decline and the magnitude of the decline as measured by the second differences of the smoothed series. Consistent with claims that 1980 marked the beginning of union decline in these countries (Pontusson 1992a; Hall 1987; Visser 1991; Griffin et al. 1990), only the low-union density countries began their accelerated decline in the 1970s. Just two countries, Sweden and Finland, show no sharp decline in unionization.

TABLE 11.1
Year and Magnitude of Union Decline, Eighteen OECD
Countries, 1973–1989

	Year of Union Decline	Magnitude of Decline
High-density countries		
Belgium	1984	−0.1
Denmark	1986	−0.8
Finland	—	—
Sweden	—	—
Middle-density countries		
Australia	1982	−0.3
Austria	1985	−0.2
Canada	1982	−0.1
Germany	1981	−0.4
Ireland	1981	−0.8
Italy	1980	−0.4
New Zealand	1983	−0.8
Norway	1983	−0.3
United Kingdom	1980	−1.2
Low-density countries		
France	1977	−0.4
Japan	1978	−0.3
Netherlands	1979	−0.6
Switzerland	1978	−0.6
United States	1980	−0.3

Note: Magnitude of decline is defined as the second difference of
the smoothed union density time series in the year of union decline.

While this design is geared to explaining the union declines that were un-
detectable with conventional models, sharply accelerating union declines (as
in Ireland or the United Kingdom) are treated as qualitatively similar to more
modest changes in trend (as in Austria or Norway). This limitation is addressed
to some degree through a sensitivity analysis that examines how the results
depend on information from each country.

If unionization downturns are treated as qualitatively new developments,
the probability of a downturn can be modeled as a function of time and some
predictor variables, which may vary over time. Following the approach of
the analysis of bargaining decentralization, discrete-time hazard rate models
provide a simple framework for examining how the probability of union
decline depends on time and explanatory variables. With this model, annual
data are collected from each country up to the year of accelerating deunionization. Each country scores 0 on the dependent variable for each year,
except the downturn year, which is coded 1. Countries with no union decline

(Finland and Sweden) are censored, scoring 0 for all years. In this specification, large unions, with the help of a healthy economy and a strong institutional presence in the labor market and state, can both delay and resist decline. I obtain estimates of the effects of the explanatory variables from a logistic regression on the stacked time series collected for each country. Diagnostics show that data are underdispersed. This means that the dependent variable has smaller variance than we would conventionally assume. I thus use quasi-likelihood methods to estimate an extra component of dispersion in the dependent variable (McCullagh and Nelder 1989, 124–28). I explore the quasi-likelihood fit by comparing its estimates to a robust fit that down-weights outlying observations (Pregibon 1982). This robust fit serves the dual purpose of providing a summary of the data that resists the influence of outliers while flagging outlying observations (with very small weights) for further analysis.

Independent Variables

I argue that the historic downturn in unionization in the 1980s was fueled by hostile world economic conditions, dwindling mobilization efforts, and labor's deteriorating institutional position in the market and the state. To capture the effects of international competition and recession, I relate changes in unionization trends to economic openness (exports and imports as a percentage of GDP) and unemployment. Increases in each variable precipitate union decline: union membership is directly eroded through job loss, and employers resist unions to remain competitive on world markets. Although produced by the pressures of global competition, work reorganization is thought to be a causally proximate source of union decline. It could be argued that more direct measures of flexible work organization should be used. Unfortunately, more direct measures of work organization are seriously incomplete (Hall 1987, 10). I investigated proxies, such as the level of Japanese direct investment, economic concentration, and average firm size, but these were either unavailable in a time series or were missing for some countries.

Mobilization efforts are measured by strike activity and preexisting organization. Following the analysis of union decline by Griffin and his colleagues (1990), I measure labor militancy by the number of days lost because of industrial action, standardized by the size of the labor force. Union organization is buoyed by strike activity, which serves as a rallying point for workers; thus increasing strike activity should hinder union decline. The preexisting level of unionization is measured with a lagged union density variable. We expect that large unions have the organizational resources to resist union decline.

TABLE 11.2
Description of Variables Used in the Analysis

Variable	Description
Dependent variable	
Union decline	A binary variable indicating the year of the union decline defined in equation (11.1)
Independent variable	
Economic openness	Annual change in exports plus imports as a percentage of GDP (Penn World Tables, Mark 5; see Summers and Heston 1991)
Unemployment	Annual change in unemployment rate (OECD 1987, 1990)
Strike activity	Annual rate of change in days lost due to industrial disputes per 1,000 employed workers (ILO 1975–1992; OECD 1987, 1990)
Union density	The percentage of the dependent labor force that is union members, lagged one year
Decentralization	A binary variable indicating the year of decentralization of collective bargaining; nine countries experienced decentralization
Left representation in government	Proportion of cabinet seats held by labor, social democratic, and communist parties (*Keesing's Contemporary Archives* 1972–1985)

Note: Four observations for Belgian strike activity were imputed, using wage, GDP growth, leftist parties' share of vote, and strike data from the Netherlands.

The decentralization of labor market institutions is indicated by a dummy variable. The bargaining-decentralization points are taken from the review of changes in industrial relations institutions in Chapter 10. For example, Sweden scores 0 in all years up to 1983, and 1 in subsequent years, following the dissolution of centralized bargaining and the establishment of independent negotiations in the metalworking industry. Decentralization of bargaining should also drive the downturn in unionization. The cabinet representation of prolabor political parties should also forestall union decline. Table 11.2 presents the definitions and sources for the independent variables.

Time series data begin at 1973—the turning point in the world economy—and end at the year of union decline in each country. Table 11.3 reports the number of years from 1973 to the unionization downturn, measured by the smoothed model. For instance, ten observations from Australia are used for analysis, covering the period from 1973 until union decline in 1982. Adding all the survival times plus the time series lengths for the two censored countries gives a total of 179 nation-years for analysis. Table 11.3 also provides some summary statistics for the explanatory variables.

TABLE 11.3
Unionization Survival Times and Summary Statistics for Independent Variables,
Eighteen OECD Countries, 1973–1989

	(1)	(2)	(3)	(4)	(5)	(6)
High-density countries						
Belgium	12	.14	65	2.8	.89	7
Denmark	14	.64	75	1.9	.33	1,279
Finland	—	.55	78	1.9	.12	149
Sweden	—	.62	86	2.2	−.07	1,259
Middle-density countries						
Australia	10	.30	52	1.4	.44	14
Austria	13	.95	58	1.3	.23	147
Canada	10	.60	32	−0.2	.47	6
Germany	9	.74	40	2.9	.41	1,121
Ireland	9	.17	56	5.5	.41	36
Italy	8	.00	49	2.4	.15	10
New Zealand	11	.27	44	1.1	.47	14
Norway	11	.91	60	0.7	.15	440
United Kingdom	8	.62	52	3.7	.31	34
Low-density countries						
France	5	.00	21	3.1	.44	−7
Japan	6	.00	34	2.1	.13	−8
Netherlands	7	.31	39	9.0	.46	641
Switzerland	6	.29	34	8.2	.05	67
United States	8	.50	23	1.5	.19	−2

Notes: Column headings are as follows: (1) Number of Years from 1973 to Union Decline;
(2) Mean Left Representation in Government; (3) Mean Lagged Union Density; (4) Mean
Change in Economic Openness; (5) Mean Change in Unemployment; and (6) Mean Percentage
Change in Strike Activity.
Finland and Sweden data are censored at 1988.

Results

Model Estimates

The results shown in Table 11.4 indicate that the hazard model provides a good
fit to the data, successfully predicting the timing of sharp union decline in ten
of the sixteen uncensored countries. In the remaining six countries, the predicted probability of decline is highest in the year of accelerating deunionization. Estimated coefficients provide strong evidence for all effects except
strike activity. The positive effect of the decentralization of collective bargaining is particularly strong. The estimate suggests that the decentralization of
collective bargaining increases the probability of union decline from about .3
to more than .8. Although the crude dummy variable may be expressing un-

TABLE 11.4
Quasi-Likelihood and Robust Coefficients from Discrete-Time Hazard Rate Model of Union Decline, Eighteen OECD Countries, 1973–1989

Independent Variable	Quasi-Likelihood Coefficient	Robust Coefficient	Cross-Validation Bounds	Extreme Bounds
Constant	−1.99	−2.68	(−3.20, −1.45)	(−5.28, −0.69)
	(2.58)	(2.59)		
Time	1.37	1.74	(1.28, 1.81)	(0.24, 1.37)
	(6.45)	(5.46)		
Economic openness	0.11	0.16	(0.06, 0.15)	(−0.01, 0.11)
	(2.75)	(2.98)		
Unemployment	1.13	1.50	(0.92, 1.40)	(0.56, 1.15)
	(3.48)	(3.39)		
Strike activity	0.42	0.84	(−8.16, 2.12)	(−0.23, 0.21)
	(0.13)	(0.22)		
Union density (lagged)	−0.23	−0.30	(−0.29, −0.21)	(−0.23, −0.11)
	(6.19)	(5.37)		
Decentralization	2.84	4.43	(1.93, 3.83)	(−0.49, 2.84)
	(3.63)	(3.90)		
Left representation in government	−3.50	−4.00	(−5.63, −3.17)	(−3.16, −1.68)
	(4.48)	(4.02)		
DISPERSION	0.36	0.42		

Notes: Numbers in parentheses below coefficients are absolute t statistics. Strike activity coefficients and bounds have been multiplied by 10^4.

measured time-dependent effects, this estimate provides strong evidence that the erosion of corporatist institutions can, by itself, make union decline quite likely. The negative coefficient for left representation in government is also consistent with expectations: social democratic cabinet representation substantially lowers the odds of a downturn in union density. This result is consistent with the historical experience of Sweden and Finland, where social democratic parties retained cabinet representation through more of the 1980s and working-class organization was maintained until the late 1980s. Despite the rightward shift of incumbent social democratic parties, unions retained membership more successfully under parties of the left than under conservatives or Christian democrats.

Supporting Freeman's (1989) claim that economic stagnation in the wake of the oil shocks created a "crisis of unionism," parameter estimates suggest that recession and increasing international competition raise the chances of accelerating union disorganization. According to these estimates, the odds of union decline more than doubled in the small European countries, where the value of imports and exports grew annually by 10 percentage points in the late 1970s and early 1980s. The effect of unemployment on the likelihood of a downturn in unionization is also substantial: an increase of a single percentage point in the annual unemployment rate—modest by the standards of 1970s recession— is estimated to multiply the odds of union decline by about three.

Consistent with the descriptive statistics and other research (Griffin et al. 1990), lagged union density is negatively related to union decline. This suggests that weakly organized union movements with few organizing resources and with membership concentrated in traditional industry sectors are highly vulnerable to unionization downturns. The magnitude of this effect can be illustrated by comparing two countries that are similar in many respects except union density. Canada and the United States are institutionally alike, but Canadian union density exceeds American union density by about 15 percentage points. A set of typical values for Canada in the late 1970s generates an estimated probability of union decline of around .3. Replacing Canadian with U.S. union density while keeping all the other values exactly the same generates an estimated probability of union decline of .8.

Finally, the effect of strike activity finds the least support from the data. Contrary to theory, the coefficient is positive and is estimated with considerable imprecision. This may be a result of the extreme volatility of the strike data: large outliers may be suppressing an accurate estimate of the effect. Outliers can be identified by examining leverages, which express the influence of observations on the coefficients. Leverages range between 0 and 1, with outliers scoring greater than about .2 in this analysis (McCullagh and Nelder 1989, 405). Diagnostics revealed a large leverage point (greater than .5) for Germany, resulting from a massive spike in the strike data in 1978. From a statistical point of view, it is useful to fit the outlier separately with a dummy variable to investigate its influence on the model estimates. While the coefficient for strike activity becomes about 20 percent larger, all other estimates change little as a result of fitting the exceptional German case.

The outlier's historical significance provides further insight into the relationship between strikes and union decline. The high level of industrial unrest in Germany in 1978 was driven in part by a large strike and retaliatory lockout in the printing industry when employers introduced new technology that allowed newspaper reporters to file their stories directly on typesetting computers, threatening redundancy of skilled typesetters and the reclassification of typesetting as a clerical job (Flanagan et al. 1983, 244–45). This outlier again illustrates that data on industrial disputes may reflect employer offensives as well as working-class militancy. Indeed, the German experience suggests a spurious positive relationship between strike activity and union decline in situations where workers are unsuccessfully protesting work force reductions.

Table 11.4 shows the results from a robust estimator that downweights poorly fitting observations. For the robust estimator, all coefficients retain their signs and precision. The two institutional variables show the greatest change. The decentralization effect becomes about two-thirds larger on the linear scale and the coefficient for left government representation displays a similar shift in the negative direction. The effect of strike activity, by contrast, approaches 0.

The weights from the robust fit show that the two censored cases, Sweden and Finland, generally fit the model less well than do the other countries. Indeed, the robust estimator practically excludes the influence of Sweden altogether. Put another way, although conditions were ripe for union decline, labor leaders in these two countries managed to avoid the losses that occurred elsewhere in the OECD. For Sweden, there is additional evidence that the model works reasonably well, but the union density series is censored before the decline is observed. Union densities in Sweden fell in 1988 and continued to decline through the early 1990s. The LO lost membership in 1988 for the first time since 1933 (EIRR 1989c, 1991b). Although censoring Finland also generates an outlier identified by the robust estimator, the model seems to capture the unusually healthy state of the unions in Finland. Finland's predicted probability of decline in 1988, the year of censoring, is only .28.

Sensitivity Analysis

Although the results seem strong, uncertainty about the data and the model specification have not been addressed. Thus, for example, the year of bargaining decentralization was specified precisely, but this is a stylization of the historical record in those countries where institutional change was not marked by a single decisive event. To assess the sensitivity of the results to information from particular countries in the data set, I report some cross-validation results based on reestimation of the model with one country omitted from the analysis. Reestimating the model this way for all eighteen countries provides a range of coefficients that indicates variability due to the influence of each country. The robustness of the results, presented in Table 11.4, is clear. The sign of each coefficient, except the one for strike activity, remains stable for many data subsets. The cross-validation results provide slightly stronger evidence for the effect of strike activity, as most of the cross-validation coefficients are in the hypothesized negative direction.

Observed effects may also depend on the reported model specification. A systematic approach to this problem of specification uncertainty involves examining how coefficients respond to changes in the model (Leamer 1983). This "extreme bounds analysis" investigates variability in a coefficient when all possible subsets of the other independent variables are included in the model. The bounds reported in Table 11.4 show the smallest and largest coefficients that result from this manipulation of the model specification. Here, the results are a little less reassuring. The signs of most coefficients are stable, although both the strike activity and decentralization effects are sensitive to the model specification. The instability of the strike effect is not surprising, since it appears to be only weakly related to union decline. On the other hand, a large positive estimate for the bargaining decentralization variable depends crucially on the inclusion of the union density predictor. Without union density in the model, the coefficients for the decentralization effect are mostly small and negative. Pessimistically, we might conclude that evidence for the decentralization effect is modest, given its sensitivity to the model specification. From a more optimistic standpoint, this sensitivity is not too troubling, because our prior belief in the union density effect is quite strong. Because it makes strong theoretical sense that union decline depends strongly on preexisting union densities, confidence in the bargaining decentralization effect is increased.

If institutional variation is used to explain the divergent paths of labor movement development, how do we explain the common pattern of union decline in the 1980s? Institutional changes rooted in shifts in the world economy have fueled the union density losses of the last two decades. Specifically, the decentralization of collective bargaining and the electoral failure of labor parties are associated with the near-universal and historically novel decline of union organization in the 1980s. During this decade, unions lacked the institutional resources to resist the pressures for decline that stemmed from recession and an increasingly uncertain economic climate. Weakly organized labor forces were most vulnerable to deunionization. On the other hand, the data suggest that strike activity does little to resist union decline.

Twelve

Conclusion

THE FUTURE of unions in the 1990s looks remarkably different from their prospects at the beginning of the 1950s. The early 1950s were a highwater mark. The importance of unions to postwar capitalism was widely recognized, and organizational strength was unprecedented. Nearly fifty years later the big industrial organizations that symbolized the power of organized labor appeared poised for obsolescence. Recession, global competition, and increasing economic uncertainty undermined unions and the institutional frameworks in which they developed.

It was not the business cycle, not the structure of the economy, not even the resistance of employers that was chiefly important for explaining the growth of postwar union movements. Instead, labor market and state institutions were critical. They provided the context in which political and economic forces on the workplace were played out. The right configuration of institutions could be found in Belgium, Denmark, Finland, and Sweden. In those countries, centralized representation in industrial relations transformed whole labor forces into union constituencies. The weakest and most vulnerable in the labor market were included in the labor movement through Ghent systems. Centralized labor markets and union-run unemployment insurance reformulated the logic of union growth. With these institutions, union density withstood recessions and extended well beyond the core manufacturing industries. Close links to working-class parties gave unions another way of uncoupling their fortunes from the market. Social democratic parties advanced union interests through the state, bypassing the market forces that conventionally constrain union growth. The impact of such parties is clearest in Scandinavia. The Belgian Socialist party was electorally weaker, and unionization among employed workers was lower than in northern Europe.

The institutional sources of union growth were more poorly approximated in other countries. In Norway and Austria, labor markets were centralized and unions shared strong ties to successful social democratic parties. However, the state, not the unions, ran unemployment insurance. Union organization was high in these countries, but both failed to achieve the near-universal union membership that we see in Sweden and Finland. In Australia, New Zealand, Ireland, and the United Kingdom, industry bargaining rather than national bargaining predominated, and Labour had not become the natural party of government in the fashion of the Nordic Social Democrats. Unions, at least until the

1980s, steadily organized about half the labor forces of these countries. From the early 1970s on, the Italian labor movement followed a similar path. The crowning moment of the Italian labor movement in the Hot Autumn of 1969 set the unions there on a new course of expansion. By the beginning of the 1980s, Italian union organization had surpassed British levels. Canada provides a diluted version of the British model: coordination in the labor market through pattern bargaining and a labor party that was strong principally at the provincial level. Under these conditions, unions organized about a third of the labor market through the postwar period.

In Germany, the institutional context was supportive of organized labor, but union representation was strongly patterned by gender. Durable industry bargaining and a politically powerful central confederation closely tied to the Social Democrats provided important mechanisms for union growth. Yet German union density was low compared to, say, that of Britain or Australia. While unions organized about half the work force in the English-speaking countries, German union density was 10 to 15 points lower. A clue here is provided by the unusually large gender gap in German union membership. Low union representation among German women significantly reduced overall density. If men and women were organized at similar rates—as in Sweden or Denmark—German union organization would be nearly 10 points higher.

The impact of gender on union membership is even stronger in the Netherlands and Switzerland. In both those countries, union membership among women was extremely low. Compounding this effect, left parties were weaker than in Germany, involved in government only through large coalitions. In Switzerland the political left was neutralized to some degree by the stable pattern of grand coalitions in the Federal Council. The Dutch Socialists were often in opposition, most critically perhaps during the hard times of the late 1970s. Recession in the Netherlands was especially severe. Unemployment had risen to over 10 percent by 1982 and remained high through the following decade. Without a compensating mechanism such as the Ghent system, union membership was seriously depleted.

In the absence of centralized labor markets, Ghent systems, or successful working-class parties, the news for organized labor was mostly bad. In France, Japan, and the United States, falling unionization dominated the postwar period. Unions in these countries reflected, rather than restructured, the distribution of power in the marketplace. The fateful influence of economic conditions—the business cycle and the industrial structure—strengthened unions in some cases but devastated them in others. Collective action in the labor market was restricted to the public sector or traditional industries, and easily unraveled through recessions. Class had no concrete institutional reality in these settings. This was clearest in Japan and the United States, where a business unionism that rejected broader political goals was woven into the surrounding institional frameworks of the state and the economy. Ironically perhaps, this business unionism was victimized by the market economy it accomodated. The model was perfected in the United States, where cutthroat competition among workers and unbridled employer resistance to unions defeated labor organization throughout the postwar period. The narrow economic role that unions filled under these conditions was reduced further by alarming falls in density and membership after the oil price shocks of 1973 and 1974.

How do we make sense of the recent period? If labor markets are institutional constructions that can build class-wide collective action under almost any economic conditions, why do we now see cracks in even the most powerful European unions, just when economic competition has intensified? If anything, the recent period takes us to the edge of the current analysis. Recent developments represent not the triumph of markets over institutions, but the limited capacity of national institutions to regulate the effects of a global institutional context. Because the institutions that promoted union growth are aligned with national boundaries, their power over market competition from abroad is weak. Once trade was liberalized, exchange rates were deregulated, and newly industrializing countries expanded manufacturing exports, competition intensified in the international marketplace. Global economic forces contributed to union decline in two ways. First, the growth in world trade eroded the competitive position of the unionized labor forces of the OECD and compelled the reorganization of mass production industries. Without an encompassing institutional framework that could nullify labor market competition from beyond national borders, unionization widely declined in the 1980s. Second, the institutional sources of union growth had themselves come under stress. Social democrats lost office in many countries through the 1980s, labor markets became more decentralized, and union density decline followed. In short, the unity of nation-class organizations rooted in national institutions was outflanked by an emergent international institutional context.

In two countries the effects of globalization were accelerated. The unparalleled political offensives of Thatcher and Reagan in the 1980s crippled the labor movements of Britain and the United States. Thatcher's innovation was to build a formal legal framework where none had previously existed. This significantly reduced the ability of unions to coordinate, and enhanced the capacity of employers to resist. Reagan, on the other hand, restaffed the existing legal machinery with staunch union opponents. As employers, both governments took a strong hand against unions, fueling hostility to labor in the private sector. In this way, the organizing principle of class was forcibly eliminated from industrial relations. In its place, the fragmented relations of the market came to dominate economic imagery in policy, management philosophy, and labor negotiations.

Although these are vivid examples of union defeat, we should be careful to distinguish level and trend as we think about the future of labor movements. Unionization was falling through the 1980s, and collective bargaining became more decentralized in about half of the eighteen countries I surveyed. Despite these convergent trends to labor movement decline, institutional divergence still dominates the working classes of the advanced capitalist countries. Union density in the 1990s varies between about 10 and 90 percent. Labor market institutions in Austria, Germany, and Scandinavia remain significantly more centralized than in Britain or the United States. By 1990, collective agreements still covered well over half of all European workers. The postwar labor movements of the capitalist democracies have thus been pushed in similar directions by the growth of world markets, but institutional variation remains strongly imprinted on the individual trajectories.

What about the future? Can the continued growth of world markets eliminate institutional differences and force the convergence of capitalist labor markets on a generic model of deregulation and unlimited competition? This is certainly a scenario discussed by students of European integration. Most obstacles to the mobility of labor, capital, and goods are now removed within Europe, exposing workers even further to market pressures. The prospect of monetary unification further darkens the picture since such unification will remove from national control an important policy instrument for protecting labor in exposed sectors. In this context, some researchers have discussed the possibility of union organization and collective bargaining across national boundaries (Tilly 1995; Visser and Ebbinghaus 1995). Transnational organization might enable unions to find an institutionalized power base that is independent of world market fluctuations. With institutions such as these, the national stories of this book could be reproduced on an international scale. International institutions could redistribute bargaining power and resources across national boundaries. While we see hints of transnational industrial relations in Europe, there are still substantial obstacles (Streeck 1993, 90–97). Regional inequality—within Europe alone—is high, so cheap labor promises big returns to capital mobility. Employer organization is also fragmented. If unions in different countries were able to present a united front, it is unclear with whom they would bargain.

Can we thus expect a convergent pattern of union decline as long as national institutions regulate industrial relations battered by global markets? Perhaps not. The analysis of bargaining decentralization suggested that similar market pressures can result in a variety of outcomes because of diverse institutional starting points. Market-driven convergence is unlikely under even the most competitive economic conditions. The examination of bargaining decentralization found an alternative source of union power in local, rather than centralized, labor market institutions. The works council was the key institution for this analysis. Through a guarantee of employee representation in the workplace, works councils offered flexibility, productivity, and political voice. These micro-institutional outcomes compensated for the rigidities of centralized labor markets. Facing a volatile world economy, institutionalized workplace representation thus contributed to the continuity of national labor market regimes. If this analysis is right, the future of labor movements may rest more with micro institutions like these, than with the barely realized possibility of globalized macro institutions. To the extent that works councils are rooted in national or European systems of industrial relations, and to the extent that they allow workers to collectively contribute to productivity and employment security, we can understand them as class institutions. That is, works councils such as these provide a a kind of universal representation that reduces competition in the labor market. In this picture, unions work for employment security and worker participation through their contribution to productivity within the firm.

Although the form is very different, the underlying institutional logic here resembles that of our macro institutions—centralized labor markets, left parties, and the Ghent system. These speculations about the future of labor movements thus brings us full circle. Novel economic conditions may trigger institutional innovation, but the fundamental mechanisms remain the same. Unions flourish where they are institutionally insulated from the market forces that drive competition among workers. Without institutional protection, collective action among workers depends on the caprice of the market. Universal, class-wide representation remains threatened by fragmented market exchange. From this perspective, class and market exist in ongoing tension in capitalist democracies, and the permanent victory of one over the other is unlikely. The future of trade unions is thus contested but secure—contested while markets offer the temptation of private rewards, but secure in the conflicting interests of bosses and workers.

Appendix _____

Data and Methods

Chapter Two. Variation in Union Membership

Data Sources

In this chapter and throughout the book unless otherwise indicated, union density figures are from Visser's (1992a) gross density series. New Zealand figures were amended with data from various years of the *New Zealand Official Yearbook*. The Japanese series was lengthened by using Kuwahara's (1987) data. The density series includes retired and unemployed members in union membership counts. Only the Italian membership series is seriously incomplete, missing Italian Confederation of Labor (UIL) confederation membership figures for years prior to 1969. The Italian membership series was adjusted by interpolating UIL figures from the 1950s and 1960s. For several countries, there are breaks in the dependent labor force series that form the denominator for the union density statistic. These were smoothed to eliminate discontinuities in the density series.

Chapter Six. Cross-Sectional Analysis
of Union Density

Bayesian Regression

The discussion focused on the selection of prior means and variances for the regression coefficients. To complete the Bayesian specification, the shapes of prior distributions for all the model parameters must also be chosen. Certain choices, called conjugate priors, are particularly computationally tractable. In the linear regression with normal errors, the conjugate analysis places Normal prior distributions on the regression coefficients and a Gamma distribution on the inverse of the variance. Regression analysis with this Normal-Gamma prior is described in Gelman et al. (1995, ch. 8).

The unusual feature of this analysis was the priors for simultaneity. Following Leamer's (1991) discussion, the regression of interest is

$$d - b_0 + b_1 g + b_2 c + b_3 l + e,$$

where d is union density, g is a dummy variable indicating countries with Ghent systems, c is labor market centralization, and l is left government. If this equation is estimated, b_3 is likely to be biased upwards because d drives up the level of l. With l depending on other exogenous variables, w, the conditional mean of d can be written as

$$d \mid g, c, l, w = (b_0 + b_1 g + b_2 c + b_3 l + e)$$
$$+ (b_0^* + b_1^* g + b_2^* c + b_3^* l + b_4^* w + e^*).$$

Here, the starred coefficients describe the bias due to simultaneity. Although there is perfect collinearity in this equation, there are no problems of estimation as long as some of the coefficients are specified to have a proper prior distribution. The problem then reduces to specifying prior distributions for the coefficients of interest, b_i, and the simultaneity coefficients, b_j^*. Leamer (1991) describes how to elicit these priors given beliefs about the size of the feedback coefficient and the prior ratio of error variances from equations for the two endogenous variables. In the current analysis, the feedback coefficient was given a prior mean of .01, and the variance ratio was .1.

Regression Analysis with Measurement Error

The simulation approach elaborates a resampling plan suggested by Chatterjee and Hadi (1988). The innovation in this chapter is the heterogeneity allowed the measurement error. Symmetric probability distributions for measurement error were represented with suitably rescaled and relocated Beta distributions, with shape parameters $\alpha = 4$ and $\beta = 4$. Skewness was introduced by resetting one of the shape parameters to 2. Inferences were based on 2,000 replications of the resampling plan. It is difficult to reconcile the resampling approach taken here with the generally Bayesian approach to inference adopted throughout the book. Still, the resampling approach seems to have some intuitive appeal and provides a way of taking account of several sources of uncertainty and bias in the analysis.

Chapter Seven. The Business Cycle and Union Growth

The Robust Hierarchical Model

Use of the t distribution in robust regression has been surveyed by Lange, Little, and Taylor (1989). Maximum likelihood estimation with the t distribution yields a redescending M-estimator of the type described by Mosteller and Tukey (1977). The likelihood justification for the t model facilitates its generalization to data with more complicated structures (Western 1995a).

The model can be formally written as follows. For each of $j = 1, \ldots, 18$ countries, we have a vector of time series coefficients, b_j with $i = 1, \ldots, 6$ elements, and a matrix of longitudinal predictors, x_j. The conditional distribution of union density growth, Δd, is given the outlier-resistant t distribution:

$$\Delta d_j \sim t\,(\mu_j, \psi_j, \nu = 4),$$

where the dispersion, ψ_j, varies across countries, and the conditional mean is written $\mu_j = x_j\,b_j$. The degrees of freedom parameter, $\nu = 4$, was chosen with a little experimentation. Degrees of freedom in this vicinity yielded very similar results, suggesting that the likelihood is flat in this region, but higher than at $\nu = \infty$, the Normal specification. As is typical in multilevel models, each of the six 18-vectors of time series coefficients, b_i, for each predictor was assumed to be Normal, conditional on the matrix of institutional data, z:

$$b_i \sim N(\eta_i, \sigma_i^2),$$

where, $\eta_i = z\gamma_i$. Diffuse Normal-Gamma priors were placed on the time series coefficients, b, and the institutional coefficients, γ.

Unfortunately, the t distribution in this specification is somewhat intractable and conventional numerical methods would be difficult to justify in this finite sample situation. The estimates reported here are based simulation from the posterior distribution using the Gibbs sampler (e.g., Tanner 1992).

Data Sources

Consumer price inflation rate. Data for all countries are from the International Monetary Fund's International Financial Statistics (International Monetary Fund 1990).

Unemployment rate. Most data are taken from OECD (1963, 1980, 1987). The Australian series was completed with data from Bain and Elsheikh (1976). Austrian data for 1950–1961 were estimated by using unemployment figures reconstructed from Visser (1989) and linear interpolation of OECD (1963) total labor force figures. The Danish series was extended with data from various years of the Danish *Statistiske Efterretninger*. Swiss data for 1969–1973 were obtained from OECD (1980). ILO (various years) data were used to complete series for the following countries: Finland (1950–1958), France (1950–1953), Italy (1950–1954), Japan (1950–1952), New Zealand (1950–1953), Switzerland (1950–1959).

Employment growth. Data for the growth in the dependent labor force were taken from Visser (1992a). For Japan, figures for the total number of employees from the *Japan Yearbook* were used for 1950–1960. For New Zealand, civilian labor force data were used, from the *Official New Zealand Yearbook* for 1950–1960 and OECD (1974, 1991b) *Labour Force Statistics*. The Danish data are based on Visser's (1989) wage- and salary-earner series. A few missing values have been interpolated.

Pro-labor cabinet representation. This was coded from information reported in Paloheimo (1984) and Woldendrop, Keman, and Budge (1993).

Strike activity. Strike data for all countries are from ILO (various years). The denominator, the number of wage- and salary-earners, is from OECD (1963, 1980, 1988b). The Australian employee series was completed with the Bain and Price (1980) dependent labor force series, adjusted by unemployment figures from the *Official Yearbook of Australia* (various years) for 1950–1963. The *New Zealand Official Yearbook* was used to complete the New Zealand series for 1954–1971. The Swedish series was completed with the Bain and Price (1980) dependent labor force series adjusted by unemployment figures from ILO (various years). The Swiss series for 1950–1959 is from ILO (various years).

Chapter Eight. The Structure of Labor Markets

The Logistic Hierarchical Model

Hierarchical logistic regression models have been proposed by researchers in statistics and the social sciences (e.g., Schall 1991; Wong and Mason 1985). In the current specification, for each of $j = 1, \ldots, 10$ countries, we have a vector of micro-level effects, b_j, with $i = 1, \ldots, 8$ elements. The binary dependent variable for each country equals 1 if a respondent is a union member, and 0 otherwise. If the micro-level covariates are collected in the matrix x_j, the distribution of the dependent variable, y_j, is Bernoulli with expectation:

$$E(y_j) = \pi_j,$$

$$\log\left(\frac{\pi_j}{1 - \pi_j}\right) = x_j\, b_j$$

The 10-vector, b_i, of effects for a particular predictor for all countries has a Normal distribution, conditional on the matrix of institutional data z:

$$b_i \sim N(\eta_i, \sigma_i^2)$$

where $\eta_i = z\,\gamma_i$. Diffuse Normal-Gamma priors were placed on the coefficients. With large random effects and a small number of macro contexts, many numerical methods based on first-order approximations to the likelihood may not be accurate (Rodríguez and Goldman 1995). Estimates reported here were obtained by directly simulating draws from the posterior, using the Gibbs sampler.

Bibliography

Adeney, Martin, and John Lloyd. 1986. *The Miners' Strike, 1984–5: Loss without Limit*. London: Routledge and Kegan Paul.

Ahlén, Kristina. 1989. "Swedish Collective Bargaining under Pressure: Inter-Union Rivalry and Incomes Policy." *British Journal of Industrial Relations* 27:330–46.

Alber, Jens. 1981. "Government Responses to the Challenge of Unemployment: The Development of Unemployment Insurance in Western Europe." Pp. 151–83 in *The Development of Welfare States in Europe and America*, edited by Peter J. Flora and Arnold J. Heidenheimer. New Brunswick, N.J.: Transaction Books.

Alestalo, Matti, and Hannu Uusitalo. 1987. "Finland." Pp. 123–90 in *Growth to Limits: The Western European Welfare States since World War II*, edited by Peter J. Flora. Berlin: De Gruyter.

Allison, Paul D. 1982. "Discrete Time Methods of the Analysis of Event Histories." Pp. 61–98 in *Sociological Methodology 1982*, edited by Samuel Leinhardt. San Francisco: Jossey-Bass.

Alvarez, R. Michael, Geoffrey Garrett, and Peter Lange. 1991. "Government Partisanship, Labor Organization, and Macroeconomic Performance." *American Political Science Review* 85:539–56.

American Federation of Labor (AFL). 1931. *Unemployment Insurance*. Washington, D.C.: AFL.

Amoroso, Bruno. 1990. "Development and Crisis of the Scandinavian Model of Industrial Relations." Pp. 71–96 in *European Industrial Relations: The Challenge of Flexibility*, edited by Guido Baglioni and Colin Crouch. Newbury Park, Calif.: Sage.

Andersen, Jürgen Goul, and Tor Bjørkland. 1990. "Structural Changes and New Cleavages: The Progress Parties in Denmark and Norway." *Acta Sociologica* 33:195–217.

Antos, Joseph, Mark Chandler, and Wesley Mallow. 1980. "Sex Differences in Union Membership." *Industrial and Labor Relations Review* 33:162–69.

Armingeon, Klaus. 1982. "Determining the Level of Wages: The Role of Parties and Trade Unions." Pp. 225–82 in *The Impact of Parties: Politics and Policies in Democratic Capitalist States*, edited by Francis Castles. London: Sage.

Armstrong, Philip, Andrew Glyn, and John Harrison. 1991. *Capitalism since 1945*. London: Blackwell.

Arthurs, H. W., D. D. Carter, H. J. Glasbeck, and J. Fudge. 1988. "Canada." In *International Encyclopedia for Labour Law and Industrial Relations*, edited by Roger Blanpain. Deventer, Netherlands: Kluwer.

Ashenfelter, Orley, and John H. Pencavel. 1969. "American Trade Union Growth: 1900–1960." *Quarterly Journal of Economics* 83:434–48.

Aubert, Gabriel. 1989. "Collective Agreements and Industrial Peace in Switzerland." *International Labour Review* 128:373–88.

Baglioni, Guido. 1991. "An Italian Mosaic: Collective Bargaining Patterns in the 1980s." *International Labour Review* 130:81–93.

Bain, George Sayers, and Farouk Elsheikh. 1976. *Union Growth and the Business Cycle*. Oxford: Blackwell.

Bain, George Sayers, and Robert Price. 1980. *Profiles of Union Growth: A Comparative Statistical Portrait of Eight Countries*. Oxford: Blackwell.

Ball, Chris. 1980. "The Resolution of Inter-Union Conflict: The T.U.C.'s Reaction to Legal Intervention." *Industrial Law Journal* 9:13–27.

Barkan, Joanne. 1984. *Visions of Emancipation: The Italian Workers Movement since 1945*. New York: Praeger.

Barnett, Vic. 1982. *Comparative Statistical Inference*. 2d ed. New York: Wiley.

Becker, Joseph M. 1959. *Shared Government in Employment Security: A Study of Advisory Councils*. New York: Columbia University Press.

Bedani, Gino. 1995. *Politics and Ideology in the Italian Workers' Movement: Union Development and the Changing Role of the Catholic and Communist Subcultures in Postwar Italy*. Oxford: Berg.

Bell, Daniel. 1973. *The Coming of Post-Industrial Society: A Venture in Social Forecasting*. New York: Basic Books.

Berenstein, Alexandre. 1993. "Switzerland." In *International Encyclopedia for Labour Law and Industrial Relations*, edited by Roger Blanpain. Deventer, Netherlands: Kluwer.

Berk, Richard A., Bruce Western, and Rob Weiss. 1995. "Statistical Inference for Apparent Populations." Pp. 421–58 in *Sociological Methodology, 1995*, edited by Peter Marsden. Oxford: Blackwell.

Bernstein, Irving. 1954. "The Growth of American Unions." *American Economic Review* 44:301–18.

———. 1969. *Turbulent Years: A History of the American Worker, 1933–1941*. Boston: Houghton Mifflin.

Beveridge, William H. 1953. *Power and Influence*. London: Hodder and Stoughton.

Beyme, Klaus von. 1985. *Political Parties in Western Democracies*. Aldershot, England: Gower.

Bjørklund, Anders, and Bertil Holmlund. 1991. "Economics and Unemployment Insurance: The Case of Sweden." Pp. 101–78 in *Labour Market Policy and Unemployment Insurance*, edited by Anders Bjørklund, Robert Haveman, Robinson Hollister, and Bertil Holmlund. Oxford: Clarendon.

Blanpain, Roger. 1970. "Recent Trends in Collective Bargaining in Belgium." *International Labour Review* 104:111–28.

———. 1984. "Recent Trends in Collective Bargaining in Belgium." *International Labour Review* 123:319–32.

———., ed. 1995. *International Encyclopedia for Labour Law and Industrial Relations*. Deventer, Netherlands: Kluwer.

Block, Fred. 1990. *Postindustrial Possibilities: A Critique of Economic Discourse*. Berkeley: University of California Press.

Bluestone, Barry, and Irving Bluestone. 1992. *Negotiating the Future: A Labor Perspective on American Business*. New York: Basic Books.

Bluestone, Barry, and Bennett Harrison. 1982. *The Deindustrialization of America: Plant Closings, Community Abandonment and the Dismantling of Basic Industry*. New York: Basic Books.

Bok, Derek C. 1971. "Reflections on the Distinctive Character of American Labor Laws." *Harvard Law Review,* no. 6:1394–1462.

Booth, Alison. 1983. "A Reconsideration of Trade Union Growth in the United Kingdom." *British Journal of Industrial Relations* 21:377–91.

Box, George E. P., and George C. Tiao. 1973. *Bayesian Inference in Statistical Analysis*. New York: Wiley.

Brody, David. 1975. "The New Deal and World War II." Pp. 267–309 in *The New Deal: The National Level*, Vol. 1, edited by John Braeman, Robert H. Bremner, and David Brody. Columbus: Ohio State University Press.

Brooks, B. T. 1988. "Australia." In *International Encyclopedia for Labour Law and Industrial Relations*, edited by Roger Blanpain. Deventer, Netherlands: Kluwer.

Bruno, Michael, and Jeffrey Sachs. 1985. *The Economics of Worldwide Stagflation*. Oxford: Blackwell.

Calmfors, Lars, and Driffill, John. 1988. "Bargaining Structure, Corporatism, and Macroeconomic Performance." *Economic Policy* 6:13–62.

Cameron, David R. 1984. "Social Democracy and Labor Quiescence: The Representation of Economic Interests in Advanced Capitalist Societies." Pp. 143–78 in *Order and Conflict in Contemporary Capitalism*, edited by John H. Goldthorpe. Oxford: Clarendon.

Castles, Francis G. 1985. *The Working Class and Welfare: Reflections on the Political Development of the Welfare State in Australia and New Zealand, 1890–1980*. Sydney: Allen and Unwin.

Chang, Clara, and Constance Sorrentino. 1991. "Union Membership Statistics in 12 Countries."*Monthly Labor Review* 114:46–53.

Chatterjee, Samprit, and Ali S. Hadi. 1988. *Sensitivity Analysis in Linear Regression*. New York: Wiley.

Clegg, Hugh Armstrong. 1976. *Trade Unions under Collective Bargaining: A Theory Based on Comparisons between Six Countries*. Oxford: Blackwell.

———. 1978. *The System of Industrial Relations in Great Britain*. Oxford: Blackwell.

———. 1979. *The Changing System of Industrial Relations in Great Britain*. Oxford: Blackwell.

Cole, Robert E. 1989. *Strategies for Learning: Small-Group Activities in American, Japanese, and Swedish Industry*. Berkeley: University of California Press.

Commons, John R. 1918. *History of Labour in the United States*. New York: Macmillan.

Congress of Industrial Organization (CIO). 1952. *Unemployment Insurance*. CIO Guidebook no. 2.

Contini, Giovanni. 1985. "Politics, Law, and Shop Floor Bargaining in Postwar Italy." Pp. 192–218 in *Shop Floor Bargaining and the State: Historical and Comparative Perspectives*, edited by Steven Tolliday and Jonathan Zeitlin. Cambridge: Cambridge University Press.

Cook, Alice. 1984. "Introduction." Pp. 3–36 in *Women and Trade Unions in Eleven Industrialized Countries*, edited by Alice H. Cook, Val R. Lorwin, and Arlene Kaplan Daniels. Philadelphia: Temple University Press.

Cox. Robert H. 1993. *The Development of the Dutch Welfare State: From Workers Insurance to Universal Entitlement*. Pittsburgh: University of Pittsburgh.

Crosland, C.A.R. 1956. *The Future of Socialism*. London: Cape.

Crouch, Colin. 1979. *Politics and Industrial Relations*. Manchester: Manchester University Press.

Crouch, Colin. 1990. "Afterword." Pp. 356–62 in *European Industrial Relations: The Challenge of Flexibility*, edited by Guido Baglioni and Colin Crouch. Newbury Park, Calif.: Sage.

———. 1992. "The Fate of Articulated Industrial Relations Systems: A Stock-Taking after the 'Neo-Liberal' Decade." Pp. 169–87 in *The Future of Labour Movements*, edited by Marino Regini. Newbury Park, Calif.: Sage.

———. 1993. *Industrial Relations and European State Traditions*. Oxford: Clarendon.

Dahl, Robert A., and Charles E. Lindblom. 1953. *Politics, Economics and Welfare: Planning and Politico-Economic Systems Resolved into Basic Social Processes*. Chicago: University of Chicago Press.

Dahrendorf, Ralf. 1959. *Class and Class Conflict in Industrial Societies*. London: Routledge.

Davis, James A., and Tom W. Smith. 1994. *General Social Survey Cumulative File, 1972–1994* [MRDF]. ICPSR no. 6217. Ann Arbor: Inter-University Consortium for Political and Social Research.

Degans, M. 1975. "Unemployment Insurance in Belgium." *International Social Security Review* 28:406–12.

Domhoff, G. William. 1967. *Who Rules America?* Englewood Cliffs, N.J.: Prentice-Hall.

———. 1990. *The Power Elite and the State: How Policy is Made in America*. New York: Aldine de Gruyter.

Dornbusch, Rudiger. 1980. "Exchange Rate Economics: Where Do We Stand?" (with discussion). *Brookings Papers on Economic Activity*, no. 1, 143–205.

Draper, Hal. 1978. *Karl Marx's Theory of Revolution*. Vol. 2. New York: Monthly Review Press.

Duda, Helga, and Franz Tödtling. 1986. "Austrian Trade Unions in the Economic Crisis." Pp. 227–68 in *Unions in Crisis and Beyond: Perspectives from Six Countries*, edited by Richard Edwards, Paola Garonna, and Franz Tödtling. Dover, Mass.: Auburn House.

Duncan, Greg J., and Frank P. Stafford. 1980. "Do Union Members Receive Compensating Wage Differentials?" *American Economic Review* 70:355–71.

Dunlop, John T. 1949. "The Development of Labor Organization: A Theoretical Framework." Pp 163–96 in *Insights into Labor Issues*, edited by Richard Lester and Joseph Shister. New York: Macmillan.

Durcan, J. W., W.E.J. McCarthy, and G. P. Redman. 1983. *Strikes in Post-War Britain: A Study in Stoppages of Work Due to Industrial Disputes, 1946–73*. London: Allen and Unwin.

Ebbinghaus, Bernhard. 1993. "Labour Unity in Diversity: Trade Unions and Social Cleavage in Western Europe 1890–1989." Ph.D. diss., European University Institute, Florence.

———. 1995. "The Siamese Twins: Citizenship Rights, Cleavage Formation, and Party-Union Relations in Western Europe." *International Review of Social History*, supp. 3, 40:51–89.

The Economist. 1985. "Tougher Nuts." *The Economist*, May 11, 53, 56.

Efron, Bradley, and Robert Tibshirani. 1993. *An Introduction to the Bootstrap*. New York: Chapman and Hall.

Efron, Bradley. 1986. "Why Isn't Everyone a Bayesian?" (with discussion). *American Statistician* 40:1–11.

Elvander, Nils. 1974. "Collective Bargaining and Incomes Policy in the Nordic Countries: A Comparative Analysis." *British Journal of Industrial Relations* 12:417–37.

———. 1990. "Incomes Policies in the Nordic Countries." *International Labour Review* 129:1–21.

Esping-Andersen, Gøsta. 1985. *Politics against Markets*. Princeton: Princeton University Press.

———. 1990. *Three Worlds of Welfare Capitalism*. Cambridge: Polity.

Esping-Andersen, Gøsta, and Kees van Kersbergen. 1992. "Contemporary Research on Social Democracy." *Annual Review of Sociology* 18:187–208.

European Industrial Relations Review (*EIRR*). 1981. "Works Council Rights in Eight Countries." *EIRR*. 88:13–25.

———. 1986. "Changes to the Works Constitution Act." *EIRR* 152:28–34.

———. 1989a. "Trends in the Level of Collective Bargaining." *EIRR* 183:24–26.

———. 1989b. "Trends in the Level of Collective Bargaining: Part 2." *EIRR* 186:20–22.

———. 1989c. "Union Membership in 1988." *EIRR* 184:9.

———. 1991a. "Collective Bargaining and the 1991 Round." *EIRR* 207:20–23.

———. 1991b. "Union Membership Down." *EIRR* 212:9.

———. 1995. "The 1995 Danish Collective Bargaining Round." *EIRR* 262:24–27.

Farber, Henry S. 1990. "The Decline of Unionization in the United States: What Can Be Learned from Recent Experience." *Journal of Labor Economics* 8:S75–S105.

Farkas, George, Paula England, and Margaret Barton. 1988. "Structural Effects on Wages: Sociological and Economic Views." Pp. 93–112 in *Industries, Firms, and Jobs: Sociological and Economic Approaches*, edited by George Farkas and Paula England. New York: Plenum.

Federal Social Insurance Office (Switzerland). 1961. "Social Security in Switzerland." *Bulletin of the International Social Security Association* 14:475–519.

Ferner, Anthony, and Richard Hyman, eds., 1992. *Industrial Relations in the New Europe*. Oxford: Blackwell.

Fiorito, Jack. 1982. "American Trade Union Growth: An Alternative Model." *Industrial Relations* 21:123–27.

Flanagan, Robert J., David W. Soskice, and Lloyd Ulman. 1983. *Unionism, Economic Stabilization, and Incomes Policies: European Experience*. Washington: Brookings Institution.

Flanagan, Robert J., Robert S. Smith, and Ronald J. Ehrenberg. 1984. *Labor Economics and Labor Relations*. Scott Foresman.

Flora, Peter J., ed. 1983–1987. *Growth to Limits: The Western European Welfare States since World War II*. Berlin: De Gruyter.

Franzosi, Roberto. 1995. *The Puzzle of Strikes: Class and State Strategies in Postwar Italy*. New York: Cambridge University Press.

Freeman, Richard B. 1986a. "Effects of Unions on the Economy." Pp. 179–200 in *Unions in Transition: Entering the Second Century*, edited by Seymour Martin Lipset. San Francisco: Institute for Contemporary Studies.

———. 1986b. "The Effect of the Union Wage Differential on Management Opposition and Union Organizing Success." *American Economic Review* 76:92–96.

Freeman, Richard B. 1988. "Contraction and Expansion: The Divergence of Public Sector and Private Sector Unionism in the United States." *Journal of Economic Perspectives* 2:63–88.

———. 1989. "On the Divergence in Unionism in Developed Countries." NBER Working Paper no. 2817. Cambridge, Mass.: National Bureau of Economic Research.

Freeman, Richard B., and Robert Gibbons. 1993. "Getting Together and Breaking Apart: The Decline of Centralised Collective Bargaining." NBER Working Paper no. 4464. Cambridge, Mass.: National Bureau of Economic Research.

Freeman, Richard B., and James L. Medoff. 1984. *What Do Unions Do?* New York: Basic Books.

Freeman, Richard B., and J. Pelletier. 1989. "The Impact of Industrial Relations Legislation on British Union Density." *British Journal of Industrial Relations* 28:141–64.

Freeman, Richard B., and Marcus Rebick. 1989. "Crumbling Pillar? Declining Union Density in Japan." *Journal of the Japanese and International Economies* 3:578–605.

Friedman, Milton. 1962. *Capitalism and Freedom*. Chicago: University of Chicago Press.

Galenson, Walter. 1986. "The Historical Role of American Trade Unionism." Pp. 39–73 in *Unions in Transition: Entering the Second Century*, edited by Seymour Martin Lipset. San Francisco: Institute for Contemporary Studies.

———. 1952. "Scandinavia." Pp. 104–72 in *Comparative Labor Movements*, edited by Walter Galenson. New York: Russell and Russell.

Gallup, George H. 1976. *The Gallup International Public Opinion Polls: Great Britain, 1937–1975*. Westport, Conn.: Greenwood.

Garfinkel, Harold. 1967 *Studies in Ethnomethodology*. Englewood Cliffs, N.J.: Prentice-Hall.

Gelman, Andrew, John B. Carlin, Hal S. Stern, and Donald B. Rubin. 1995. *Bayesian Data Analysis*. New York: Chapman and Hall.

Golden, Miriam, Peter Lange, and Michael Wallerstein. 1993. "Trends in Collective Bargaining and Industrial Relations in Non-Corporatist Countries: A Preliminary Report." Paper presented at the annual meeting of the American Political Science Association, Washington, D.C.

Goldfield, Michael. 1987. *The Decline of Organized Labor in the United States*. Chicago: Chicago University Press.

Goldman, Alvin L. 1983. "United States of America." In *International Encyclopedia for Labour Law and Industrial Relations*, edited by Roger Blanpain. Deventer, Netherlands: Kluwer.

Goodall, Colin. 1990. "A Survey of Smoothing Techniques." Pp. 126–76 in *Modern Methods of Data Analysis*, edited by John Fox and J. Scott Long. Newbury Park, Calif.: Sage.

Gordon, Andrew. 1985. *The Evolution of Labor Relations in Japan: Heavy Industry, 1853–1955*. Cambridge: Council on East Asian Studies, Harvard University.

Gould, William B. 1993. *Agenda for Reform: The Future of Employment Relationships and the Law*. Cambridge.: MIT Press.

Grais, Bernard. 1983. *Lay-Offs and Short-Time Working in Selected OECD Countries*. Paris: OECD.

Greenstone, J. David. 1977. *Labor In American Politics*. New York: Knopf.

Griffin, Larry J., Christopher Botsko, Ana-Maria Wahl, and Larry W. Isaac. 1991. "Theoretical Generality and Case Particularity: Qualitative Comparative Analysis and Trade Union Growth and Decline." *International Journal of Comparative Sociology* 32:10–36.

Griffin, Larry J., Holly J. McCammon, and Christopher Botsko. 1990. "The 'Unmaking' of a Movement? The Crisis of U.S. Trade Unions in Comparative Perspective." Pp. 169–94 in *Change in Societal Institutions*, edited by Maureen Hallinan, David Klein, and Jennifer Glass. New York: Plenum.

Haber, William, and Merrill G. Murray. 1966. *Unemployment Insurance in the American Economy: An Historical Review and Analysis*. Homewood, Ill.: Irwin.

Hall, Peter A. 1987. "European Labor in the 1980s: Introduction." *International Journal of Political Economy* 17:3–25.

Hancke, Bob. 1991. "The Crisis of National Unions: Belgian Labor in Decline." *Politics and Society* 19:463–87.

Hancock, Keith, and J. E. Isaac. 1992. "Australian Experiments in Wage Policy." *British Journal of Industrial Relations* 30:213–36.

Hardimann, Niamh. 1988. *Pay, Politics, and Economic Performance in Ireland 1970–1987*. Oxford: Clarendon.

Harris, José. 1984. *Unemployment and Politics: A Study in English Social Policy 1886–1914*. Oxford: Oxford University Press.

Headey, Bruce. 1970. "Trade Unions and National Wages Policy." *Journal of Politics* 32:407–39.

Heckscher, Charles C. 1988. *The New Unionism: Employee Involvement in the Changing Corporation*. New York: Basic Books.

Heclo, Hugh. 1974. *Modern Social Politics in Britain and Sweden: From Relief to Income Maintenance*. New Haven: Yale University Press.

Hibbs, Douglas A. 1987. *The Political Economy of Industrial Democracies*. Cambridge: Harvard University Press.

Hicks, Alexander. 1988. "Social Democratic Corporatism and Economic Growth." *Journal of Politics* 50:677–704.

Hince, Kevin, and Martin Vranken. 1991. "A Controversial Reform of New Zealand Labour Law: The Employment Contracts Act 1991." *International Labour Review* 130: 475–94.

Hines, A. G. 1964. "Trade Unions and Wage Inflation in the United Kingdom 1948–1962: A Disaggregated Study." *Economic Journal* 79:66–89.

Hirsch, Barry T., and John T. Addison. 1986. *The Economic Analysis of Unions: New Approaches and Evidence*. London: Allen and Unwin.

Hirsch, Barry T., and Mark Berger. 1984. "Union Membership Determination and Industry Characteristics." *Southern Economic Journal* 50:665–79.

Horowitz, Gad. 1968. *Canadian Labour in Politics*. Toronto: University of Toronto Press.

Howell, Chris. 1992. *Regulating Labor: The State and Industrial Relations Reform in Postwar France*. Princeton: Princeton University Press.

Howells, John M. 1982. "New Zealand." In *International Encyclopedia for Labour Law and Industrial Relations*, edited by Roger Blanpain. Deventer, Netherlands: Kluwer.

Hyman, Richard. 1992. "Trade Unions and the Disaggregation of the Working Class."
    Pp. 150–68 in *The Future of Labour Movements*, edited by Marino Regini. Newbury
    Park, Calif.: Sage.
Inagami, Takeshi. 1988. *Japanese Workplace Industrial Relations*. Tokyo: Japan
    Institute of Labor.
International Labor Office (ILO). 1955. *Unemployment Insurance Schemes*. Geneva:
    ILO.
ILO. Various years. *Yearbook of Labour Statistics*. Geneva: ILO.
International Monetary Fund. 1990. International Financial Statistics [MRDF]. Wash-
    ington, D.C.: International Monetary Fund.
Irving, Ronald E. M. 1979. *The Christian Democratic Parties of Western Europe*.
    London: Allen and Unwin.
Jacobsen, Per. 1989. "Denmark." In *International Encyclopedia for Labour Law and
    Industrial Relations*, edited by Roger Blanpain. Deventer, Netherlands: Kluwer.
Jacoby, Sanford M. 1991. "American Exceptionalism Revisited: The Importance of
    Management." Pp. 173–241 in *Masters to Managers: Historical and Comparative
    Perspectives on American Employers*, edited by Sanford M. Jacoby. New York:
    Columbia University Press.
———. 1995. "Social Dimensions of Global Economic Integration." Pp. 3–29 in *The
    Workers of Nations: Industrial Relations in a Global Economy*, edited by Sanford
    Jacoby. New York: Oxford University Press.
Janoski, Thomas. 1990. *The Political Economy of Unemployment: Active Labor Market
    Policy in West Germany and the United States*. Berkeley: University of California
    Press.
Johansen, Lars Nørby. 1987. "Denmark." Pp. 191–246 in *Growth to Limits: The West-
    ern European Welfare States since World War II*, Vol. 2, edited by Peter Flora.
    Berlin: De Gruyter.
Kanawaty, George, Alan Gladstone, Joseph Prokopenko, and Gerry Rodgers. 1989.
    "Adjustment at the Micro Level." *International Labour Review* 128:269–98.
Katz, Harry C. 1993. "The Decentralization of Collective Bargaining: A Literature
    Review and Comparative Analysis." *Industrial and Labor Relations Review*
    47:3–22.
Katz, Harry C., Thomas A. Kochan, and Robert B. McKersie. 1990. "A Reaction to the
    Debate." Pp. 189–201 in *Reflections on the Transformation of Industrial Relations*,
    edited by James Chelius and James Dworkin. Metuchen, N.J.: Institute of Manage-
    ment and Labor Relations.
Katzenstein, Peter J. 1984. *Corporatism and Change: Austria, Switzerland, and the
    Politics of Industry*. Ithaca, N.Y.: Cornell University Press.
———. 1985. *Small States in World Markets: Industrial Policy in Europe*. Ithaca,
    N.Y.: Cornell University Press.
Keesing's Contemporary Archives. 1972–1988. Vols. 18–34. London: Longman.
Kelly, John. 1988. *Trade Unions and Socialist Politics*. London: Verso.
Keohane, Robert. 1984. "The World Political Economy and the Crisis of Embedded
    Liberalism." Pp. 15–38 in *Order and Conflict in Contemporary Capitalism: Studies
    in the Political Economy of Western Nations*, edited by John H. Goldthorpe. Oxford:
    Clarendon.

Kiehel, Constance. 1932. *Unemployment Insurance in Belgium: A National Development of Ghent and Liege Systems.* New York: Industrial Relations Counselors.

King, Desmond. 1995. *Actively Seeking Work? The Politics of Unemployment and Welfare Policy in the United States and Great Britain.* Chicago: University of Chicago Press.

Kitschelt, Herbert. 1994. *The Transformation of European Social Democracy.* New York: Cambridge University Press.

Knoellinger, Carl Erik. 1960. *Labor in Finland.* Cambridge: Harvard University Press.

Kochan, Thomas A., Harry C. Katz, and Robert B. McKersie. 1986. *The Transformation of American Industrial Relations.* New York: Basic Books.

Korpi, Walter. 1978. *The Working Class in Welfare Capitalism.* London: Routledge.

———. 1983. *The Democratic Class Struggle.* London: Routledge.

———. 1989. "Power, Politics and State Autonomy in the Development of Social Citizenship: Social Right during Sickness in Eighteen OECD Countries since 1930." *American Sociological Review* 54:309–28.

Korpi, Walter, and Gøsta Esping-Andersen. 1984. "Social Policy as Class Politics in Post-War Capitalism: Scandinavia, Austria and Germany." Pp. 189–208 in *Order and Conflict in Contemporary Capitalism: Studies in the Political Economy of Western European Nations,* edited by John H. Goldthorpe. Oxford: Clarendon.

Korpi, Walter, and Michael Shalev. 1979. "Strikes, Industrial Relations and Class Conflicts in Capitalist Societies." *British Journal of Sociology* 30:164–87.

Kuwahara, Yasuo. 1987. "Japanese Industrial Relations." Pp. 211–31 in *International and Comparative Industrial Relations,* edited by Greg J. Bamber and Russell D. Lansbury. London: Allen and Unwin.

Lange, Kenneth L., Roderick J. A. Little, and Jeremy M. G. Taylor. 1989. "Robust Statistical Modelling Using the *t* Distribution." *Journal of the American Statistical Association* 84:881–95.

Lange, Peter, George Ross, and Maurizio Vannicelli. 1982. *Unions, Change, and Crisis: French and Italian Union Strategy and the Political Economy 1945–80.* London: Allen and Unwin.

Lange, Peter, Michael Wallerstein, and Miriam Golden. 1995. "The End of Corporatism? Wage Setting in the Germanic and Nordic Countries." Pp. 76–100 in *The Workers of Nations: Industrial Relations in a Global Economy,* edited by Sanford Jacoby. New York: Oxford University Press.

Lash, Scott. 1985. "The End of Neo-Corporatism? The Breakdown of Centralised Bargaining in Sweden." *British Journal of Industrial Relations* 23:215–39.

Lash, Scott, and John Urry. 1987. *The End of Organized Capitalism.* Cambridge: Polity.

Layard, Richard, Stephen Nickell, and Richard Jackman. 1991. *Unemployment: Macroeconomic Performance and the Labour Market.* Oxford: Oxford University Press.

Leamer, Edward E. 1983. "Let's Take the Con out of Econometrics." *American Economic Review* 23:31–43.

———. 1991. "A Bayesian Perspective on Inference from Macro-Economic Data." *Scandinavian Journal of Economics* 93:225–48.

Lehmbruch, Gerhard S. 1984. "Concertation and the Structure of Corporatist Networks." Pp. 60–80 in *Order and Conflict in Contemporary Capitalism: Studies in the*

Political Economy of Western European Nations, edited by John H. Goldthorpe. Oxford: Clarendon.

Lenin, V. I. 1968 [1902]. *Lenin on Politics and Revolution: Selected Writings*, edited by James Connor. Indianapolis: Pegasus.

Levine, Stephen. 1979. *The New Zealand Political System: Politics in a Small Society.* Sydney: Allen and Unwin.

Lipset, Seymour Martin. 1986. "Labor Unions in the Public Mind." Pp. 287–321 in *Unions in Transition: Entering the Second Century*, edited by Seymour Martin Lipset. San Francisco: Institute for Contemporary Studies.

Lipset, Seymour Martin, and Joan Gordon. 1953. "Mobility and Trade Union Membership." Pp. 491–500 in *Class, Status and Power: A Reader in Social Stratification*, edited by Reinhard Bendix and Seymour Martin Lipset. Glencoe, Ill.: Free Press.

Locke, Richard M. 1991. "The Resurgence of the Local Union: Industrial Restructuring and Industrial Relations in Italy." *Politics and Society* 18:347–79.

———. 1992. "Industrial Restructuring and Industrial Relations in the Italian Automobile Industry." Pp. 247–76 in *Bargaining for Change: Union Politics in North America and Europe*, edited by Miriam Golden and Jonas Pontusson. Ithaca, N.Y.: Cornell University Press.

Lorwin, Val. 1975. "Labor Unions and Political Parties in Belgium." *Industrial and Labor Relations Review* 28:243–81.

Maddox, Graham. 1978. "The Australian Labor Party." Pp. 159–316 in *Political Parties in Australia*, edited by Graeme Starr, Keith Richmond, and Graham Maddox. Richmond, Australia: Heinemann Educational.

Maier, Charles S. 1988. *Recasting Bourgeois Europe: Stabilization in France, Germany and Italy in the Decade after World War I.* Princeton: Princeton University Press.

Markovits, Andrei S. 1986. *The Politics of the West German Trade Unions: Strategies of Class and Interest Representation in Growth and Crisis.* Cambridge: Cambridge University Press.

Marsh, David. 1992. *The New Politics of British Trade Unionism: Union Power and the Thatcher Legacy.* Ithaca, N.Y.: ILR Press.

Mason, William M., G. Y. Wong, and Barbara Entwistle. 1983. Pp. 72–103 in *Sociological Methodology 1983–1984*, edited by S. Leinhardt. San Francisco: Jossey-Bass.

Masters, Marick F., and John D. Roberston. 1988. "The Impact of Organized Labor on Public Employment: A Comparative Analysis." *Journal of Labor Research* 9:347–62.

McCarthy, Charles. 1984. *Elements in a Theory of Industrial Relations.* Dublin: Irish Academic Press.

McCullagh, Peter and John A. Nelder. 1989. *Generalized Linear Models.* 2d ed. London: Chapman Hall.

Meulders, Danièle, Robert Plasman, and Valèrie Vander Stricht. 1993. *The Position of Women on the Labour Market in the European Community.* Aldershot, England: Dartmouth.

Ministry of Social Affairs (Finland). 1953. *Social Legislation and Work in Finland.* Helsinki: Ministry of Social Affairs.

Misra, Joya, and Alexander Hicks. 1994. "Catholicism and Unionization in Affluent Postwar Democracies."*American Sociological Review* 59:304–26.

Molitor, Michel. 1978. "Social Conflicts in Belgium." Pp. 21–51 in *The Resurgence of Class Conflict in Western Europe since 1968*, Vol. 1, edited by Colin Crouch and Alessandro Pizzorno. London: Macmillan.

Mosteller, Frederick, and John W. Tukey. 1977. *Data Analysis and Regression: A Second Course in Statistics*. Reading, Mass.: Addison-Wesley.

Negrelli, Serafino, and Ettore Santi. 1990. "Industrial Relations in Italy." Pp. 154–98 in *European Industrial Relations: The Challenge of Flexibility*, edited by Guido Baglioni and Colin Crouch. Newbury Park, Calif.: Sage.

Nelson, Daniel. 1969. *Unemployment Insurance: The American Experience 1915–1935*. Madison: University of Wisconsin Press.

Neufeld, Maurice. 1961. *Italy: School for Awakening Countries*. Westport, Conn.: Greenwood.

Neumann, George, Peder J. Pedersen, and Niels Westergaard-Nielsen. 1989. "Long Run Trends in Aggregate Unionization." Center for Labor Economics Working Paper no. 90–4. Denmark: University of Aarhus and Aarhus School of Business.

New Zealand Official Yearbook. Various years. Wellington, New Zealand: Department of Statistics.

Nilstein, Arne. 1966. "White Collar Unionism in Sweden." Pp. 261–304 in *White Collar Trade Unions: Contemporary Developments in Industrialized Societies*, edited by Adolf Sturmthal. Urbana: University of Illinois Press.

Norris, Pippa. 1987. *Politics and Sexual Equality: The Comparative Position of Women in the Western Democracies*. Boulder, Colo.: Wheatsheaf.

Northrup, Herbert R., and Amie D. Thornton. 1988. "The Federal Government as Employer: The Federal Labor Relations Authority and the PATCO Challenge." Labor Relations and Public Policy Series, no. 32. Wharton School, Industrial Research Unit, Philadelphia.

Official Australian Yearbook. Various years. Canberra: Australian Bureau of Statistics.

Oliver, Nick, and Barry Wilkinson. 1989. "Japanese Manufacturing Techniques and Personnel and Industrial Relations Practice in Britain: Evidence and Implication." *British Journal of Industrial Relations* 27:73–91.

Olsson, Sven. 1986. "Sweden." Pp. 1–116 in *Growth to Limits: The Western European Welfare States since World War II*, Vol. 1, edited by Peter J. Flora. Berlin: De Gruyter.

———. 1987. "Sweden." Pp. 1–64 in *Growth to Limits: The Western European Welfare States since World War II*, Vol. 4, edited by Peter J. Flora. Berlin: De Gruyter.

Organisation for Economic Cooperation and Development (OECD). 1963. *Manpower Statistics*. Paris: OECD.

———. 1974. *Labour Force Statistics*. Paris: OECD.

———. 1979a. *Collective Bargaining and Government Policies in Ten OECD Countries*. Paris: OECD.

———. 1979b. *Unemployment Compensation and Related Unemployment Policy Measures*. Paris: OECD.

———. 1980. *Labour Force Statistics*. Paris: OECD.

———. 1982. *Historical Statistics*. Paris: OECD.

———. 1987. *Labour Force Statistics*. Paris: OECD.

Organisation for Economic Cooperation and Development (OECD). 1988a. *Employment Outlook*. Paris: OECD.

———. 1988b. *Labour Force Statistics*. Paris: OECD.

———. 1988c. *Historical Statistics*. Paris: OECD.

———. 1989. *Historical Statistics*. Paris: OECD.

———. 1990. *Labour Force Statistics*. Paris: OECD.

———. 1991a. *Employment Outlook*. Paris: OECD.

———. 1991b. *Labour Force Statistics*. Paris: OECD.

———. 1992a. *Historical Statistics*. Paris: OECD.

———. 1992b. *Labour Force Statistics*. Paris: OECD.

———. 1993. *Main Economic Indicators, Historical Statistics: Prices, Labour, Wages*. Paris: OECD.

———. 1994. *The OECD Jobs Study: Labour Market Trends and Underlying Forces of Change*. Paris: OECD.

———. 1995. *Labour Force Statistics*. Paris: OECD.

Paloheimo, Heikki. 1984. *Government in Democratic Capitalist States, 1950–1983: A Data Handbook*. Turku: Finnish Political Science Association.

Panitch, Leo. 1981. "Trade Unions and the Capitalist State." *New Left Review* 125:21–44.

Pedersen, Peder J. 1982. "Union Growth in Denmark 1911–39." *Scandinavian Journal of Economics* 84:583–92.

———. 1990. "Arbejdsløshedsforsikring og faglig organerisering, 1911–85." *Nationaløkonomisk Tidsskrift* 128:230–46.

Pelling, Henry. 1993. *A Short History of the Labour Party*. 10th ed. New York: St. Martin's.

Perlman, Selig. 1928. *A Theory of the Labor Movement*. New York: Augustus.

Peterson, Richard B. 1987. "Swedish Collective Bargaining: A Changing Scene." *British Journal of Industrial Relations* 25:31–48.

Piore, Michael, and Charles Sabel. 1984. *The Second Industrial Divide: Possibilities for Prosperity*. New York: Basic Books.

Piven, Frances Fox. 1992. "Introduction." In *Labor Parties in Postindustrial Societies*, edited by Frances Fox Piven. Cambridge: Polity.

Polanyi, Karl. 1957. "The Economy as Instituted Process." Pp. 243–70 in *Trade and Market in the Early Empires*, edited by Karl Polanyi, Conrad M. Arensberg, and Harry W. Pearson. Glencoe, Ill.: Free Press.

Pontusson, Jonas. 1992a. "Introduction: Organization and Political-Economic Perspectives on Union Politics." Pp. 1–44 in *Bargaining for Change: Union Politics in North America and Europe*, edited by Miriam Golden and Jonas Pontusson. Ithaca, N.Y.: Cornell University Press.

———. 1992b. "The Role of Economic-Structural Change in the Decline of European Social Democracy: Some Hypotheses and Cross-National Evidence." Paper presented at the annual meeting of the American Political Science Association, Chicago, August.

———. 1992c. "At the End of the Third Road: Swedish Social Democracy in Crisis." *Politics and Society* 20:305–32.

Pontusson, Jonas, and Peter Swenson. 1992. "Markets, Production, Institutions, and Politics: Why Swedish Employers Have Abandoned the Swedish Model." Paper presented at the Eighth International Conference of Europeanists, Council for European Studies, Chicago.

Pregibon, Daryl. 1982. "Resistant Fits for Some Commonly Used Logistic Models with Medical Applications." *Biometrics* 38:485–98.

Ragin, Charles C. 1987. *The Comparative Method: Moving Beyond Qualitiative and Quantitative Strategies.* Berkeley: University of California Press.

Reder, Melvin, and Lloyd Ulman. 1993. "Unionism and Unification." Pp. 13–44 in *Labor and an Integrated Europe*, edited by Lloyd Ulman, Barry Eichengreen, and William Dickens. Washington, D.C.: Brookings Institution.

Regalia, Ida. 1995. "Italy: The Costs and Benefits of Informality." Pp. 217–41 in *Works Councils: Consultation, Representation, and Cooperation in Industrial Relations*, edited by Joel Rogers and Wolfgang Streeck. Chicago: University of Chicago Press.

Regalia, Ida, Marino Regini, and Emilio Reyneri. 1978. "Labour Conflicts and Industrial Relations in Italy." Pp. 101–58 in *The Resurgence of Class Conflict in Western Europe since 1968*, Vol. 1, edited by Colin Crouch and Alessandro Pizzorno. London: Macmillan.

Regini, Marino. 1984. "The Conditions for Political Exchange: How Concertation Emerged and Collapsed in Italy and Great Britain." Pp. 124–42 in *Order and Conflict in Contemporary Capitalism*, edited by John Goldthorpe. Oxford: Clarendon.

———. 1987. "Industrial Relations in the Phase of 'Flexibility.'" *International Journal of Political Economy* 17:88–107.

Reynaud, Jean-Daniel. 1974. "Trade Unions and Political Parties in France: Some Recent Trends." *Industrial and Labor Relations Review* 28: 208–25.

Richardson, Bradley M., and Scott C. Flanagan. 1984. *Politics in Japan*. Boston: Little, Brown.

Riddell, W. Craig. 1993. "Unionization in Canada and the United States: A Tale of Two Countries." Pp. 109–48 in *Small Differences That Matter: Labor Markets and Income Maintenance in Canada and the United States*, edited by David Card and Richard B. Freeman. Chicago: University of Chicago Press.

Roche, William K., and Joe Larragy. 1990. "Cyclical and Institutional Determinants of Annual Trade Union Growth in Ireland: Evidence from the DUES Data Series." *European Sociological Review* 6:49–72.

Rodríguez, Germán, and Noreen Goldman. 1995. "An Assessment of Estimation Procedures for Multilevel Models with Binary Responses." *Journal of the Royal Statistical Society,* ser. A, 158:73–89.

Roebroek, Joop, and Theo Berben. 1987. "Netherlands." Pp. 671–752 in *Growth to Limits: The Western European Welfare States since World War II*, edited by Peter J. Flora. Berlin: De Gruyter.

Rogers, Joel, and Wolfgang Streeck. 1994. "Workplace Representation Overseas: The Works Councils Story." Pp. 97–156 in *Working under Different Rules*, edited by Richard Freeman. New York: Russell Sage Foundation.

Rojot, Jacques. 1986. "The Development of French Employers' Policy Towards Trade Unions." *Labour and Society* 11:1–16.

Rood, Max Gustaaf. 1993. "Netherlands." In *International Encyclopedia for Labour Law and Industrial Relations*, edited by Roger Blanpain. Deventer, Netherlands: Kluwer.

Rosenfeld, Rachel, and Arne L. Kalleberg. 1991. "Gender Inequality in the Labor Market: A Cross-National Perspective." *Acta Sociologica* 34:207–25.

Roth, H. 1973. *Trade Unions in New Zealand: Past and Present*. Wellington, New Zealand: Reed.

Rothstein, Bo. 1989. "Marxism, Institutional Analysis and Working-Class Power." *Politics and Society* 18:317–46.

―――. 1992. "Labor-Market Institutions and Working-Class Strength." Pp. 35–56 in *Structuring Politics: Historical Institutionalism in Comparative Analysis*, edited by Sven Steinmo, Kathy Thelen, and Frank Longstretch. Cambridge: Cambridge University Press.

Royal Commission on Poor Laws and Relief of Distress. 1910. *Reports from Commissioners, Inspectors and Others*. App. Vol. 9, *Minutes of Evidence*. Cd. 5068. London: His Majesty's Stationery Office.

Sabel, Charles. 1987. "A Fighting Chance: Structural Change and New Labor Strategies." *International Journal of Political Economy* 17:26–57.

―――. 1995. "Bootstrapping Reform: Rebuilding Firms, the Welfare State and Unions." *Politics and Society* 23:5–48.

Schall, Robert. 1991. "Estimation of Generalized Linear Models with Random Effects." *Biometrika* 78:719–27.

Scharpf, Fritz. 1987. *Crisis and Choice in European Social Democracy*. Ithaca, N.Y.: Cornell University Press.

Schmitter, Philippe C. 1981. "Interest Intermediation and Regime Governability in Contemporary Western Europe and North America." Pp. 287–330 in *Organizing Interests in Western Europe: Pluralism, Corporatism, and the Transformation of Politics*, edited by Suzanne Berger. New York: Cambridge University Press,

Schumpeter, Joseph A. 1954. *History of Economic Analysis*. New York: Oxford University Press.

Scriven, Jeannie. 1994. "Women at Work in Sweden." Pp. 153–82 in *Working Women: An International Survey*, edited by Marilyn Davidson and Cary Cooper. New York: Wiley.

Shalev, Michael. 1992. "The Resurgence of Labour Quiescence." Pp. 102–32 in *The Future of Labour Movements*, edited by Marino Regini. London: Sage.

Sharp, William L. 1992. "Collective Negotiations: An Historical Perspective." *Journal of Collective Negotiations in the Public Sector* 21:231–37.

Sharpe, Ian G. 1971. "The Growth of Australian Trade Unions: 1907–1969." *Journal of Industrial Relations* 13:144–62.

Sheflin, Neil, Leo Troy, and C. Timothy Koeller. 1981. "Structural Stability in Models of American Trade Union Growth." *Quarterly Journal of Economics* 96:77–88.

Skocpol, Theda. 1984. "Emerging Agendas and Recurrent Strategies in Historical Sociology." Pp. 356–91 in *Vision and Method in Historical Sociology*, edited by Theda Skocpol. New York: Cambridge University Press.

Snyder, David. 1976. "Institutional Setting and Industrial Conflict: Comparative Analyses of France, Italy, and the United States." *American Sociological Review* 40:259–78.

Soskice, David W. 1978. "Strike Waves and Wage Explosions, 1968–1970: An Economic Interpretation." Pp. 221–46 in *The Resurgence of Class Conflict in Western Europe since 1968*, Vol. 2, edited by Colin Crouch and Alessandro Pizzorno. New York: Holmes and Meier.

Spates, T. G., and G. S. Rabinovitch. 1931. *Unemployment Insurance in Switzerland: The Ghent System Nationalized with Compulsory Features*. New York: Industrial Relations Counselors.

Spineux, Armand. 1990. "Trade Unionism in Belgium: The Difficulties of a Major Renovation." Pp. 42–70 in *European Industrial Relations: The Challenge of Flexibility*, edited by Guido Baglioni and Colin Crouch. Newbury Park, Calif.: Sage.

Starr, Paul. 1987. "The Sociology of Official Statistics." Pp. 7–57 in *The Politics of Numbers*, edited by William Alonso and Paul Starr. New York: Russell Sage Foundation.

Stephens, John D. 1979. *The Transition From Capitalism to Socialism*. Urbana: University of Illinois Press.

———. 1991. "Industrial Concentration, Country Size and Trade Union Membership." *American Political Science Review* 85:941–49.

Stewart, Bryce M. 1930. *Unemployment Benefits in the United States: The Plans and Their Setting*. New York: Industrial Relations Counselors.

Stinchcombe, Arthur. 1968. *Constructing Social Theories*. New York: Harcourt Brace.

Strasser, Rudolf. 1982. "Austria." In *International Encyclopedia for Labour Law and Industrial Relations*, edited by Roger Blanpain. Deventer, Netherlands: Kluwer.

Streeck, Wolfgang. 1984. "Neo-Corporatist Industrial Relations and the Economic Crisis in West Germany." Pp. 291–314 in *Order and Conflict in Contemporary Capitalism*, edited by John H. Goldthorpe. Oxford: Clarendon.

———. 1993. "The Rise and Decline of Neocorporatism." Pp. 80–101 in *Labor and an Integrated Europe*, edited by Lloyd Ulman, Barry Eichengreen, and William Dickens. Washington, D.C.: Brookings Institution.

———. 1995. "Works Councils in Western Europe: From Consultation to Participation." Pp. 313–48 in *Works Councils: Consultation, Representation, and Cooperation in Industrial Relations*, edited by Joel Rogers and Wolfgang Streeck. Chicago: University of Chicago Press.

Summers, Robert, and Alan Heston. 1991. "The Penn World Tables (Mark 5): An Expanded Set of International Comparisons 1950–88." *Quarterly Journal of Economics* 106:327–68.

Suvinanta, Antti. 1987. "Finland." In *International Encyclopedia for Labour Law and Industrial Relations,* edited by Roger Blanpain. Deventer, Netherlands: Kluwer.

Swenson, Peter. 1989. *Fair Shares: Unions, Pay and Politics in Sweden and West Germany*. Ithaca, N.Y.: Cornell University Press.

———. 1991. "Managing the Managers: The Swedish Employers' Confederation, Labor Scarcity, and the Suppression of Labor Market Segmentation." *Scandinavian Journal of History* 16:335–56.

Swindinsky, R. 1974. "Trade Union Growth in Canada, 1911–1970." *Relations Industrielles* 29:435–51.

Tanner, Martin. 1992. *Tools for Statistical Inference: Methods for the Exploration of Posterior Distributions and Likelihood Functions*. 2d ed. New York: Springer Verlag.

Teague, Paul. 1995. "Pay Determination in the Republic of Ireland: Towards Social Corporatism." *British Journal of Industrial Relations* 32:253–75.

Thelen, Kathleen. 1991. *A Union of Parts: Labor Politics in Postwar Germany.* Ithaca,
N.Y.: Cornell University Press.
————. 1993. "West European Labor in Transition: Sweden and Germany Compared."
World Politics 46:23–49.
Therborn, Gøran. 1977. "The Rule of Capital and the Rise of Democracy." *New Left
Review* 103:3–41.
Thomas, Robert J., and Thomas A. Kochan. 1992. "Technology, Industrial Relations
and the Problem of Organizational Transformation." Pp. 210–31 in *Technology and
the Future of Work,* edited by Paul S. Adler. New York: Oxford University Press.
Tilly, Charles. 1986. *The Contentious French.* Cambridge: Belknap Press.
————. 1995. "Globalization Threatens Labor's Rights." *International Labor and
Working Class History* 47:1–23.
Tokuichi, Utada. 1993. *Labour Unions and Labour-Management Relations.* Japan:
Japan Institute of Labour.
Traxler, Franz. 1994. "Collective Bargaining Levels and Coverage." *OECD Employ-
ment Outlook,* 167–94. Paris: OECD.
Treiman, Donald S., and Patricia Roos. 1983. "Sex and Earnings in Industrial Society:
A Nine Nation Comparison." *American Journal of Sociology* 89:612–50.
Treu, Tiziano 1991. "Italy." In *International Encyclopedia for Labour Law and Indus-
trial Relations,* edited by Roger Blanpain. Deventer, Netherlands: Kluwer.
Trowbridge, Alexander B. 1986. "A Management Look at Labor Relations." Pp. 405–
18 in *Unions in Transition: Entering the Second Century,* edited by Seymour Martin
Lipset. San Francisco: Institute for Contemporary Studies.
Troy, Leo. 1986. "The Rise and Fall of American Trade Unions: The Labor Movement
from FDR to RR." Pp. 75–109 in *Unions in Transition: Entering the Second Century,*
edited by Seymour Martin Lipset. San Francisco: Institute for Contemporary Studies.
————. 1990. "Is the U.S. Unique in the Decline of Private Sector Unionism?" *Journal
of Labor Research* 11:111–43.
Tsiganou, Helen A. 1991. *Workers' Participative Schemes: The Experience of Capitalist and Plan-Based Societies.* New York: Greenwood.
Turner, Lowell. 1991. *Democracy at Work: Changing World Markets and the Future of
Labor Unions.* Ithaca, N.Y.: Cornell University Press.
United Nations. 1985. *The Economic Role of Women in the EEC Region: Developments
1975–1985.* New York: United Nations.
Verma, Anil. 1990. "Comments: A Comparative Perspective on the Strategic Choice
Framework." Pp. 174–88 in *Reflections on the Transformation of Industrial Rela-
tions,* edited by James Chelius and James Dworkin. Metuchen, N.J.: IMLR Press/
Rutgers University.
Vilrokx, Jacques, and Jim Van Leemput. 1992. "Belgium: A New Stability in Industrial
Relations?" Pp. 357–92 in *Industrial Relations in the New Europe,* edited by An-
thony Ferner and Richard Hyman. Oxford: Blackwell.
Visser, Jelle. 1989. *European Trade Unions in Figures.* Boston: Kluwer.
————. 1990a. "In Search of Inclusive Unionism." *Bulletin of Comparative Labour
Relations* 18 Special issue.
————. 1990b. "Continuity and Change in Dutch Industrial Relations." Pp. 199–242
in *European Industrial Relations: The Challenge of Flexibility,* edited by Guido
Baglioni and Colin Crouch. Newbury Park, Calif.: Sage.

———. 1991. "Trends in Trade Union Membership." *OECD Employment Outlook*, July, 97–134.

———. 1992a. "Trade Union Membership Database." Unpublished data file. Department of Sociology, University of Amsterdam.

———. 1992b. "The Strength of Union Movements in Advanced Capitalist Democracies: Social and Organizational Variations." Pp. 17–54 in *The Future of Labour Movements*, edited by Marino Regini. Newbury Park, Calif.: Sage.

Visser, Jelle, and Bernhard Ebbinghaus. 1992. "Making the Most of Diversity? European Integration and Transnational Organization of Labour." Pp. 206–76 in *Organized Interests and the European Community*, edited by Justin Greenwood, Jürgen Grote, and Karsten Ronit. London: Sage.

Waddington, Jeremy. 1992. "Trade Union Membership in Britain, 1980–1987: Unemployment and Restructuring." *British Journal of Industrial Relations* 30: 287–323.

Wallerstein, Michael. 1989. "Union Organization in Advanced Industrial Democracies." *American Political Science Review* 83:483–501.

———. 1991. "Reply to Stephens." *American Political Science Review* 85: 949–53.

Webb, Paul. 1992. *Trade Unions and the British Electorate*. Aldershot, England: Dartmouth.

Weiler, Paul C. 1990. *Governing the Workplace: The Future of Labor and Employment Law*. Cambridge: Harvard University Press.

Weitz, Peter R. 1975. "Labor and Politics in a Divided Movement: The Italian Case." *Industrial and Labor Relations Review* 28:226–42.

Western, Bruce. 1993. "Postwar Unionization in Eighteen Advanced Capitalist Countries." *American Sociological Review* 58:266–82.

———. 1994a. "Unionization and Labor Market Institutions in Advanced Capitalism, 1950–1985." *American Journal of Sociology* 99:1314–41.

———. 1994b. "Institutional Mechanisms for Unionization in Sixteen OECD Countries: An Analysis of Social Survey Data." *Social Forces* 73:497–519.

———. 1995a. "Concepts and Suggestions for Robust Regression Analysis." *American Journal of Political Science* 39:786–817.

———. 1995b. "A Comparative Study of Working Disorganization: Union Decline in Eighteen Advanced Capitalist Countries." *American Sociological Review* 60: 179–201.

Western, Bruce, and Simon Jackman. 1994. "Bayesian Inference for Comparative Research." *American Political Science Review* 88:412–23.

Whiteside, Noel. 1987. "Social Welfare and Industrial Relations 1914–1939." Pp. 211–242 in *A History of British Industrial Relations*, Vol. 2., edited by Chris Wrigley. Brighton, England: Harvester.

Wilson, Graeme K. 1982. "Why Is There No Corporatism in the United States?" Pp. 219–36 in *Patterns of Corporatist Policy-Making*, edited by Gerhard Lehmbruch and Philippe C. Schmitter. London: Sage.

Windmuller, John P. 1969. *Labor Relations in Netherlands*. Ithaca, N.Y.: Cornell University Press.

———. 1981. "Concentration in Trends in Union Structure: An International Comparison." *Industrial and Labor Relations Review* 35:43–57.

Windmuller, John P. 1984. "Employers Associations in Comparative Perspective: Organization, Structure, Administration." Pp. 1–23 in *Employers Associations and Industrial Relations*, edited by John Windmuller and Alan Gladstone. Oxford: Clarendon Press.

Windolf, G. Paul, and Joachim Haas. 1989. "Who Joins the Union? Determinants of Union Membership in West Germany 1976–1984." *European Sociological Review* 5:147–65.

Winterton, Jonathan, and Ruth Winterton. 1989. *Coal Crisis and Conflict*. Manchester: Manchester University Press.

Woldendorp Jaap, Hans Keman, and Ian Budge. 1993. "Parties and Governments in Industrialized Parliamentary Democracies." *European Journal of Political Research* 24:1–120.

Wolman, Leo. 1924. *The Growth of American Trade Unions, 1880–1923*. New York: National Bureau of Economic Research.

Wong, George Y., and William M. Mason. 1985. "The Hierarchical Logistic Regression for Multilevel Analysis." *Journal of the American Statistical Association* 80:513–24.

Wood, Adrian. 1994. *North-South Trade, Employment, and Inequality: Changing Fortunes in a Skill-Driven World*. Oxford: Clarendon.

Wright, Erik Olin. 1990. Comparative Project on Class Structure and Class Consciousness: Core and Country–Specific Files [MRDF]. Madison: University of Wisconsin, Institute for Research on Poverty [producer]; Ann Arbor: Inter-University Consortium for Political and Social Research [distributor].

Zysman, John. 1983. *Governments, Markets and Growth: Financial Systems and the Politics of Industrial Change*. Ithaca, N.Y.: Cornell University Press.

Index